GRAMMAR TO ENRICH & ENHANCE WRITING

CONSTANCE WEAVER

WITH JONATHAN BUSH

HEINEMANN
Portsmouth, NH

Heinemann

361 Hanover Street
Portsmouth, NH 03801–3912
www.heinemann.com

Offices and agents throughout the world

The authors and publisher wish to thank those who have generously given permission to reprint borrowed material:

"Errorwocky" from "Welcoming Errors as Signs of Progress" by Connie Weaver in *Language Arts,* Vol. 59, 1982. Copyright © 1982 by the National Council of Teachers of English. Reprinted and used with permission.

(continues on page x)

Library of Congress Cataloging-in-Publication Data
Weaver, Constance.
    Grammar to enrich and enhance writing / Constance Weaver with Jonathan Bush.
      p. cm.
    Includes bibliographical references and index.
    ISBN-13: 978-0-325-00758-8
    ISBN-10: 0-325-00758-6
    1. English language—Grammar—Study and teaching (Middle school).
2. English language—Grammar—Study and teaching (Secondary).　3. English language—Composition and exercises—Study and teaching (Middle school).
4. English language—Composition and exercises—Study and teaching (Secondary).
I. Bush, Jonathan.　II. Title.
    LB1631.W347 2008
    428.0071—dc22

2007030659

Editor: Lisa Luedeke
Production management: Sarah V. Weaver
Production coordination: Abigail M. Heim
Typesetter: Publishers' Design and Production Services, Inc.
Interior and cover design: Catherine Hawkes, Cat & Mouse
Manufacturing: Jamie Carter and Steve Bernier

Printed in the United States of America on acid-free paper
Sheridan 2018

Contents

Preface   xi
Acknowledgments   xv
Overview of Grammar Basics   xvii

PART ONE   Teaching Grammar for Writing: Principles to Practice

Toward a Middle Way   1

Teaching grammar to enrich and enhance writing   3
    Grammar to enrich writing   3
    Grammar to enhance writing   4
Grammar in the writing process: A quick overview   5
Our perspective on teaching grammar: Positive, productive, and
  practical   6

Grammar, Grammars, and the Traditional Teaching of Grammar   9

Expanding the basic definition of grammar   10
Concepts of grammar and grammars   12
What's wrong with how grammar has traditionally been taught?   13
    1. Teaching grammar in isolation produces little if any
       improvement   14
    2. Traditional grammars define parts of speech in inconsistent
       and confusing ways   15
    3. Traditional grammar books have focused mostly on
       analyzing language and eliminating errors   18
    4. Traditional grammars urge writers to follow archaic and
       arbitrary rules   20
Why not teach grammar traditionally? A reprise   23

3   **What Works in Teaching Grammar to Enrich and Enhance Writing**   25

Twelve principles supporting our approach   26
    1. Teaching grammar divorced from writing doesn't strengthen writing and therefore wastes time   26
    2. Few grammatical terms are actually needed to discuss writing   27
    3. Sophisticated grammar is fostered in literacy-rich and language-rich environments   27
    4. Grammar instruction for writing should build on students' developmental readiness   31
    5. Grammar options are best expanded through reading and in conjunction with writing   32
        Grammar and authentic reading   32
        Grammar and authentic writing   33
    6. Grammar conventions taught in isolation seldom transfer to writing   35
    7. Marking "corrections" on students' paper does little good   37
    8. Grammar conventions are applied most readily when taught in conjunction with editing   38
    9. Instruction in conventional editing skills is important for all students but must honor their home language or dialect   40
    10. Progress may involve new kinds of errors as students try to apply new writing skills   45
    11. Grammar instruction should be included during various phases of writing   50
    12. More research is needed on effective ways of teaching grammar to strengthen writing   50
A better way   52

 4   **Teaching Grammar Throughout the Writing Process**   53

How can we teach grammatical options while students are working on a piece of writing?   57
Playing with grammar, becoming a writer   58
A framework for teaching grammar throughout the writing process   62
What about writing workshop?   *with Patricia Bills*   65
    Minilessons   66
    Focus lessons   66

Teacher conferences   67
Demonstrations   67
A note about conventions and editing   67
Editing: Every teacher's bugaboo   68
Our "model" of grammar in the writing process   68

PART TWO   Teaching Grammar to Enrich and Enhance Writing

From Ice Cream to Dragons: Adjectival Modifiers at Work   71

Adding modifiers via key grammatical options   74
Understanding present participials   75
Another Emily teaches present participials   *with Emily Mihocko*   76
An extended lesson with sixth graders   83
Basic approaches to teaching modifiers and helping students
 revise   89
Modifiers in nonfiction   90
Remembering our purpose   91

Bringing in the Rest of the Gang: More Adjectival Modifiers   93

Connecting sentence chunking to art: Some examples   94
Playing with adjectivals out of order   *with Rebecca Schipper*   97
Out-of-order adjectival phrases: The motley crew   98
Rebecca teaches adjectives out of order to ninth graders   99
Renaming or categorizing with appositives   103
Teaching appositives to sixth graders   103
Absolutes, absolutely!   106
Teaching absolutes with the novel Good Night, Mr. Tom   *110*
Free modifying adjectivals in poetry   112
Free modifying adjectivals in nonfiction prose   115
Present participials   116
Other adjectivals out of order   118
Appositives   118
Absolutes   120
To keep in mind   121

Revision to the Rescue   123

Noticing when sentences can be combined   124
Noticing when sentences can be expanded   127

Editing Begins with Observation: Adverbial Clauses and the AAAWWUBBIS   by Jeff Anderson   131

Facing the error of our ways   132
Working editing into the writing process: The AAAWWUBBIS comes alive!   133
 Making the AAAWWUBBIS stick   136
 Enhancing meaning with the AAAWWUBBIS: What condition are your transitions in?   137
Making editing a positive experience   138

Editing: Approaching the Bugaboo in Diverse Classrooms   141

Deciding what editing skills to teach   142
Teaching writers to code-switch from African American English to standard   146
Promoting the acquisition of English: Editing in language-rich and literacy-rich classrooms   148
 Second language acquisition   150
 Behavioral versus constructivist approaches to teaching and learning   151
 Understanding interlanguage   152
 Are there developmental phases in the acquisition of English?   154
 Interlanguage and teaching English grammatical patterns: A review   156
 Promoting a low "affective filter"   157
 Principles to guide the teaching of standard English features   157

Rescuing Expository Writing from the Humdrum: From Rhetoric to Grammar   159

Following a formula for persuasive writing   161
Abandoning the formula to make writing more persuasive   163
 Stylistic options that enrich the writing   165

Contrasting these two approaches to persuasion   166
    Use of ethos and pathos in service of logos: A rhetorical
      decision   167
    Cohesion in "Coaches: 'Sit Down'"   169
Rules that don't rule   171
    The "frumious fragament"—or fragments reconsidered   171
    Rhetorical/stylistic use of but *or* and *to start a sentence   175*
      In journalism   176
      In creative and expository writing   177
What does all this mean for teachers of writing?   180
A final word   183

Grammar: Rocks and Mortar   185

Adjectivals   186
Adverbials   189
An aside on prepositional phrases   190
The mortar: Meanings of cohesive and transitional devices   191
The mortar: Grammatical categories   192
    Coordinating conjunctions, correlative conjunctions, and
      conjunctive adverbs   193
    Joining and separating independent clauses   194
    Creating adverbial clauses   196
    Creating adjectival clauses   197
    Creating noun clauses   197
Choosing your rocks and mortar   198

Making Decisions That Make a Difference: Grammar and the "6 Traits" of Writing   201

What should we teach when?   203
Interpreting the guide   206
    Enriching writing through grammar   207
      Grammatical options   207
      Organization/structure   208
      Parallelism   208
      A note about infinitives and gerunds   209
      "Cleft" and other inverted sentences   210
    Enriching writing through word choice   212
      "Just right" words   212
      Forms of the verb *to be*   214
    Enhancing writing through punctuation and usage   214

Using the "nonrubric" with caution 215
Applying the guide 216
    Paper 1: The Silent Assassin 217
    Applying the guide to paper 1 218
    Paper 2: Smelling Like a Dirty Ashtray 219
    Applying the guide to paper 2 220
    Paper 3: Polygamy Good or Bad 221
    Applying the guide to paper 3 222
    Further notes on using the guide 223
    Paper 4: The First Time I Got Bit by a Cat and Went to the Hospital 224
    Applying the guide to paper 4 225

PART THREE Teaching Grammar to Enhance Writing:
Focus on Editing

Rethinking How to Respond to Students' Errors
by Sharon Moerman 227

Considering and reconsidering Chasity's piece 228
Chasity and research as my teachers 232
Working with Chasity 233

Code-Switching: Teaching Standard English in African American Classrooms by Rebecca S. Wheeler 235

Key sociolinguistic concepts relevant to the writing classroom 239
    Vernacular grammar patterns in student writing 240
Teaching standard English in African American classrooms:
  Code-switching and contrastive analysis 242
Contrastive analysis and code-switching: Powerful tools for standard
  literacy 244
Code-switching in the classroom 245
    Setting the stage 245
    Code-switching minilessons illustrated 248
Making code-switching work for you and your students 250
    Seeing student writing as data 250
    Deciding where to start 252
    Making stylistic choices 252
    Endgame code-switching to standard English 253
    Grading student writing for standard usage and mechanics 253
    Deciding what comments to make in the margin 255

Linguistically informed responses to reading aloud   256
In conclusion   257

 15   **The Transformative Classroom: Rethinking Grammar Instruction for English Language Learners**
by Jason Roche and Yadira Gonzalez   259

A challenge to traditional teaching   259
    Changing demographics   260
  · *The diversity of English language learners   260*
Toward the transformative classroom   261
    Deficits versus assets   262
    Lifting the burden of failure   263
    Rethinking "errors" and building on what students can *do   263*
Interlanguage and students' increasing command of English   264
Behavioral versus transformative approaches to interlanguage   266
The writing process   266
    Immersion   266
    Using authors as models for our own writing   267
    Prewriting/drafting   268
    Revising   272
    Editing   275
        Informal editing conversations   278
        Group or class minilessons   279
    Celebrating   280

References   283
Contributors   294
Index   296

We started this book three years ago as what appeared to be a fairly simple task: to create an updated version of Connie's *Teaching Grammar in Context*. Oh, how plans can go awry! And what interesting things can happen when well-made plans do collapse. What we've developed has gone far beyond what we first planned. We think it's far better as well. Though clearly a continuation of Connie's work, this book is considerably more than a new edition of *Teaching Grammar in Context*: more comprehensive, more reader friendly, and more concretely focused on teachers' practical needs. Readers familiar with Connie's work will recognize in this new book, too, her deep understanding of grammar, theoretical approaches to language study, and pedagogical strategies for the teaching of grammar—the teaching stance and grammatical analysis found in *Grammar for Teachers*, the commitment to theory and research seen in *Teaching Grammar in Context,* and the focus on classroom pedagogy seen in *Lessons to Share* and her recent *Grammar Plan Book*. Readers will also see Jonathan's commitment to making classroom writing "real," and to developing techniques and skills that teachers can immediately implement for teaching grammar in conjunction with and in the context of writing. In short, although this book is based in theory and research, we wrote it *as* teachers, *for* teachers. This is a book with ideas and techniques that can immediately be put into practice, based on the work of thoughtful, skilled teachers we've admired and worked with over the years.

Grammar to Enrich and Enhance Writing is a snappy title, but we don't like it just because it has alliteration (although we admit that we like it for that reason too). We also like it because it includes two key terms—*enrich* and *enhance*—that aptly describe our approach to teaching grammar. Grammar can be a way to e*nrich* student writing—a way to make writing better, more complex, more exciting, and overall, more rich and interesting. Grammar can be a toolbox for the writer, or as Stephen King (2000) says, one of the tools in the top shelf of a writer's toolbox. The more the writer knows about his or her tools and the more practice—and guidance from a teacher—in using them, the more expert the student writer becomes at using those tools in crafting words, phrases, sentences, paragraphs, transitions, images, and eventually complete, polished writings. Grammar is also a way to *enhance* student writing—not only in terms of correctness and conventions, but, when appropriate, going beyond correctness for effect: with purpose and for specific stylistic reasons.

For us, grammar is not only inherently connected to the teaching of writing, it is, broadly construed, the *essence* of writing. The following key themes permeate the text:

- *Grammar can address all of the popular "6 traits" of writing* (Spandel, 2005; Culham, 2003). These, more broadly worded, are ideas/details, organization, word choice, voice/style/tone, conventions, and of course sentence sense, variety, and fluency.
- *Often, in teaching grammar, less is more.* Grammar is not something to be "covered" in writing class. Nor is it something that writing teachers need to teach in a way that ensures understanding of every language feature, skill, and tool. Rather, we suggest that teachers be selective, concentrating on aspects of grammar that enrich and enhance student writing and minimizing the use of grammatical terminology.
- *The teaching of grammar should be positive, productive, and practical.* Grammar is more than correctness, and the teaching of grammar should emphasize and open up possibilities for expression. Students should be able to see grammar as a way to strengthen writing, and as something that has immediate and clear implications for writing in real genres, for real purposes and real audiences. Grammar examples can and should be drawn from real sources—literary, journalistic, others.
- *The teaching of grammar should occur throughout the writing process.* Too often, grammar allegedly taught "in context" is completely separated from the actual process of writing, and n'er the twain do meet—at least instructionally. Teaching grammar, both to enrich and enhance, has a natural place within all writing phases, from planning through revision and editing, in preparation for ultimate publication.

The book is organized into three main sections. Part 1, Teaching Grammar for Writing: Principles to Practice, integrates theories of grammar and the teaching of grammar with classroom practices, creating our overall vision of teaching grammar specifically for writing. Part 2, Teaching Grammar to Enrich and Enhance Writing, manifests that vision with specific grammatical tools and teaching ideas, implemented within specific classroom contexts. It culminates with a chapter that invites teachers to consider different aspects of grammar to enrich and enhance writing and to make decisions about their own priorities and goals in relation to a guide we have developed and tested.

Part 3 highlights individual teachers as they consider several ways of helping students edit their grammar to enhance their writing, with emphasis on working with students who have severe editing needs, teaching African American speakers to code-switch, and guiding English language learners to edit their grammar.

There's plenty of grammar in this book—a teacher seeking a better understanding of basic aspects of the English language won't be disappointed—but we mostly deal with teaching limited aspects of grammar in conjunction with writing: how to apply this principle in positive, productive, and practical ways. And since this is a book about teaching, for teachers, we rely on our readers—capable, knowledgeable teachers of writing and literacy—to read and respond, learn and understand, and, most important, consider, adapt, and improve upon the ideas in this book.

Constance Weaver and Jonathan Bush
Western Michigan University
January 2007

Acknowledgments

Our grateful acknowledgment and thanks to:

Patricia Bills, faculty specialist, Western Michigan University, for the section "What About Writing Workshop?" in Chapter 4.

Carol McNally, literacy coach, Springfield Middle School, Battle Creek, Michigan, and Amanda Schripsema, language arts teacher at Mattawan (Michigan) Middle School, for their contributions to Chapter 4.

Max Baird, for his "I Am" poem in Chapter 4.

Emily Mihocko, first-grade teacher at Round Elementary School in Hartland, Michigan, for her section on present participials in Chapter 5. Thanks also to her students, especially Noah Tappen, Margaret Nied, and Madeline Cooper, whose "I am" poems and drawings are reproduced here.

Jeff Henderson, sixth-grade teacher at Baldwin Middle School, Hudsonville, Michigan, for team-teaching a lesson with one of us, and his students Julia and Caleb for their writings in Chapter 5.

Rebecca Schipper, a secondary teacher in the Hudsonville, Michigan, public schools, for her lesson description and plan and her journal entry, and her students for examples from their writings (Chapter 6).

Betty Roberts, sixth-grade teacher at the Greenwich (Connecticut) Country Day School, and her students Lucy Williams, Annaliesa Routh, Thomas Galluccio, and Robert Said for their "I Am" poems in Chapter 6.

John Weaver for his drawings (Chapter 3) and poem "A War Death" (Chapter 6).

Eda (Liesbeth) Koning, Kim Jay, and Michelle Jackson-Long for their sentence-chunking drawings in Chapter 6.

Diane Mayfield, seventh-grade teacher at Moreland Middle School, Blue Springs, Missouri, and her student Julie Nickelson for an excerpt from her writing in Chapter 7.

Jeff Anderson, Rayburn Middle School and Trinity University, San Antonio, for Chapter 8, "Editing Begins with Observation: Adverbial Clauses and the AAAWWUBBIS," and his student Samantha for her writing.

Gretchen Rumohr-Voskuil, a former high school teacher who also taught composition methods, literature, and English methods as a doctoral student at Western Michigan University, for quotes from her multigenre paper on teaching grammar (Chapter 10).

Maridella Carter, Diane Mayfield, and Katie Arnold-Clow, teachers in Blue Springs, Missouri, for papers we used in establishing the guide in Chapter 12 (and to Ruth Culham for making this possible).

Sharon Moerman, eighth-grade teacher at Watervliet (Michigan) Middle School, for Chapter 13, "Rethinking How to Respond to Students' Errors."

Rebecca Wheeler, Christopher Newport University, Newport News, Virginia, for Chapter 14, "Code-Switching: Teaching Standard English in African American Classrooms."

Jason Roche and Yadira Gonzales of Roosevelt High School in Fresno, California (formerly at Reedley, California, High School), for Chapter 15, "The Transformative Classroom: Rethinking Grammar Instruction for English Language Learners." Thanks also to Oscar Hernandez at Reedley for his contributions to the chapter, which Roche and Gonzales gratefully acknowledge. Roche and Gonzales teach also at Fresno Pacific University and Roche also teaches for the University of Phoenix.

I (Connie) especially want also to thank the wonderful people at Heinemann. Lisa Luedeke, my editor, never failed to encourage me through her positive responses to my work; she is an absolute gem. Alan Huisman is, quite simply, the best developmental editor I have ever had: He has tightened my writing—our writing—to a degree I never would have believed possible. Editorial coordinator Stephanie Colado's diligent assistance helped me tie up various loose ends. Special gratitude goes also to Abby Heim, Sarah Weaver, and Cathy Hawkes, the best production coordinator, production manager, and designer I have ever had.

Overview of Grammar Basics

W e offer this overview of basic definitions knowing full well that definitions alone do not teach. These definitions and examples simply provide a review for some teachers and a nudge to others to gain a grasp of these concepts, all of which can appropriately be taught to students—but preferably in the context of teaching more complex grammatical constructions in conjunction with writing itself. The more complex constructions are addressed throughout this book.

Basic parts of speech

1. A *noun* designates someone or something: *girl, puppy, flower, money, idea, honesty*. Any word or group of words that works like a single noun is a *nominal*.

2. A *pronoun* can "take the place of" or "stand for" a noun (or noun phrase): *he, me, your, his, this, that, which, who, someone, anything, nobody*, etc. Therefore a pronoun is also a nominal. (Nominals have several basic functions, discussed in other chapters only as needed.)

3. A *verb* expresses action or state of being. For example, a verb tells what a subject noun does, is doing, or did: *he skis, he is skiing, he skied*. When two or more words work together as a verb, they are usually called a *verb phrase*. (It would be more logical to call such a phrase a "verbal," but that's not traditional.) Here are the forms of the verb *to be: am, is, are, was, were, be, being, been*. This is the major verb, though not the only one, that expresses a state of being.

4. An *adjective* is a word that modifies a noun. Any word or group of words working like a single adjective is an *adjectival*.

That was a <u>corny</u> joke.

Herb wrote some poems <u>about working in a grocery store</u>.

The excitement <u>that was generated by Superman's appearance</u> couldn't be quelled.

5. An *adverb* is a word that modifies a verb. Any word or group of words working like a single adverb is an *adverbial*. Sometimes an adverbial seems to modify the whole action specified in a sentence. Adverbials usually tell in what manner (how); to what extent (how long, how far, and so on); where; when; or why with respect to the action.

<u>Ironically</u>, I've been getting stressed <u>while editing materials on stress reduction</u>.

<u>With a steady hand</u>, Kim retraced the drawing <u>in darker ink</u>.

Mark <u>quickly</u> zoomed <u>into the one empty parking space</u>.

We waited <u>twenty-four hours</u>.

<u>Then</u> we called the police, <u>because we didn't know what else to do</u>.

6. A *preposition* is a word like *in, on, by, to,* or *around* when it introduces a noun, pronoun, or noun phrase (nominal). Examples: *in the box, <u>on</u> it, <u>by</u> the brightly colored box, <u>to</u> the big box, <u>around</u> the mysterious box*. Together, the preposition + the following nominal constitute a *prepositional phrase*.

7. A *coordinating conjunction* joins two grammatical elements of the same kind. *And* and *but* are the most common, followed by *or, so,* and *yet*. Other words that sometimes conjoin two sentences are *for* and *nor*, and the pairs *either . . . or, neither . . . nor*. (Some people have learned an acronym for remembering the basic coordinating conjunctions: FANBOYS, which stands for *for, and, nor, but, or, yet, so*.)

8. *Subordinating conjunctions* are words that begin adverb clauses. Or to put it another way, when we place a subordinating conjunction in front of a sentence, we have made it into a subordinate clause: a piece of a sentence. Example: *When you're through*, put your materials away; I had to quit, *though I wasn't finished yet*. (See the explanation that follows under "Clauses and Phrases.")

Basic parts of a sentence: Subject + predicate

1. The verb is crucial to a sentence. (See the preceding definition of verbs.) The verb or verb phrase can stand alone as a *predicate,* but many verbs require something to follow them: *I petted the dog* (direct object); *Marvin was my first dog* (predicate nominal); *my dog was very rambunctious* (predicate adjectival).

2. The *subject* usually (but not always) specifies who or what is doing the action or is in the state specified by the verb. The subject may be any word or group of words that can work as a noun: a nominal, in other words. Here are some basic two-word sentences, subject plus verb:

Computers quit. Hope endures. Zack left. Malcolm grinned.
They laughed. She smirked. Nobody cried. Everyone smiled.

Clauses and phrases

1. A *clause* contains a subject plus a complete verb unit. In the following example, *being* is not a complete verb: *Jack being ready now.* Thus these words do not constitute a clause.

   a. A clause that can stand alone as a grammatically complete sentence is an *independent (main) clause.* (A sentence that has only one clause, an independent clause, is called a *simple sentence.* A sentence with two or more independent clauses is a *compound sentence.*)

   b. A clause that is grammatically tied to, or part of, another clause is a *subordinate (dependent) clause.*

   For example:

   I can't wait until you are ready to leave.

   Although the champ was stronger, his opponent was more clever.

   This is the one that I wanted.

   That was his secret, which he finally told me.

   I know what you mean.

   She knew that she shouldn't do it.

   She knew it was wrong.

A *complex sentence* contains one independent clause and at least one subordinate clause.

2. A *phrase* is a group of words that functions together as a unit but does not contain a subject plus a complete verb. In this example, the underlined phrase modifies *plane*: *The plane <u>taxiing down the runway</u> was designed by Peter's father*. Many modifiers are phrases.

Toward a Middle Way

When the public demands that we teach grammar in the schools, what is it that they want? Sometimes they—especially the "successful" members of middle-aged and older generations—vaguely remember learning rules for writing or memorizing definitions of parts of speech, different kinds of verbs, and maybe gerunds or participles. Often, the nostalgists don't remember much about these aspects of grammar, but they think that grammar somehow must have been good for them or that students today should be subjected to the same trials they themselves were. Though some of us—especially English teachers—can point to some of what we learned and explain how we use it effectively in our writing, the public in general tends to view grammar merely as prohibitive rules: Don't do this, don't do that. Many English teachers can attest to this perception from social interactions with strangers. How often have you been introduced to someone as an English teacher—or an English major or minor—and gotten the reaction, "Oh, I'd better watch my grammar"?

What *is* grammar? The grammar of a language is its structure, which enables us to communicate whether or not we or anybody else consciously understands that structure. Word order, for instance, tells us that "George loves Alanna" does not necessarily mean that Alanna loves George. Basically, *grammar* means roughly the same thing as *syntax*, a more technical term for *how*—not what—words combine to make meaning. The grammar of a language just *is*.

Rarely do people outside the university or the classroom talk about this basic meaning of grammar, which underlies all other meanings. Given the popular conceptions and misconceptions about grammar, even teachers are often confused about what grammar is and uncertain about their appropriate role in teaching—or not teaching—grammar to students. Connie's 1979 publication *Grammar for Teachers*, the all-time best seller of the National Council of Teachers of English (NCTE), has been a landmark text in the debate about what to teach. Reading it, many English teachers or future teachers absorbed the message that over the decades, most student writers have benefited little from plowing their way through grammar books. Most teachers seemed to have missed the message, though, that teachers themselves need to know enough about grammar to help students focus on interesting grammatical features in literature and to draw on a very limited number of grammatical concepts to help students enrich and enhance their writing. Truthfully, *Grammar for Teachers* did little to demonstrate how teachers might accomplish this aim.

In education, as in other fields, the pendulum—in our case, the pendulum of pedagogy—tends to swing from one extreme to the other. In the teaching of grammar, English teachers have swung from teaching grammar out of a grammar book during much or most of a semester each year, grades 7 through 12, to the opposite extreme of teaching almost nothing at all about grammar.

These unproductive extremes surfaced again in a phone call Jonathan recently received regarding grammar. It was from Joy, a local high school teacher whom we respect and know—a pillar of our local teaching community, a leader among her colleagues. Yet here she was, asking for help. "So," she began, "what about grammar? Have I missed something? I must be missing something. Am I?" She went on to describe a newer teacher at her school who believed that grammar should be totally banished from English language arts instruction. This teacher championed a no-grammar approach that relies on writing practice and revision for generating fluency with language, without explicit attention to syntax and sentence-level features. Joy contrasted this teacher with another colleague who built writing around the study of grammar as the most important feature of her writing classroom.

"I know I'm in the middle of these two," Joy continued. "But what should that middle be?"

A short, pithy response to Joy's question is simply, "Teach grammar in the context of writing," as advised in Connie's *Teaching Grammar in Context* (1996a) and a related article (1996b). However, some teachers have claimed that not everything writers need to know about grammar is best taught while students are engaged in the writing process—and for just a few grammatical concepts, we can agree. Critics, often linguists, have latched onto the phrase "teaching grammar in context," misunderstood the concept, and denounced the approach as ineffective in teaching grammar. We say, "Of course. Teaching grammar for its own sake was never the aim." Rather than promoting the teaching of writing as a vehicle for learning grammar, Connie was urging teachers to draw selectively on those aspects of grammar that actually can make writing more effective. Many teachers got this message but still needed more help.

Teaching grammar to enrich and enhance writing

As a first step in clarifying what we mean by teaching grammar in context, we offer a middle ground between the extremes of Joy's colleagues. Our advice, slightly rephrased: Empower students to draw on those aspects of grammar that will enrich and enhance their writing. In other words, we encourage teachers to focus on writing and, in the process, guide students in using whatever grammatical options and features will make their writing more interesting and more appreciated by their audience.

Grammar to enrich writing

By focusing on certain grammatical constructions as they draft or revise, students—indeed, all of us—can write more interesting, more detailed sentences. We can thereby also write with greater rhetorical effectiveness. To paraphrase Aristotle, rhetoric is the use of all available means to persuade an audience (1991, Book 1, Ch. 2); today, we would say that rhetoric involves not only persuading an audience to do or believe something, but also engaging them deeply through the use of language and a distinctive style or voice. Insightfully, noted stylist Francis Christensen claimed we need a rhetoric that will not merely express ideas but also *generate* them (1965, 1967). Grammar, along with word choice, is a cornerstone of rhetoric. As later chapters will demonstrate, focusing on certain aspects of grammar and their effective use can generate ideas and their development—in other words, content.

In fiction or poetry, grammar can help us create a *persona*, a narrator or character with a distinctive *style,* or *voice.* Think, for instance, of the narrator of Edgar Allan Poe's "The Telltale Heart." Or consider Holden Caulfield, the first-person narrator of J. D. Salinger's *Catcher in the Rye* (1951/1991), who deliberately parodies the first-person narrator of Charles Dickens' *David Copperfield.* Or compare the third-person narrative voice in Gary Paulsen's *Hatchet* (1991) with that of *Dogsong* (1999): Paulsen's deft and deliberate use of grammar is part of what makes the difference. Or listen to the first-person narrators of popular songs, particularly those telling a story or expressing beliefs. In all such instances, even some with supposedly impersonal third-person narrators, style reflects the main character or the setting or events. Style and voice

Smart teaching of grammar with and for writing

Connie's most recent publication, *The Grammar Plan Book: A Guide to Smart Teaching* (2007), includes not only an idealized framework for teaching selected aspects of grammar (updated here in Chapter 4), but also several extended teaching examples. In this book, we provide a much more detailed rationale, along with many more illustrations of what "teaching grammar in context" can mean when strengthening writing is the goal.

can be modified for different purposes and audiences in informative and persuasive writing and speaking, too—as, for instance, in Martin Luther King's cherished "I have a dream" speech.

But the deliberate use of grammar is found in more than such canonized settings. We also see the same traits—grammar used for effects and with rhetorical purpose—in road signs, fast-food menus, instruction manuals, and all other commonplace forms of communication that nevertheless reflect complex decisions about style, voice, and even correctness.

Regarding correctness, the text *Spoken Soul* (Rickford & Rickford, 2000) offers numerous historical examples of spoken and written English in which the use of "Black English" features is rhetorically "correct"—that is, appropriate to depict characters and situation, to engage and move an audience, and/or to emphasize a given sociopolitical perspective. Today, we still see rhetorical grammatical and stylistic features, along with "Black English," used spontaneously but deliberately in composed-on-the-spot genres like sermons and rap, as the preacher conveys passion and exhorts his congregation and as the rapper belts out his rap. Thus "correctness," too, is a matter of using grammar appropriate to the desired effect.

Obviously our concept of grammar to enrich writing includes rhetoric, or "rhetorical grammar," as Martha Kolln (2006) calls it: the use of particular grammatical options to create certain effects. As Frances Christensen wrote long ago, "Grammar maps out the possible; rhetoric narrows the possible down to the desirable or effective" (1965; 1967, p. 39). Overall, conscious attention to grammatical options, their placement, and variation in their use will naturally enhance a writer's sentence sense, or what is sometimes called "sentence fluency." All these aspects of writing—ideas/development, style/voice, and sentence fluency/sense—show up in many rubrics for assessing writing. They are often assessed but not always taught. Seldom, in fact, do we teach the effective use of grammar as students draft and revise. Clearly, teachers need more help in learning to teach the conscious and constructive use of grammar to enrich writing—to make it more lively and rhetorically effective.

Grammar to enhance writing

But what about teaching grammar to *enhance* writing? By this we mean using grammatical options that are conventional, or deliberately nonconventional, but in either case effective for particular purposes and audiences: the decorations on the cake, so to speak. We *emphatically* do not subscribe to the school of thought that "grammar" is avoiding or correcting "errors," or making grammatical choices mistakenly thought to be universally "right" rather than "wrong." There is no single variety of English that's appropriate for all purposes and situations, as we will further explain in Chapter 3. Nevertheless, we know that for many occasions, using the conventions of mainstream English is profitable for writers and speakers, and these conventions are best taught while students are editing their writing, rather than in isolation. That way, there is little or no wasteful teaching: first teaching a concept or form in an isolated unit of grammar study, then reteaching the same thing in conjunction with the editing process. Some reteaching is necessary in any case, as teachers must repeatedly help students apply an editing concept—such as some aspect of subject-verb agreement—even if that concept is understood when first presented. But the concept will be better grasped and remembered if first taught at the point of need.

Teaching students to enhance their writing by editing for appropriate words and grammar is an essential part of guiding students throughout the writing process.

Grammar in the writing process: A quick overview

Teaching grammar to enrich writing may occur not only when students are preparing to write but also when they are drafting and revising; these processes overlap and occur cyclically. So, too, with editing to enhance writing: Writers may edit for the desired conventions of language use not only after they've revised but during the drafting process as well. Given the intertwining of various phases in the writing process, no visual model can do it justice, as we emphasize at the end of Chapter 4. For now, though, we share our enhancement of the 1990s Michigan model of writing (Michigan State Board of Education, 1994), which is more satisfactory than most, given its two-way arrows to indicate multidirectionality and the loops to indicate recursiveness—that is, recurring, though unpredictable, cycles. As an overview of our intent and progression in this book, we have added our notion of where the teaching of grammar to enrich and enhance writing can profitably occur (see Figure 1–1).

We admit that a few grammatical concepts, such as subject and verb, may be best taught in separate lessons, perhaps right before a lesson on punctuating sentences or on making verbs "agree" with their subjects. Finally, we emphasize that writing for publication, for an audience beyond the classroom and in genres not limited to school, encourages students to enrich their content and enhance their writing to a degree that nothing else can do.

For teachers with little conscious knowledge of grammar, we offer a short overview of basic definitions before Chapter 1. For those seeking more, *The Grammar Plan Book* (Weaver 2007) is a grammar handbook that doubles as a planner for making decisions about teaching grammar.

While we are firmly convinced that teachers should respect and honor the natural language of students, we are also firmly convinced that student writers should be offered guidance in using language conventions that are widely accepted in mainstream society: the "language of wider communication," as it has been called by the Conference on College Composition and Communication (1988).

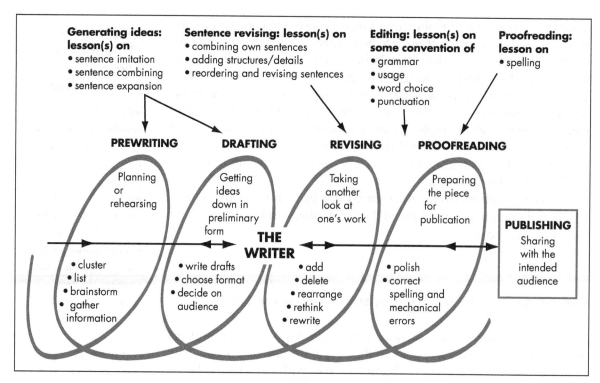

FIGURE 1–1. The basic recursive model of the writing process—the loops and the text within—was prepared for the Michigan Proficiency Examination Framework for Writing by the Michigan Council of Teachers of English in 1993. For this book, Connie has added suggestions on the teaching of grammar above the basic MCTE/MDE model.

Our perspective on teaching grammar: Positive, productive, and practical

Overall, then, teaching grammar to enrich and enhance writing is teaching grammar as *possibility*. We see it as *positive*, the offering of options rather than the avoidance of errors; as *productive*, especially in the sense that it produces effective sentences and paragraphs; and as eminently *practical*. Teaching a minimal amount of grammar, mostly while guiding students throughout the writing process, not only enriches and enhances writing, but empowers writers.

Chapters 2 and 3 offer our rationale for this positive, productive, and practical approach. In Chapter 2, we elaborate on our premise that teaching grammar traditionally is not the best way to help students make their writing more effective through conscious use of grammatical tools. We give several reasons, the most important of which is this: There is hardly any research evidence that teaching grammar traditionally, in isolation from writing, enhances the quality or conventional "correctness" of student writing. We repeat: The hope that teaching grammar in isolation will improve writing is not supported by research. For most students, the two—grammar and its use in writing—must be explicitly connected. Thus we believe teaching grammar as a separate subject primarily wastes valuable time that could be spent in helping writers use grammatical options and conventions more appropriately. This leaves more time for students to write and for teachers to guide them in their writing.

Chapter 3 further explains the rationale for our approach to teaching grammar by presenting a dozen elaborated statements about what works and what we recommend. Since you may want to think ahead about these topics, we list here these guiding observations and principles for teaching grammar to enrich and enhance writing:

1. Teaching grammar as a separate subject divorced from writing wastes valuable instructional time because few students transfer their grammar study to writing without teacher guidance.

2. Most of the grammatical terms used in traditional grammar books are not really needed to explain grammatical options and conventions.

3. The acquisition and development of students' grammatical repertoire—the emergence of more sophisticated grammar—is fostered in literacy-rich and language-rich environments and classrooms.

4. Grammar instruction should not be limited to the scope and sequence found in a textbook series, but should build on students' developmental readiness.

5. Grammar to *enrich* students' writing—options for adding detail, structure, voice/style, and fluency—is partly learned through extensive, authentic reading and is most readily taught and learned in conjunction with literature and authentic writing.

6. There is minimal value in teaching the conventional prescriptions for grammar, usage, punctuation, and other aspects of mechanics in complete isolation from writing.

7. Teachers do little good and often a great deal of harm by making numerous "corrections" on students' papers.

8. Conventions to *enhance* writing can be taught more efficiently and learned more effectively during and in conjunction with the editing process than in completely isolated lessons on grammar, usage, and mechanics.

Research on the teaching of grammar for writing

The most recent summary of research on teaching grammar to improve writing has concluded, as have other summaries for at least seventy-five years, that there is "no high-quality evidence" that teaching grammar to improve the quality or accuracy ("correctness") of writing has a positive effect on many students' writing when the grammar is taught as a separate subject, in isolation from writing (Andrews et al., 2004b). See Chapters 2 and 3 for more discussion of research on the teaching of grammar for writing.

9. It is important to teach *all* students relevant skills for editing their writing according to the conventions widely accepted in mainstream society—while still honoring each student's home language or dialect.

10. When students experiment with new grammatical options or try out new skills in their writing, their efforts often result in new kinds of errors that are signs of progress.

11. Grammar taught in conjunction with writing will be most effective when reinforced through more than one phase of the process and with numerous writing situations and assignments.

12. There is need for more research on differing approaches to teaching grammar when the primary goal is to strengthen students' writing.

Overall, we believe that by teaching grammar in positive, productive, and practical ways, teachers can make a significant difference in how, and how well, their students write.

You'll notice that we've replaced the phrase *teaching grammar in the context of writing* with *teaching grammar in conjunction with writing* to allow for a slightly greater range of possibilities. Nevertheless, the thrust of this book is basically the same: teaching useful aspects of grammar as we help students enrich and enhance their writing.

Overall, we believe that by teaching grammar in positive, productive, and practical ways, teachers can make a significant difference in how, and how well, their students write. It's a goal worth serious pursuit.

This book, then, is the beginning of the answer we offer to Joy and to other teachers of writing who want to know "what to do with grammar."

Grammar, Grammars, and the Traditional Teaching of Grammar

2

When we ask teachers what they think grammar is, we typically end up with a list like this:

- Parts of speech (noun, verb, adjective, adverb, pronoun, preposition, conjunction, interjection)
- Sentence structures (subject + verb; phrases; clauses)
- Sentence types (declarative, interrogative, imperative, exclamatory; simple, compound, complex, compound/complex)
- "Correct" syntax (subject-verb agreement, pronoun-antecedent agreement, etc.)
- "Correct" usage (appropriate use of *affect*, *effect*, etc.)
- "Correct" punctuation and use of mechanics (perhaps including spelling)

These categories are not entirely consistent, and indeed, different grammar books, language arts series, and writing textbooks do not categorize the topics in exactly the same way. For example, what's listed here as syntax is sometimes listed under usage, punctuation is sometimes listed under mechanics, and so forth.

The notable thing about such lists is that they focus on two kinds of topics: (1) elements of the language and how they occur as parts of sentences and (2) the use of what we call not "correct" English but rather the commonly taught conventions of English—how to use certain aspects of the language as highly educated people do (or as we think they do), particularly in public writing. Typically absent from such lists is a notion of grammar as options—different grammatical constructions that can help the writer add descriptive details and create different styles, voices, and rhetorical effects.

Teachers' concepts of grammar often derive from the instructional materials they experienced as a student or the materials they now use or see used in English and language arts instruction. Almost always, these materials share the same kind of content because they are based on previous grammars of the same nature, what we call *traditional grammars*: that is, materials for teaching traditional grammatical explanations and rules and teaching them traditionally, as a separate subject isolated from writing. Traditional grammars are partly *descriptive*, in that they describe language elements and patterns (though often inaccurately or unhelpfully), and partly *prescriptive*, in that they tell writers what to do and what not to do with language—especially what *not* to do. Books on "errors" to avoid or correct abound in today's bookstores, reflecting this thrust of traditional grammar.

Expanding the basic definition of grammar

The grammar of a language is its structure, whereby communication is made possible; that structure exists whether or not anybody can describe it.

A language, any language, consists of elements and rules for combining them. These rules are akin to the "rules" for how our digestive system works or how our eyes work with our brains to enable us to see: They are operations that we ordinarily aren't conscious of. For that reason, the rules of language that make communication possible might be called operational rules, and this grammar that we unconsciously use might be called *operational grammar*.

Curious about what kinds of rules contribute to the structure of English? Immediately we must shift from operational grammar, which we use automatically, to *descriptive grammar*, an examination of what structural features make language work. In English, there are three structural features: *word order*, the most important; *function words* (also called structure or signal words), which glue the major kinds of content-bearing words together; and *inflectional word endings*, which are absent or present or change according to the sentence. Here are some examples:

- *Word order:* "George loves Alanna" can't be changed to "Alanna loves George" without changing the meaning. Similarly, "Jennifer squeezed the snake" does not mean the same as "The snake squeezed Jennifer." Or again, we might say, "They sat on the floor," but "Floor the they on sat" is such unnatural word order that the sentence is difficult to understand.

- *Function words:* The following sentences, with the function words underlined, include at least one example of each kind of function word:

  <u>After</u> it <u>had</u> rained <u>for</u> <u>an</u> hour, <u>the</u> young people gave up <u>their</u> idea <u>of</u> camping out. Instead they rented <u>a</u> room <u>at</u> <u>a</u> motel where they <u>could</u> swim <u>in</u> <u>a</u> pool <u>and</u> eat <u>by</u> <u>the</u> poolside.

  If you aren't familiar with so-called function words, don't be surprised if certain other words also seem to perform the function of gluing words together. Interestingly, the exact function word or a close equivalent can often be predicted from the words being glued together, called *content words.* This demonstrates that function words are not as important as word order.

- *Inflectional word endings:* Inflectional endings change to indicate grammatical meaning—plural or possessive for nouns; tense or aspect for verbs (the latter having to do with the completion, ongoing nature, or possibility of the action); degree of comparison for adjectives or adverbs. However, inflectional endings do not change a word's part of speech. Notice the different forms of the noun *bike* and the verbs *borrow* and *ride* in the following sentences, as well as the superlative adjective *fastest*:

  Elana <u>borrows</u> the boys' <u>bikes</u> every spring. She <u>borrowed</u> Amos's <u>bike</u> last week and <u>rode</u> it over broken glass. Elana can't <u>ride</u> it now because the <u>bike's</u> tires are shot. Amos is <u>rid</u>-<u>ing</u> a motorcycle now. Unfortunately, he <u>rides</u> too fast. He hasn't <u>ridden</u> his old, pedal-powered <u>bike</u> all year.

  Such endings and internal changes are less important grammatical signals in English than word order.

What we find so intriguing about these grammatical signals in English is not merely their existence, but also that toddlers and preschoolers mostly learn these aspects of grammar without any direct instruction.

What we find so intriguing about these grammatical signals in English is not merely their existence, but also that toddlers and preschoolers mostly learn these aspects of grammar without any direct instruction. The child is an unconscious grammar machine, producing new elements and generating increasingly sophisticated rules for combining words into sentences. Eventually, without any adult explanation, children learn more than just the basic patterns—or "rules"—of their native language. In fact, a research study in the 1960s showed that by the end of kindergarten, children may use in their speech almost all the basic sentence patterns and grammatical constructions found in the speech of older children (O'Donnell, Griffin, & Norris, 1967). And by the end of first grade, children use this variety of grammatical constructions more fully and more flexibly.

This research should give us pause when we're tempted to think that children won't know grammar unless we teach it to them. They "know" it unconsciously, because they use a wide variety of grammatical constructions and rules in their utterances. They use far more than most of us are able to describe.

Concepts of grammar and grammars

Patrick Hartwell's "Grammar, Grammars, and the Teaching of Grammar" (1985) inspired not only the title of this chapter but our decision to discuss different kinds of grammars. These terms are defined and described briefly below, starting with the basic definition of grammar that we have already articulated.

- *Grammar:* The structural elements and patterns of a language, regardless of whether anyone is conscious of them; the "rules" that make a sentence not just a random string of words but a structure capable of communicating meaning.
- *Operational grammar:* The grammar that native speakers of a language naturally use in speaking; the grammar—language structures and patterns—we intuitively "know" and use but usually aren't aware of knowing or using; our unconscious knowledge of grammar that enables us to communicate with other speakers of the same language. This is the same as the preceding basic definition, except that calling it *operational grammar* emphasizes that this is grammar in use. Scholars of language acquisition investigate how such patterns develop within and across individuals and languages.
- *Traditional school grammar:* The grammatical descriptions and prescriptive rules that have been taught in schools for centuries and that have changed surprisingly little over the years. *Traditional grammars*—the grammar books themselves—are self-perpetuating: New grammar books stray little from the previous generation's, preserving not only some inaccurate and unhelpful definitions but even the fossilized rules made up by some grammarian several centuries ago (including rules that never did reflect how prominent writers of any era wrote, but rather somebody's idea of rules that writers "ought" to follow). Thus

traditional grammars are known for their *prescriptive rules* stating what writers allegedly should and shouldn't do.

- *Descriptive grammars:* The grammars developed by linguists, who attempt to describe the structure of the language as it is used by native speakers—not just highly educated speakers of the language, but all speakers and their language varieties (dialects). Scholars who have developed descriptive grammars are called *linguists*, and their branch of study is *linguistics*, derived from the Latin word for *tongue*, a synonym for *language*. To put it the other way around, *linguistic grammars* are basically descriptive, though there are some subcategories and clarifications to be made. For example, in addition to describing particular language varieties, sociolinguists have discovered socially determined variations within these dialects.

All the schools of linguistics we draw on fall within the descriptive tradition, though structural linguists of the 1950s—notably Charles Fries (1952), Paul Roberts (1956), and W. Nelson Francis (1958)—attempted to describe the language without any reference to meaning; *transformational/generative* linguists in the tradition of Noam Chomsky (1957, 1965) attempted in the 1960s to account for how we understand sentences; and *functional* linguists in the tradition of M. A. K. Halliday's work in the 1970s and 80s (e.g., 1985) have emphasized the social functions and rhetorical uses of grammatical constructions (e.g., Collerson, 1994; Fairclough, 1989).

For a fuller treatment of the differences between traditional and linguistic grammars, which primarily describe the language, see Brock Haussamen's *Revising the Rules: Traditional Grammar and Modern Linguistics* (2000).

For now, however, we turn our attention to traditional school grammar and the traditional grammar books in which the explanations and prescriptive rules of traditional grammar are enshrined. It should be obvious by now that we do not believe that teaching grammar traditionally, or teaching traditional grammars, is the best way to offer grammar-based help to writers.

What's wrong with how grammar has traditionally been taught?

Though everyone unconsciously knows a great deal about grammar and employs grammatical elements and rules automatically, teachers can help students use the grammatical resources of the language more extensively

It should be obvious by now that we do not believe that teaching grammar traditionally, or teaching traditional grammars, is the best way to offer grammar-based help to writers.

A current book that deals with English grammar more traditionally than otherwise but does incorporate some modern insights is the inexpensive *McGraw-Hill Handbook of English Grammar and Usage* (Lester & Beason, 2005). The authors recommend their book for "consenting adults" who "value ideas, evidence, and explanations" (p. 1); they present it as a "painless prescription for proper English" (back cover) that contains two parts, "Grammar 101" and "How to Find and Correct Mistakes."

and more effectively in their writing. Often, though, the grammatical "help" teachers have offered hasn't proved very helpful. There are many reasons for this, including the nature of traditional grammar taught in schools, the comprehensive grammar books sold to the public, and the writer's handbooks with hefty chunks of grammar sold to schools and college students. Examples of the former are *English Grammar for Dummies* (Woods, 2001) and *The Complete Idiot's Guide to Grammar and Style* (Rozakis, 1997). Examples of the latter include the famous—and infamous—*Warriner's English Grammar and Composition* series (1986, with predecessors dating back to 1948), which is no longer in print. The books themselves are often called "traditional grammars." The twenty-first century has seen the publication of some big, heavy, and expensive hardback handbooks for college classes. The *Simon & Schuster Handbook for Writers* (Troyka, 2004) and the *St. Martin's Handbook* (Lunsford, 2003) are two.

Following are some major reasons for not teaching traditional grammar as presented in the more thorough textbooks, as well as reasons for not teaching grammar traditionally—that is, reasons for not teaching grammar as a separate subject, regardless of the "kind" of grammar taught.

1. Teaching grammar in isolation produces little if any improvement

Teaching grammar in isolation from writing—that is, teaching the grammar book instead of helping writers write—has been found again and again to have little if any positive effect on most students' writing. In a 1986 study, George Hillocks found that of several methods teachers employed to help students write more effectively, the only method that had a negative effect was teaching grammar as a separate subject!

The most recent, most comprehensive review of the research on the effects of teaching traditional grammar concludes, once again, that "the clear implication, based on the available high quality research evidence, is that the evidence base to justify the teaching of grammar in English to 5- to 16-year-olds in order to improve writing is very small" (the "York" study: Andrews et al., 2004b, p. 4). When taught in isolation, neither traditional nor other kinds of grammar were effective in improving writing. *The authors of the York study suggest, therefore, that teaching any kind of grammar in isolation with the intent "to improve the quality and/or accuracy" of students' writing is not worth our instructional time.*

They conclude their review with a call for more research:

> We now know that there is no high quality evidence that teaching of traditional grammar or syntax (or the direct teaching of formal

or generative/transformational grammars) is effective with regard to writing development. Having established that much, we can now go on to research what is effective, and to ask clearer and more pertinent questions about what works in the development of young people's literacy. (p. 5)

We appreciate this call for more research: well-designed, high-quality, longitudinal experimental studies that consider the effects of other grammatical approaches to enriching students' writing and enhancing their use of conventions. With longitudinal studies, though, come more variables that cannot be controlled. There is also a serious need for well-designed, high-quality qualitative teacher research.

Given the current evidence that teaching grammar as an isolated school subject does not improve writing for many students, we hope you can see why we don't want the pendulum to swing back to the earlier extreme of teaching grammar extensively and exhaustively. It simply isn't productive enough to be practical. But for readers who aren't yet convinced that teaching grammar traditionally is unnecessary and impractical, we offer additional reasons.

2. Traditional grammars define parts of speech in inconsistent and confusing ways

Traditional grammars define parts of speech in inconsistent and confusing ways, focusing too much attention on grammatical form and analyzing language, but not enough on employing the grammatical structures that can convey precise descriptions and clarifying information—particularly the modifying functions that add details to bare-bones writing.

For example, here are the definitions of the major grammatical elements—parts of speech—from *Warriner's High School Handbook* (1992):

A noun is a word used to name a person, place, thing, or idea.
A pronoun is a word used in place of a noun or of more than one noun.
A verb is a word that expresses action or otherwise helps to make a statement.
An adjective is a word used to modify a noun or a pronoun.
An adverb is a word used to modify a verb, an adjective, or another adverb.

In order to become familiar with these definitions and—especially if you have little or no background in traditional grammar—to gain some idea of why using such definitions to identify parts of speech can be difficult, label the underlined words in the following sentences as to part of speech (N for noun, V for verb, P for pronoun, J for adjective, or A for adverb). Then discuss your answers and difficulties with friends or colleagues:

1. We should <u>team</u> up for the race.
2. The <u>match</u> is wet.
3. <u>Which</u> team will win?
4. There's a <u>short</u> in the wire.
5. Sort those socks and <u>match</u> them, please.
6. Drive <u>slow</u>, Charles.
7. Amos and Joseph have a lot of <u>team</u> spirit.
8. Carmen scored the <u>match</u> point.
9. Who won the <u>match</u>?
10. We took a <u>slow</u> trip around the lake.
11. Line up our <u>team</u>.
12. It wasn't a <u>short</u> trip.
13. You did <u>what</u>?
14. The <u>slow</u> will lose the race.
15. You'd better not <u>short</u> me on my order.

If you weren't always certain of the answer, it may be because nouns and verbs are defined in terms of meaning, while pronouns, adjectives, and adverbs are defined in terms of function. This is like defining apples by their colors and oranges by their taste.

Perhaps the inconsistency arises partly because, in traditional grammar, nouns have five major and some minor functions—and a noun sometimes functions as an adjective or an adverb. Furthermore, some verbs can function as a verb, an adjective, or a noun. Students—and their teachers—often find it hard to identify a noun or a verb or a pronoun in a sentence because they focus on meaning or a list of pronoun forms, not on how the word functions. Often, a word is mistakenly identified as a noun, pronoun, or verb when it is working the way an adjective or an adverb does.

Macauley (1947) used a similar fifty-item list in an extensive sequence of research studies undertaken in Scotland in the 1940s (see Weaver, 1996a, pp. 16–20, for a discussion). Parts of speech and their functions were taught extensively during the primary and secondary grades—about thirty minutes a day at both levels. Even after three years of intensive teaching at the secondary level, the results were dismal: The only classes scoring 50 percent or above on all five parts of speech were the two classes studying a foreign language! We suspect this result derives partly from the directions, which asked for labeling parts of speech instead of determining the word's function in its sentence. Then again, that is part of our point: Traditional grammar is confusing as commonly taught and tested.

By the way, the answers to the preceding activity are 1,V; 2, N; 3, J; 4, N; 5, V; 6, A; 7, J; 8, J; 9, N; 10, J; 11, N; 12, J; 13, P; 14, N; 15, V.

In the long run, it is far more useful for writers to focus on the functions of words and groups of words than to analyze sentences in order to identify the parts of speech. Thus, for example, a *nominal* is any word or group of words that functions the way a noun does, and the most important function of a nominal is the subject function. We don't use the term *verbal* in this book—not only because we don't need it, but also because its use in traditional grammar differs from its definitions in certain linguistic grammars.

The various parts of speech—eight, according to traditional grammars—are not all equally important for writers. In fact, the modifying functions add most of the detail to sentences: An *adjectival* is any word or group of words that modifies a noun or pronoun, and an *adverbial* is any word or group of words that modifies a verb or the entire subject-verb unit. (As writers, we don't need to know the other functions of adverbials.) *The primary noun and verb of a sentence are simply the scaffolding from which the clarifying details of the sentence, the modifiers, will arise.* This point is illustrated in the following excerpt from a piece by one of Harry Noden's eighth graders (Noden, 1999). We added underlining to highlight the modifying constructions that are set off by commas:

> An elderly man sits next to the creek. <u>Heart aching</u>, <u>eyes watering</u>, he thinks of his deceased wife. <u>Touching the water as if it were part of her</u>, he reflects. The water, <u>a calmer of people</u>, helps comfort the man. It sheds tears for him, <u>as it streams along by his fingers</u>. (p. 82)

Such "free modifiers"—as Francis Christensen (1965/1967) calls those set off by commas—help make writing come alive. They are useful, to varying degrees, not only in narrative/descriptive writing but also in informative/persuasive writing. They are taught only minimally in traditional grammars but emphasized in this book, in Christensen's *Notes Toward a New Rhetoric* (1967, reprinted in Christensen & Christensen, 1978), and in such currently available texts as:

- Constance Weaver's *The Grammar Plan Book* (2007).
- Harry Noden's *Image Grammar* (1999) and his *Image Grammar Activities Book* (2007).
- Don and Jenny Killgallon's *Grammar for Middle School: A Sentence-Composing Approach* (2006) and *Grammar for High School: A Sentence-Composing Approach* (2007).

Prove it to yourself

Through several activities, Ed Schuster, in *Breaking the Rules* (2003), further demonstrates how grammar definitions are inaccurate or misleading, why grammar study quickly becomes confusing, and—therefore—why traditional grammar teaching simply frustrates students, seems irrelevant to them, and wastes valuable class time. Try his activities—we think you'll be convinced.

- William Strong's *Sentence Combining: A Composing Book* (1994) and *Writer's Toolbox: A Sentence-Combining Workshop* (1996).

3. Traditional grammar books have focused mostly on analyzing language and eliminating errors

Traditional grammar books for schools have focused on analyzing language and rooting out errors, initially errors in speech and later those in writing. Even today's handbooks for college writing courses give comparatively little attention to writing effective sentences.

Historically, the grammar taught in our schools reflects centuries of commitment to teaching grammar for its own sake, not to help writers. The concept of grammar as training the mind reached its peak during the Middle Ages. Grammar became the chief subject of the trivium (grammar, rhetoric, and logic), studied intensively because it was considered the foundation of all knowledge. Indeed, grammar was viewed as the gateway to sacred as well as secular knowledge; conscious knowledge of grammar was thought to be a prerequisite for understanding theology and philosophy as well as literature. Furthermore, "grammar was thought to discipline the mind and the soul at the same time" (Huntsman, 1983, p. 59).

Because of these broad humanistic goals, grammar was taught as a separate subject, with an emphasis on grammatical categories of words, identifying the part of speech of each word in a sentence, and—for nouns, pronouns, and verbs—specifying their "case, gender, number, tense, or person in a given sentence" (Woods, 1986, p. 18, fn. 2). Such activities derive not just from the English grammars of the Middle Ages, but from the Latin grammars that preceded them and the Greek grammars that date back to the second century BC. Thus, for centuries, there never was a direct connection between teaching grammar and writing, or even the expectation that teaching grammar would improve writing.

The Industrial Revolution in the eighteenth century saw an additional claim for the benefits of grammar instruction: to enable the lower classes to move up to the middle class, in manners as well as in income. At least, this was a claimed intent for such grammars as Bishop Lowth's *A Short Introduction to English Grammar* (1762/1967), which was enormously influential. Like the English grammars from the Middle Ages, Lowth's *Short Introduction* took Latin as the prestige standard and prescribed certain "rules" for English that were based on the structure of Latin, not the structure of English. Based on Lowth's own preferences, he cited "errors" in the works of Shakespeare, Milton, Pope, and Swift, among others. Schuster (2003) writes that Lowth was "as obsessed with rooting out errors as a Puritan minister with rooting out sin" (p. 10). And indeed, one suspects that alleged errors in writing were viewed almost as sins. Influenced by Lowth's grammar text, Lindlay Murray's *English Grammar* (1795), with its accompanying exercises, was even more influential, selling an estimated 15.5 million books during the first decade of the nineteenth century (Monaghan, 1998, p. 135).

By the end of the nineteenth century, educators began to teach grammar with the unsupported expectation—or at least the claim—that grammar study would not only standardize speech and enable people to move up to the middle class but would improve writing as well. All too often, though, the most obvious effect of teaching grammar was to continue giving the middle and upper classes ammunition for looking down on those who did not change their use of language in response to the teaching of grammar.

Note, too, that while the expectation for the effects of grammar instruction changed, the traditional grammars themselves did not. From the twentieth century, consider as exemplars the famed Warriner's textbooks on grammar and composition, which began in the late 1940s and culminated in 1992 as *Warriner's High School Handbook*. A look at its contents clarifies the focus: Part 1, Grammar, includes seventy-two pages on the parts of speech, the parts of a sentence, and then phrases and clauses. Under parts of speech, five kinds of nouns are identified, along with eight kinds of pronouns, yet the functions of nouns and pronouns are not discussed until later subsections on the parts of the sentence, the phrase, and the clause. In a total of ninety-five pages, Part 2, Usage, focuses on "correct" use of certain grammatical constructions and words—mostly grammatical "don'ts" rather than what to do to write effective sentences. Part 3 devotes another seventy-five pages to mechanics. Even Part 4, Sentence Structure, focuses mostly on what not to do, though there are chapters on parallel structure and sentence combining that are more positive than negative.

While this 1992 Warriner's text is now out of print, the twenty-first century *McGraw-Hill Handbook of English Grammar and Usage* (Lester & Beason, 2005) likewise focuses on grammar and "grammatical mistakes," with hardly any attention to ways of using syntactic structures and grammatical options more effectively.

With "grammar" focusing primarily on the details of sentence elements and parts, along with what to avoid or correct as writers, is it any wonder that many students have been turned off by grammar instruction, scarcely trying to learn what's taught, much less remember and apply it in their writing? Indeed, is it any wonder that the emphasis on avoiding or correcting "errors" has discouraged many students—and their teachers—from writing, because it has made them afraid to write and thereby possibly be "wrong"? We haven't yet created a nation of writers, and the traditional focus on "errors" is one of the major reasons.

We haven't yet created a nation of writers, and the traditional focus on "errors" is one of the major reasons.

Traditional grammars urge writers to follow prescriptive rules that are sometimes not only archaic and arbitrary but in contrast to what many professional writers actually do.

The prescriptive "rules" often don't coincide with the reality of how language is used—quite effectively—by professional writers.

The prescriptive "rules" often don't coincide with the reality of how language is used—quite effectively—by professional writers. There is a long history to this, stemming from the previously mentioned eighteenth-century grammarians like Bishop Lowth and Lindlay Murray, who advocated aligning English with Latin rules of usage and severely limiting what was acceptable as "good English." Even today, the "language mavens"—as Steven Pinker (1994) calls extreme language purists like William Safire and John Simon—virtually equate their own concepts of language "errors" with sin.

The end results of these attempts were—and are—handbooks and guides that often try to control language into "correct" and "incorrect" usages based on what the guides say rather than what is effective or what published and prominent writers actually do. This role reminds us of the role we all have sometimes played as parents with our children—"do it because I say so." Susan and Stephen Tchudi (2001) describe this position as that of the language "enforcer" and urge teachers to avoid this role. Lynne Truss and her popular *Eat, Shoots and Leaves* (2003) is a current example of the enforcer, and many other examples are often found in community bookstores. A time-honored text in the same vein is Strunk and White's legendary *Elements of Style* (1935/2000).

Major problems with the "enforcers" are that some of the rules are counterproductive to writing effectively and that there are so many exceptions to when the rules are appropriate, given different guidelines and audiences, situations and purposes. In *Under the Grammar Hammer*, a text that unabashedly teaches "the 25 most important grammar mistakes and how to avoid them," author Douglas Cazort (1997) states that some grammar rules are "taught as holy revelation when they were [William Strunk's] personal 'likes and dislikes that were almost as whimsical as the choice of a necktie'" (Cazort, 1997, p. 113, citing E. B. White in Strunk and White, 2000, p. xvi).

So: many of these rules are not as immutable as we may at first have thought. Take, for example, the "rule" for using commas in a list or series. Taken from a standard American middle school grammar textbook, the "rule" tells us, "When there are three or more items in a series, use a comma after each one, including the item that precedes the conjunction (*Writer's Choice: Grammar and Composition, Grade 7*, 1996, p. 316). Thus a grammatically correct sentence might read: *They went to the park to eat ice cream, play on the swings, and go down the slide.*

But is this way of punctuating always "correct"? Consider this: *The Associated Press Stylebook* (what might be considered the *Elements of Style* for journalists, only with much more authority) states the following about commas before the conjunction in a simple series: "Use commas to separate items in a series, but do not put a comma before the conjunction in a simple series" (2002, p. 329). Thus a grammatically correct sentence, according to the AP, would be: *They went to the park to eat ice cream, play on the swings and go down the slide.*

So which is "correct," the *Writer's Choice* rule or the AP rule? The answer, of course, is *both*. If someone is writing journalistically, then the AP rule is correct. For writing in an academic setting in America, then the *Writer's Choice* is correct. To confuse things even more, Lynne Truss (*Eats, Shoots and Leaves*) describes the AP version as the correct usage in British English.

We hope we've muddied the situation enough that you begin to see the point—that there are multiple problems with traditional views of correctness.

. . .

There are many other examples of grammatical rules that do not hold up under scrutiny. For example, in *Grammar Alive!* (Haussamen et al., 2003), the authors identify, describe, and debunk six "superstitions" about grammar—six most commonly misunderstood and mistaught "rules" about writing (see Haussamen 2000 for a fuller treatment). They believe, as we do, that these "rules" prevail in many English classes "because English teachers learned them and feel an obligation to pass them on" (p. 71). Among these rules, these superstitions (rules E. B. White might call "whimsical"), are the "dreaded sentence-ending preposition" and the "abhorred split infinitive" (still perceived as an error because it's "easy to spot"); both have been construed as errors in the attempt to align English with Latin grammars. Also decried by language purists is the "contraction of ill repute" (*I'm, he's, doesn't, wouldn't*), avoidance of which the *Grammar Alive!* authors see as leading to "a standoffish, unrhythmical, overly formalized style" (p. 73). The traditional advice to avoid *I* (or *we*) in writing, another of the superstitions, can—if scrupulously followed—lead to stilted and awkward sentences as the writer struggles to avoid using first person. The same is true for the advice to avoid *you:* There are many times when addressing readers directly, even in informative and persuasive prose, is helpful in establishing rapport.

The other superstition that *Grammar Alive!* addresses is the "rule" not to start a sentence with *and*, *but*, or *so*. However, using such connectors to begin a sentence—especially the pithy, contrasting *but*—is so common in published writing that this fact alone should make us wonder why the "rule" persists. As the authors of *Grammar Alive!* write, "*But* if we slash our students' papers in red for writing in the style they read, we

We hope we've muddied the situation enough that you begin to see the point—that there are multiple problems with traditional views of correctness.

send them one of two absurd messages: Either all of these professionals are wrong and never learned their sentence-starting rules, or there must be some kind of graduate club of writers that students are denied access to" (p. 73). Sadly, the latter is the stance that many teachers take, but since the rule isn't a good one—it stifles effective writing—why insist that students demonstrate mastery of it before they can be allowed to break it?

Teachers with purist tendencies may have noticed that we have flaunted all of these so-called rules in this text. But if you didn't notice—well, think about Joseph Williams' article "The Phenomenology of Error" (1981), which many teachers are well into reading before they begin noticing alleged "errors," many of which reflect the breaking of mythological "rules" like these. What does that insensitivity to error tell us about how we praise effective published writers but criticize students for doing some of the same things, grammatically speaking? Are we actively trying to keep students from becoming good writers?

In general, we teachers need to look at grammar "rules" with a critical eye, teaching some and rejecting others that are not appropriate for the audiences, purposes, and situations addressed by our student writers. In fact, we can invite our students to compare some of the superstitions and "living dead" rules—the myths about effective usage—with what various published writers do, examining how these authors use grammatical devices to most effectively convey their messages to their audiences. Our students—collaboratively, we suggest—can then develop their own, more appropriate list of grammar dos and don'ts based on what is actually acceptable and effective in current published American writing.

More resources

For the curious, we suggest the "Grammar Superstitions" chapter in *Grammar Alive!*; "Usage: Rules That Do Not Rule (and a Few That Do)," in Ed Schuster's *Breaking the Rules* (2003); and "The Living Dead," in O'Connor's *Woe Is I* (2003). For solid treatment of current grammar, usage, spelling, and punctuation in American English today, we suggest Bryan Garner's *The Oxford English Dictionary of American Usage and Style* (2000). For an interesting and comprehensive overview of various attempts to "control" the English language, we recommend Pinker's chapter on the language mavens in *The Language Instinct* (1994); Joan Beal's *English in Modern Times* (2004); *The Story of English* (McCrum, Cran, & MacNeil, 2003); or MacNeil and Cran's *Do You Speak American?* (2005). The latter two books accompany PBS series by those names.

Why not teach grammar traditionally? A reprise

Encouraged to think we are teaching well if we teach the grammar book, we English teachers have historically treated grammar as a separate course of study, typically isolating it from writing. Yes, students were and sometimes still are required to "do grammar": to complete exercises in texts and worksheets, most of which require analyzing and labeling words and parts of sentences, with additional practice in correcting one kind of "error" at a time in sets of sentences. And yes, traditionally the students have then been given tests over the material practiced.

But with such an approach, with grammar study divorced from actual writing, is it any wonder that many students, probably most, have been bored by grammar study? Any wonder that they view grammar as irrelevant to their lives? Any wonder that even those students who *can* learn to analyze and label grammatical elements often see no reason to do so and don't long remember what they have learned? Or any wonder that many of us who *did* learn and *do* apply some aspects of grammar to our own writing still wish our teachers had spent more time guiding us in the writing process instead of subjecting us to the same repetitive grammar exercises year after year?

Let's be perfectly clear: If students write well, it is mostly due to wide reading, the rich use of language in the home and classroom, and the continued efforts of teachers to guide their students through the writing process. *Good writing is not, however, produced by mere grammar study, as research has shown again and again.* Historically, most students have not learned grammar well, fewer have remembered much after being tested on it, and fewer still have independently applied the relevant aspects of grammar study to their own writing.

It's time for a change.

What Works in Teaching Grammar to Enrich and Enhance Writing

Teaching grammar in conjunction with writing is a pedagogy of possibility that is *positive*, *productive*, and *practical*. Our approach—and increasingly that of other teachers of writing—involves teaching selected aspects of grammar, primarily within the context of the writing process, and giving students explicit guidance to help them make their writing:

- More complex and more effective syntactically (grammatically)
- More detailed and interesting
- More clearly structured and organized (appropriate connectors and transitions, effective cohesive devices)
- More effective stylistically (appropriate voice for purpose and audience)
- More effective rhetorically (sentences constructed and varied for particular effects)
- When appropriate, more conventional according to mainstream standards of "correctness"

Indeed, grammar is connected, in one way or another, to all the "6 traits" of writing commonly taught (Spandel, 2005; Culham, 2003).

Positive, *productive*, and *practical* grammar instruction treats grammar as a way to add detail, enhance style, and produce rhetorical effects—all of which are noticeably lacking in traditional grammar instruction. Traditional grammar instruction is a shotgun, one-time-only approach to mastering isolated skills. In contrast, our three Ps approach directs instructional attention to a few selected constructions and techniques sustained

> **Grammar instruction as positive, productive, and practical**
>
> Teaching grammar to enrich and enhance writing is teaching grammar as possibility. We see it as *positive*, offering options rather than focusing on errors; as *productive*, especially in the sense that it produces effective sentences and paragraphs that flow; and as eminently *practical*.

Instruction in grammar itself is minimal; application of grammar to writing is maximal.

over time. Instruction in grammar itself is minimal; application of grammar to writing is maximal.

Twelve principles supporting our approach

Twelve principles, based on research and observation, form the theoretical backbone of our three Ps approach.

1. Teaching grammar divorced from writing doesn't strengthen writing and therefore wastes time

Teaching grammar as a separate subject divorced from writing wastes valuable instructional time because few students transfer their grammar study to writing without teacher guidance.

Every twenty years or so, a new summary of research on the teaching of grammar indicates yet again that teaching grammar as a subject separate from writing does little to improve students' writing. The most recent and most extensive summary is what's known as the York study (Andrews et al., 2004b). Of course, new summaries usually build on previous ones, they tend to omit most research that hasn't been published in prominent journals, and they seldom include the important descriptive studies done by teachers, on the grounds that these haven't involved rigorous experimental procedures or statistical analysis. Research studies clearly have shortcomings, both practically and philosophically (MacLure, 2005). Nevertheless, the results accord with many teachers' experience: They've found that when grammar has been taught separately from writing, few students make the connection themselves.

Rei Noguchi (1991) has argued that less grammar study leaves more time for other, more important topics in the English language curriculum, including more time "to teach and engage students in the writing process, and, of course, more time for actual writing. In the end, less is more" (p. 121). We agree completely.

2. Few grammatical terms are actually needed to discuss writing

Most of the grammatical terms used in traditional grammar books are not really needed to explain grammatical options and conventions.

Detailed categorizing and subcategorizing of words is not necessary for writers to use the language effectively and appropriately. As writers, do we really need to know that *I* is in the subjective case, *me* in the objective case? Better to teach the conventional forms as the need arises, using examples and practical strategies rather than terms and rules. When a student produces a sentence like "Jimmy and me went to the mall," teachers often clarify the conventional form by saying, "Try the sentence without *Jimmy*. Would you say, 'Me went to the mall'? Well, then, don't use 'Jimmy and me,' either; say, 'Jimmy and I.'" Patterns are usually much easier to grasp than terms and rules, and examples often clarify better than detailed explanations. Though admittedly some students will appreciate a deeper explanation, many will simply turn a deaf ear to the details of pronoun cases, noun subcategories, and the vagaries of different "kinds" of verbs.

In case you're thinking that studying the number, case, and gender of English pronouns helps students learn another language (as it did for us), research suggests that the mere *teaching* of English grammar does *not* help most students in learning another language—partly because they see no need for the information about English at the time it's presented. Informally, when Connie has asked audiences of teachers whether learning English grammar helped them learn the grammar of another language, overwhelmingly the answer has been no. Those of us who *did* find our study of English grammar helpful in learning another language seem to be the exception—perhaps because few others learned or retained what they were taught about English. In fact, many teachers say it was studying the grammar of another language that clarified the structure of English for them.

Patterns are usually much easier to grasp than terms and rules, and examples often clarify better than detailed explanations.

3. Sophisticated grammar is fostered in literacy-rich and language-rich environments

The acquisition and development of students' grammatical repertoire— the emergence of more sophisticated grammar—is fostered in literacy-rich and language-rich environments, including classrooms.

Of course, not all students absorb grammatical options—constructions for enriching their writing—equally well, and not all constructions are equally well absorbed, nor need they be. This is why we advocate helping students learn to use the most productive grammatical options in their writing. Nevertheless, it is important for teachers to realize that another way they can "teach" the use of a wider range of constructions is by brainstorming possible topics and ideas and selecting and discussing the effective grammatical options in well-written literature. Art is another powerful stimulator for writing (e.g., Noden, 1999, 2007).

With such teaching, the use of grammatical terminology is not necessary! Two examples should suffice.

In her first year of teaching, Sarah Woltjer (1998, as recounted in Weaver et al., 2001, pp. 20–21) had taught her seventh graders grammar from a grammar book and exhorted students to use adjectives and adverbs in order to add interesting detail to their writing—all with little effect. In her second year, while she was taking Connie's grammar-in-writing course, Sarah experimented with two "treatments." First, she asked students to write about fall (autumn is a beautiful season in Michigan) and to use adjectives and adverbs. The results were dull and lifeless. Nearly two months later, she took another approach. One Monday, students brought in one or two leaves that had fallen to the ground. On Wednesday, Sarah told them they would be writing a "five senses" poem about fall. First, they brainstormed for how fall looks, sounds, smells, tastes, and feels, using and playing with the leaves (they took turns placing their leaves on the hot air register and watching the leaves blow upward). Then they moved around the room sharing a favorite Thanksgiving memory with classmates. Finally they wrote poems about fall. Throughout, Sarah had said nothing about grammar. The result? Students didn't use a lot of adjectives and adverbs, yet some students used more descriptive verbs and nouns than before, and a few students used adjectival -*ing* words and phrases—groups of words—to describe certain things in their poems. Here is an example:

Amy's Poem

I can smell the apple pie baking in the oven.
I can smell the burning leaves in the neighbor's yards.
I hear the leaves crackling under my feet as I trudge through the yard.
I hear children yelling as they jump in a pile of leaves.
I see blended colors on the leaves like someone painted them.
I touch the leaves and I feel the veins.
I touch the leaves and sometimes they break in my hands.
I taste the turkey as the grease runs down my throat.
I taste the pumpkin pie and now I know it is fall!

Amy's earlier fall poem was much shorter and did not have any -*ing* participial phrases. Using the leaves to brainstorm about fall and talking about a memory of fall simply allowed Amy's grammatical knowledge to surface in her writing.

A related but different example of what Connie calls "grammar emerging" comes from the classroom of Judy Davis, a fifth-grade teacher at the Manhattan New School. Connie tells about visiting Judy's class (taken almost verbatim from Weaver et al., 2001, pp. 21–22):

As I walked past her classroom, I was struck by the beauty of the student paintings hung high on the corridor wall. Curious about the notebook resting on a table beneath the pictures, I opened it and found smaller, photocopied versions of the same paintings, each accompanied by a creative piece of writing and an expository piece describing how the creative piece was written.

It was not only the paintings that seemed exceptional, it was the writings—and yes, I'll admit it—the use of sophisticated grammatical constructions conveying concrete detail. Alexandra, for example, used some especially effective features in the poem she wrote to accompany her painting [see Figure 3–1]. With apologies to the author, I have labeled and marked these phrases [the grammatical terms will be explained in Chapter 5]:

FIGURE 3–1. Alexandra's painting

Alone

In my mind
people walk by
participial → pretending
phrase   not to see me.
             I slowly walk past them
participial phrase → hiding behind trees,
absolute → my head
phrase   pointed to the ground.
             The sun folds
             its rays into
             the sunset.
             My mind
             reads tangled thoughts   ← three parallel phrases,
three parallel items,   about *the previous day,*   each headed by
each an object of → *the books I've read,*   "thoughts"
"about"   and *home.*
             Thoughts that separate me
             from other people
             that drift through my sleep.
             Thoughts that make me
             alone.

While this was my favorite piece, several other students' creative writings—many of them poems—also showed exceptionally effective details and structure, most commonly using the -*ing* phrases that are called present participial phrases.

When I asked Judy whether she had explicitly taught such grammatical constructions, she said no. In fact, she admitted she didn't know the names of the grammatical constructions herself; she had simply immersed her students in reading and discussing good literature, including poetry. Constructions like those Alexandra used had simply "emerged" in their writing, as a result of their engagement with art and especially literature.

These and many other examples show that (1) students have a grammatical repertoire that often exceeds what they demonstrate when they haven't explored their topics; (2) brainstorming and orally rehearsing possible topics are important means of generating not only ideas but effective grammar; and (3) students' use of effective grammatical options to convey details can be especially enhanced by reading and discussing the craft of well-written literature. None of these has to involve the explicit teaching of grammar or the use of grammatical terms!

Grammar emerging

- Students' grammatical repertoire is not fully evident when they have no opportunity to explore their topics before writing.
- Brainstorming topics, reading and discussing literature, talking about topics, creating artwork, and representing concepts through other visual means (such as clusters, webs, and charts) tend to generate not only more ideas but also a wider range of grammatical structures.
- Grammar emerges in writing as well as in speaking within literature-rich and language-rich classrooms—without the conscious study of grammar, much less the use of grammatical terms.

4. Grammar instruction for writing should build on students' developmental readiness

Grammar instruction should not be limited to the scope and sequence found in a textbook series, but should build on students' developmental readiness.

If a child is not old enough to ride a bicycle, it would be foolish—not to mention impossible—to try to teach the child to drive a car. Likewise, no one would advocate teaching a toddler to run before he or she can walk. We need to address children's grammatical needs within their "zone of proximal development," as psychologist Lev Vygotsky (1962/1986) called it. That means we need to draw on what is known about both general and individual developmental patterns in writing to help writers take the next steps in their use of grammar. What might this mean? Well, we know a kindergartner whose teacher taught him to use the colon to introduce lists, as well as some high schoolers who can't consistently put periods in appropriate places, no matter how hard they try.

Building on students' current stage of language use and development is especially important because some students clearly have difficulties with written language and its conventions—difficulties severe enough, in some cases, for them to be said to have language-learning disabilities. These students often have not only a more limited repertoire of complex sentence structures (Scott, 1999), but also more difficulty avoiding grammatical errors (Wong, 2000), and may benefit from a writing lab approach like that described by Nelson, Bahr, and Van Meter (2004).

Understanding developmental readiness is also important because, in the current educational/political climate, the U.S. government is developing policies in many aspects of literacy education that insist on treating students in a more standardized way. This is not productive relative to grammar (or anything!), especially if we then hold the same expectations

We need to draw on what is known about both general and individual developmental patterns in writing to help writers take the next steps in their use of grammar.

for everyone. On the other hand, when traditional instruction in grammar is parceled out over several years in a language arts or English program, many constructions and punctuation marks are not dealt with until long after they are learned naturally or could have been taught productively. Readiness and appropriate teaching are the keys.

The chapter on editing skills in *The Grammar Plan Book* (Weaver, 2007) and the Grammar Planner that constitutes the second part of that book encourage and enable teachers to make wise decisions about what editing skills to teach and when. See also Chapters 9 and 12 in this book.

5. Grammar options are best expanded through reading and in conjunction with writing

Grammar to *enrich* student writing—options for adding detail, structure, voice/style, and fluency—is partly learned through extensive, authentic reading and is most readily taught and learned in conjunction with authentic writing.

First, we want to make it clear that we believe students are severely and unjustifiably shortchanged if they are limited to reading texts wherein they can "correctly" pronounce all the words (see Weaver, 2003, and Krashen, 2004) and if they are not provided with language-rich books on tape that have beautiful and complex language. Similarly, we believe that students are equally shortchanged if, as writers, they are taught only the conventions of language that are sometimes considered—not always accurately—to lie within the realm of grammar: conventions of grammar, usage, punctuation, and other aspects of mechanics.

Students who are weak in reading and writing are all too often stunted in their language use by "basics first" teaching. Such teaching holds students back. Years ago, Connie taught a demonstration lesson in a "basic" college writing class in which the students only completed grammar exercises from a "programmed" text that provided answers in the back. Connie, however, guided the class in writing an "I am" participle poem (Weaver, 2007, Chapter 4) and then had the students write individual poems, after which they shared some aloud. "I didn't know they could write like that!" the teacher exclaimed afterward. Precisely our point.

Grammar and authentic reading

Authentic reading is reading whole novels, short stories, plays, essays, and such—not reading mere paragraphs in texts designed for reading instruction.

Authentic, wide reading can promote writers' use of a variety of grammatical constructions. This claim is supported by research on students' learning major grammatical constructions through reading (Krashen, 2004). The effects are especially clear in studies involving second language learning (Elley and Mangubhai, 1983; Elley, 1991). As these researchers report, students in a "book-flood" program (in which students were "flooded" with lots of books to read but no reading instruction) showed greater mastery of certain grammatical constructions than others who had studied those constructions directly and practiced them rotely, with extensive imitation and repetition.

Students who report reading more tend to be better writers (Applebee et al., 1990, and several other references cited in Krashen, 2004). The differences are most noticeable in writing style. Both of us have had students who were effective writers though they had never had any instruction in grammar. They have claimed, and we agree, that their effective use of grammatical constructions derived from their wide reading. On the other hand, we, our students, and researcher Stephen Krashen (2004, pp. 129–130) all note that even voracious readers do not necessarily learn concepts like subject-verb agreement or conventional punctuation through reading, though they do learn ways to put words together effectively.

Grammar and authentic writing

Grammar for writing is best taught in conjunction with authentic writing: that is, writing for an audience that is broader than just the teacher or even the teacher and peers, one that might include other adults in the school and the broader community. Such writing may include narration and description, even short vignettes, but also poetry and plays; letters to the principal or the editor of a newspaper; editorials, columns, or short articles in a school or community newspaper; business letters; and the like.

Most of our evidence that grammar is best taught with authentic writing is offered under principle 6, which deals with the teaching of conventions in writing. Here we'd like to call attention to research on children's oral and written language development. According to landmark studies from the 1970s, children's command of grammatical constructions in writing does not catch up with their oral language until about the seventh grade (O'Donnell et al., 1967) or even later (Loban, 1976). We suspect that this lag in development has a lot to do with our observation that not much is typically done in the earlier grades to promote children's use of grammatical options in writing. But having seen sophisticated language use among young writers who are wide readers (see also our principle 3, dealing with "grammar emerging") and/or who have had assistance in using a wider range of grammatical resources, we are confident that for many students this gap between spoken and written language can be narrowed much sooner. We are confident that teachers can guide writers to employ grammatical constructions that they would otherwise seldom if ever use.

A few words about sentence combining. One time-honored method of getting students to write more sophisticated sentences with a greater variety of grammatical options—at least temporarily—is the technique called "sentence combining." There is substantial research evidence (recently analyzed and summarized by Andrews et al., 2004a) that sentence combining, as an instructional technique, produces at least temporary benefits in richer sentences—which is all that any technique for teaching grammar for writing does, unless the teacher follows up by repeatedly guiding students to apply what they have learned. Basically, sentence combining involves the combining of two or more sentences into a single more sophisticated and more effective sentence. For example:

> Harry lived under the stairs. Harry's uncle forced him to live there.

might be combined into

> Harry's uncle forced him to live under the stairs.

While sentence-combining may be initially taught through preset, published activities, its use during revision leads us to consider this technique as, potentially, an aspect of teaching grammar in the context of writing.

Recommended texts on sentence combining

- Don and Jenny Killgallon's *Grammar for Middle School: A Sentence-Composing Approach* (2006) and *Grammar for High School: A Sentence-Composing Approach* (2007).
- William Strong's *Sentence Combining: A Composing Book* (1994) and *A Writer's Toolbox: A Sentence-Combining Workshop* (1996).

However, reading richly written texts may be at least as beneficial for many writers. Both published and unpublished research have demonstrated, in fact, that in classrooms where kids read literature, discuss it, and write a lot (with feedback), the students develop new grammatical resources, as illustrated under principle 3. See also Hartwell and LoPresti (1985).

When teachers give students specific help in imitating model sentences and generating their own sentences more freely, we are convinced that the results will be more lasting than in sentence-combining programs, and more substantial than in classrooms where students read, discuss, and write a lot, but have no specific help in playing with grammatical options.

One of our favorite freely generated examples comes from an eighth grader's piece featured in Harry Noden's *Image Grammar* (1999), a must-have resource for teachers of writing in middle school and beyond. In this student's scary description of a spider invasion, Noden highlighted instances of the grammatical constructions he had explicitly taught:

> Then it crawled in. A spider, *a repulsive, hairy creature, no bigger than a tarantula,* crawled into the room. It crawled across the floor up onto his nightstand and stopped, as if it were staring at him. He reached for a nearby copy of *Sports Illustrated*, rolled it up, and swatted the spider with all his might.
>
> He looked over only to see a hideous mass of eyes and legs. He had killed it. Just then, another one crawled in, *following the same path as the first.* He killed that one too. Then another one came, and another and another. There were hundreds of them! *Hands trembling, sweat dripping from his face,* he flung the magazine left and right, *trying to kill the spiders,* but there were too many. He dropped the magazine.
>
> Helpless now, his eyes darted around the room. He could no longer see the individual spiders. He could just see a thick, black blanket of movement. He started squirming as he felt their fang-like teeth sink into his pale flesh like millions of tiny needles *piercing his body.* (p. 12)

Even a number of our college students say that this description is better than things they write—or could have written before they, too, received similar instruction.

6. Grammar conventions taught in isolation seldom transfer to writing

There is minimal value in teaching the conventional prescriptions for grammar, usage, punctuation, and other aspects of mechanics in complete isolation from writing.

This point is especially important because we'll admit we do see a need to help students learn to take multiple-choice tests on items of conventional usage: in grammar and diction, punctuation and spelling, and even style. The ACT and SATs demand such skill, as do the College Board exams, and now, in at least a brief section, many of our state assessments of writing. *Although it is not grammar itself—the ability to analyze sentences and label parts of speech or phrases or clauses—that's usually being tested*, we and our students are increasingly faced with multiple-choice tests of skill in revising and editing isolated sentences and paragraphs.

Even so, we do not believe that teaching editing skills in isolation is the best way to get students to employ such skills in their writing. There is both negative evidence, showing the ineffectiveness of such isolated teaching, and positive evidence, showing the greater effectiveness of teaching students to employ such skills while drafting, revising, and especially while editing their writing. As Lucy Calkins noted in *The Art of Teaching Writing* (1986, pp. 94–96), what's first learned during revision and editing may later be applied while drafting. In other words, the skills are recursive and become automatic.

First, let's consider a study conducted by Findlay McQuade (1980), a secondary teacher who taught an elective editing skills course that was considered successful by students, parents, and other teachers. While McQuade was not able to exercise replicable experimental controls over the students, the teachers, or all of the teaching—controls that, if possible, would have made the study experimentally rigorous—the results are striking.

In his course, McQuade first taught parts of speech and basic sentence structure, then dealt with the "application of such principles as agreement, reference, parallel construction, tense, case [and] subordination . . . to the task of finding errors in sentences written expressly for that purpose." A similar approach was taken to punctuation, diction, and—if time permitted—spelling. Students completed dozens of exercises and five mastery tests; there were also interim and final exams, each testing "everything previously studied and, presumably, mastered" (p. 27).

When McQuade discovered that some students who had passed his course were being assigned to a mechanics competence course because of insufficient attention to conventions in their writing, he began to wonder whether, or to what extent, the editing skills class helped students write better, or at least "more correctly" according to the patterns of standard Edited American English. This led to an extensive set of comparisons in subsequent years, with results that were disappointing, if not devastating. Students who *hadn't* taken the editing skills class showed as much difference between the SAT and the later College Board test in composition as did the students who *had* taken it. His own students improved as much on their Cooperative English tests in the years they *hadn't* taken the editing skills class as in the year they *had* taken it. His students' essays at the end of the editing skills class contained almost as many errors as their pretest essays did. Most important, the students' posttest essays were much more

Disappointing results

In McQuade's study, not only did the isolated teaching of editing skills have little positive effect on the students' use of writing conventions and a definite negative effect on the overall quality of their writing, but such isolated skills teaching did not even have a demonstrably positive effect on later tests of editing skills.

poorly written: "awkwardly and I believe self-consciously constructed to honor correctness above all other virtues, including sense" (p. 29).

7. Marking "corrections" on students' papers does little good

Teachers do little good and often a great deal of harm by making numerous "corrections" on students' papers.

We too have been guilty of overcorrecting students' papers until they could hardly recognize, beneath our ink, the piece they had originally written. And for what? Our students typically made most of the same errors on the next paper . . . and the next . . . and the next. Instead of *fixing papers*, we now realize, teachers should be *guiding student writers*.

Edgar Schuster, in *Breaking the Rules* (2003), includes an important discussion of a phrase developed by Bill Strong—the "Jonathan Edwards syndrome." Jonathan Edwards, an early American Puritan preacher, wrote the often-anthologized sermon "Sinners in the Hand of an Angry God." Schuster explains:

> Strong's analogy is between this wrathful Calvinistic god and the typical English composition teacher. As we read and react to writing, *we* are like that wrathful god, we cannot keep our flaming pens off the papers of our sinning congregation. (p. 92)

Others have called this the red-pen syndrome. In any case, it is an inappropriate role. It is also one that empowers the teacher at the expense of her or his students. The teacher has all the "right" answers, leaving students in the role of ignorant novice, relying on the "expert" to "correct" their work. This doesn't motivate students to learn to do their own editing. Rather, it makes the teacher-student relationship a dependent one: Instead of empowering students to recognize, analyze, and then work with their own grammar and stylistic issues, it leaves them at the mercy of the teacher's red pen.

We suggest, instead, that teachers take a four-pronged approach:

- Guide students to eliminate from their final drafts at least some of the inappropriate features or conventions.
- Develop—ideally, in conjunction with students—evolving editing checklists based on what has been taught or what students have more or less mastered and then require students to consult these checklists when editing their papers.
- Mark no more than one or two major *patterns* of grammar, usage, or mechanics (including punctuation and spelling) for the

Instead of fixing papers, teachers should be guiding student writers.

student to work on, follow up with additional teaching, and add these patterns to a checklist for the individual student.

- Provide additional help, when needed, if a particular piece of writing is to "go public."

Depending on the climate within the school and community, teachers may very occasionally wield the famed editor's blue pencil instead of the dreaded teacher's red pen. That is, there may be circumstances under which it is appropriate for the teacher to do some final editing on the student's final draft before the piece goes public. But this practice should always be approved by the student (indeed, done with the student if possible) and should not become a substitute for teaching editing skills to the student.

8. Grammar conventions are applied most readily when taught in conjunction with editing

Conventions to enhance writing can be taught more efficiently and learned more effectively during and in conjunction with the editing process than in completely isolated lessons on grammar, usage, punctuation, and other mechanics.

McQuade's investigations failed to support the teaching of editing skills in isolation, and the York survey of the research likewise did not find support for this practice. On the other hand, two teacher studies are among the evidence that teaching skills in the context of writing can have greater effect.

The first of these studies was undertaken by teacher-researcher Lucy Calkins (1980). While producing important numerical comparisons, the study is most valuable for its rich qualitative information. In one third-grade classroom, the teacher taught simple sentences, periods, and other aspects of mechanics directly, through pretests, exercise sheets, and posttests. Though they practiced punctuation extensively, her students rarely wrote. In a second third-grade classroom, students never studied punctuation formally, but instead wrote for an hour a day, three days a week, learning punctuation as needed to make their meaning clear and learning it from the teacher, their peers, and the books they were reading.

At the end of the year, Calkins interviewed all the children in each class to determine what they knew about punctuation. The children who had studied punctuation day after day could explain, on average, only 3.85 marks of punctuation, typically by reciting the rules they had learned for the period, question mark, and exclamation mark. The students who wrote instead of studying punctuation in isolation could explain, on average, 8.66 marks of punctuation. More than half of these students explained the period, question mark, exclamation mark, apostrophe, dash,

Third graders explain punctuation

Students who learned punctuation through teacher guidance while writing had this to say (Calkins, 1980):

Alan: "If you want your story to make sense, you can't write without punctuation. . . . Punctuation tells people things—like if the sentence is asking, or if someone is talking, or if you should yell it out." (p. 569)

Chip: "[Punctuation] lets you know where the sentence ends, so otherwise one minute you'd be sledding down the hill and the next minute you're inside the house, without even stopping." (p. 569)

Andrea: "I keep putting in new kinds of punctuation because I need them. Like sound effects—it takes weird punctuation to put *thud-thud* or *splat!* onto my paper." (p. 571)

Calkins's summary: "When children need punctuation in order to be seen and heard, they become vacuum cleaners, sucking up odd bits from books, their classmates' papers, billboards, and magazines. They find punctuation everywhere, and make it their own." (pp. 572–573)

quotation marks, and commas, along with the paragraph sign and caret editing symbols. Nearly half could explain the colon, parentheses, and the asterisk. These children tended to explain the marks of punctuation not by reciting memorized rules, but by explaining or demonstrating how the marks were used in their own writing.

The second teacher study is experimental (a study the York researchers, in personal correspondence, say they accidentally overlooked). Whereas Calkins' study was primarily qualitative and did not have pre-set experimental and control groups, a study by DiStefano and Killion (1984) was constructed to test the hypothesis that students would apply writing conventions better if the conventions were taught in conjunction with their writing rather than in isolation. The study was undertaken by a group of teachers in Colorado, in grades four through six. Six elementary schools participated in the study. Three schools (the experimental group) were randomly chosen to teach the skills during the writing process; the remaining three schools (the control group) taught the skills in isolation. The skills to be tested were capitalization, punctuation, spelling, sentence structure, format, usage, and organization. These conventions, as used in actual pieces of writing on an assigned topic in September and again in May, were the criteria for determining to what degree students' writing had improved.

The key finding: "The control group did not do better than the experimental group on any criterion at any of the three grade levels" (p. 207). Differences in sentence structure favored the experimental group at the two higher grade levels, grades five and six; this criterion involved using a variety of sentence types, with no fragments or run-ons. Usage and spelling also favored the experimental group at all three grade levels, and the experimental group did significantly better on organization. DiStefano and Killion conclude:

> Overall, the process model was a huge success when the results of those schools participating in the [experimental writing process] program are compared with the results of the control group. This study also demonstrates that traditional skills can be measured by looking closely at actual writing. (p. 207)

We agree. We also emphasize that this study came about when teachers stood up for what they believed. Faced with district writing skills objectives and "objective" tests of these skills, teachers who believed in teaching skills in context challenged the district's intent to teach and test writing skills in isolation, and the district agreed to the study.

Knowledgeable and committed teachers *can* make a difference.

9. Instruction in conventional editing skills is important for all students but must honor their home language or dialect

It is important to teach all students relevant skills for editing their writing according to the conventions widely accepted in mainstream society, while still honoring each student's home language or dialect.

It is absolutely crucial for teachers to demonstrate genuine respect for each student's home language or dialect. This is the morally right thing to do, it is educationally productive, and *not* to do so can be educationally disastrous, as Herbert Kohl demonstrates in *I Won't Learn from You!* (1991). When teachers demonstrate a lack of respect for students' language usage, calling it "nonstandard," "incorrect," or even "wrong," students often reject not only the teacher but what the teacher is trying to get them to learn (Larson, 1996). Our aim in this case is especially difficult: to help such students learn to replace certain features of their written language with more widely acceptable forms—the "language of wider communication" (Conference on College Composition and Communication, 1988). Chapter 14, by Rebecca Wheeler, posits a respectful and successful approach for teaching students to "code-switch" to these mainstream forms.

In a 1980 study, Maxine Hairston found that certain features of writing generated especially negative reactions from businesspeople who inter-

From "Correcting" Students' Language to Exploring Choices

Mark Larson (1996), an English teacher who was assigned to a "Hurdles" English class when he was a high school student, confesses that he still feels inadequate in speaking and writing because of the Hurdles label and the correctionist approach. He writes: "In Hurdles, I completed a blizzard of worksheets and memorized a lot of rules, most of which are now lost to time, but I did not learn much about *language*. I learned even less about writing, except that it is as easy as crossing a mine field" (p. 91). Now, in his role as an English teacher, Larson recommends exploring language options instead of dictating one-size-fits-all "standards":

> Teach students to observe language and provide them with a vocabulary for openly discussing its many colorful, richly textured variations. Then help them recognize the place standard English, among other language variations, holds in the array of devices we humans find to "give voice accurately and fully to ourselves and our sense of the world" (Hoffman, 1989). (p. 93)

viewed and hired job applicants. Those features considered the most serious and "status marking" were:

1. Nonstandard verb forms in past or past participle: *brung* instead of *brought*; *had went* instead of *had gone.*
2. Lack of subject-verb agreement: *we was* instead of *we were*; *Jones don't think it's acceptable* instead of *Jones doesn't think it's acceptable.*
3. Double negatives: *There has never been no one here. State employees can't hardly expect a raise.*
4. Objective pronoun as subject: *Him and Richard were the last ones hired.*

Each of these features is associated with a language variety—a dialect—that is not considered mainstream within its region, particularly within the cities of the region. Despite the biases and limitations of the 1980 study (discussed in Weaver, 1996, pp. 108, 110), there is no reason to suppose that these features of language—especially when produced in writing—are any less indicative today of social class, except when they have clearly been chosen by acknowledged professionals to reflect their ethnic identity. Mastering the conventional forms of "mainstream" English will not guarantee a job, much less a high-paying job, but it is still true that the use of what Hairston called status marking forms will be used as an excuse, if not a genuine reason, to eliminate candidates from the job applicant pool.

In an article about making grammar relevant to students who speak a nonmainstream dialect, Roda Byler Yoder (1996) asks rhetorically, "Do I need to teach grammar to these inner-city students in Jackson, Mississippi? Absolutely. . . . I teach my students grammar because these young minds have big plans. They are going somewhere with their lives, and they know they need Standard American English (SAE) to get there" (p. 82). We agree that students, of whatever dialect or native language background, deserve the opportunity to be taught not only the mainstream features that are acceptable in the world of business and government, but the other forms that students of all language varieties most need to employ in the final, edited versions of their public writing.

There are several caveats, though—warnings or disclaimers we would like to make about teaching mainstream features of Edited American English (EAE):

- There is no single "Standard American English," despite what Yoder says. Wolfram and Schilling-Estes (2005) make this clear when they discuss a continuum of standardness, define a "standard" dialect as one free of structures that can be identified as nonstandard, and mention the more neutral term "mainstream" dialects instead of "standard" (pp. 8–12). Lippi-Green devotes an entire chapter of her provocative *English with an Accent* (1997) to "the standard language myth," ultimately settling for the term "mainstream US English" (MUSE), even though that too differs among educated users from different regions and ethnic backgrounds. The PBS program, book, and interactive DVD titled *Do You Speak American?* (MacNeil and Cran, 2005) make abundantly clear that our spoken language varies considerably and that even the language of well-educated Americans is not uniform in grammar, much less in pronunciation or vocabulary.

- Edited American English comes closer to being uniform, but it still is not entirely so. Certain verb forms acceptable in one part of the country, for example, are not the mainstream form in another part (for instance, the past tense of *dive* has two mainstream forms, *dove* and *dived*). Do you explain that something is *two feet long* or *two foot long*? Do you go *toward the building* or *towards the building*? Again, educated usage varies, and at one time differed regionally, though our current mobility and ubiquitous media have blurred these regional distinctions. Although editors may have been trained to replace one form with

What features of EAE are *truly* mainstream?

We advocate eliminating the term *error* to describe features not considered mainstream, noting that

> teachers' ideas about error definition and classification have always been absolute products of their times and cultures. . . . Teachers have always marked different phenomena as errors, called them different things, given them different weights. Error-pattern study is essentially the examination of an ever-shifting pattern of skills judged by an ever-shifting pattern of prejudices. (Connors & Lunsford, 1988, p. 399)

We think it is time—indeed, well past time—for teachers to be more realistic about what the conventions of Edited American English really are.

another, even they are not consistent—as Connie has found with different editors' handling of *toward* and *towards*, for instance.

- The *alleged* features of Edited American English are not necessarily the features found in *actual* EAE. In 1981, Joseph Williams published a fascinating article, "The Phenomenology of Error," in which he showed that writers of grammar handbooks—even the venerable Strunk and White, whose 1935 *Elements of Style* is in its fourth edition—made some of the same grammatical "errors" that they counseled against. Williams cites White's use of "faulty" parallelism and an inappropriate choice between *that* and *which* (p. 156). As Louis Menand pointed out humorously in *The New Yorker* (2004), even Lynne Truss' popular *Eats, Shoots and Leaves* (2003) violates some of the very rules she insists on. After purchasing a *Webster's Guide to English Usage* published by Barnes & Noble (2004), Connie read the front and back flap, finding what most traditional grammarians would consider an "error" in pronoun agreement, along with the omission of both a comma and a hyphen in situations traditional grammar books insist they be used. When even the cover of a book on usage violates the old-style rules, we must surely question what is *really* mainstream in Edited American English and what isn't. Clearly, the times, they are a-changin'.
- We teachers must keep in mind that nonmainstream varieties of English meet the needs of their users and are appropriate in many circumstances. Such language varieties—called "vernaculars" by Wolfram and Schilling-Estes (2005)—are maintained across the generations not only by the language passed on from

parent to child, but—in some cases much more important—by peer groups that convey to younger peers the language variety that is required in the schoolyards and on the street. Connie remembers a colleague from Africa who, upon returning to her native country for a visit, was told by a friend not to use her educated English when going into a certain area, or she might not leave with her head attached to her shoulders! The importance of using nonmainstream features in certain situations is underscored by an episode of the sitcom *Fresh Prince of Bel-Air*, built around contrasting language and cultural differences in a household featuring a young man, Carlton, who speaks mainstream English, and his cousin Will, who speaks primarily African American Vernacular English (AAVE). In one episode of this show, Carlton finds himself among gang members in an urban setting of Los Angeles. Will discovers what he assumes must be Carlton's predicament, and fearing for Carlton's safety, rushes to his rescue—only to find that Carlton has successfully code-shifted away from mainstream English, the "correct" grammar for his school, home, and cultural setting, into AAVE, the "correct" grammar for his current context. Clearly the grammar of mainstream English is not appropriate for all occasions. What's not so clear is that even highly educated individuals may use features of their ethnic dialect—especially when among persons of their own ethnic group. Denise Troutman explains such usage of AAVE among educated African Americans (1998). Geneva Smitherman is among the scholars who have used such features in certain essays, such as "English Teacher, Why You Be Doin' the Thangs You Don't Do?" (1972, reprinted in Smitherman, 1999). Not only are ethnic and social dialects here to stay, they are the most appropriate in certain circumstances.

- Nevertheless, we do believe students should have sympathetic guidance in learning to edit their public writing—letters to the editor, essays, and such—and that teachers should teach students not only to replace nonmainstream forms with mainstream ones, but to edit for the conventions of English that are still observed in most published informative or persuasive writing. The key is to teach *only* these conventions, not those that should have been mothballed long ago because they are seldom observed. We reiterate that "correctness" in grammar varies according to audience, context, and purpose. As a wise teacher once told Jonathan, "Remember, there is no such thing as *correct* grammar, just as there is no such thing as *good* writing. There is only appropriate grammar and effective writing, for

We reiterate that "correctness" in grammar varies according to audience, context, and purpose.

3: What Works in Teaching Grammar to Enrich and Enhance Writing

different audiences and purposes." While we accept and appreciate standards of Edited American English, we also believe that grammar taught in limited shades of right and wrong does a disservice to student writers. As Janet Alsup and Jonathan Bush state in *But Will It Work with REAL Students?* (2003), "The reality of language is that it changes and evolves over time and meets the needs of a [particular] rhetorical situation" (p. 84). Grammar changes over time, and appropriate grammar varies according to situation. We teachers need to be up to date on what really works, when and where, how and why.

10. Progress may involve new kinds of errors as students try to apply new writing skills

When students experiment with new grammatical options or try out new skills in their writing, their efforts often result in new kinds of errors that are signs of progress.

Making new kinds of errors is inevitably part of the learning process. When children are learning to ride a bicycle, they may occasionally crash into something or fall off: Their hypothesis about how to stop or how to keep the bike upright is not yet accurate, or they are simply trying to do too many new things at one time. When we adults get a new operating system for our computer, we may make new kinds of errors when we try to master new commands and procedures. At any age, we typically cannot master something—anything—all at once; we make new errors that we—of course!—didn't make when we weren't trying to do whatever it is we are now attempting.

Making new kinds of errors is inevitably part of the learning process.

So it is with writing. We could illustrate this point generously from our own students' writing, as could any of you who already teach. That being the case, we have chosen instead to illustrate the point with examples that may give you a chuckle—the point being that we should respond positively, as well, to new kinds of errors that stem from growth in using, or attempting to use, grammatical options and editing skills. The examples are taken from Connie's *Teaching Grammar in Context* (1996), pages 61 and 71.

Figure 3–2 includes six drawings that were collected in the sequence they are presented, left to right, top to bottom. In the first drawing we notice that the figure has arms, legs, and hair, but no body. The second figure shows progress, with fingers added to the hands and feet added to the legs. The third figure has "lost" its arms, while gaining another body feature. The fourth figure has arms, hands, legs, feet, shoelaces, and a body. However, it has "lost" the hair. The fifth figure includes two-dimensional legs and bodies that may be differentiated for male (dad and son) and female (mother, in the middle); however, it too shows no hair on the

FIGURE 3–2. Developmental sequence in John's drawings

people. The sixth figure is much more sophisticated, with a neck, two-dimensional arms and legs, a beard, a crown, and, yes, hair.

The first grader who wrote the piece in Figure 3–3 had been taught apostrophes, apparently, or he absorbed their use from reading. However, the child overgeneralized by putting an apostrophe in "heads" (*had's*), which is a simple plural and not a possessive. Occasionally we have found that same kind of error even in college seniors' writing after we've taught a lesson on using the apostrophe with possessives. This suggests that, for complete understanding, we must not only teach examples of a concept but also contrast them with potentially confusing nonexamples (Harris & Rowan, 1989). It also suggests our general point here: that at first, new learning is often incomplete and therefore accompanied by new kinds of errors.

The first grader who wrote the piece in Figure 3–4 had just been taught the use of commas in a series, then shown examples of a "poem" with a series of items that are a specific color, and finally asked to select a color and write a poem structured the same way. Aren't the details interesting and the commas beautifully made? Who would dare downgrade that child's writing and squelch her risk-taking by insisting that these marks were apostrophes instead of commas, and therefore "wrong"?

Incidentally, the new kinds of errors that reflect grammatical progress often involve punctuation. The examples above—the drawings and the first graders' writings—prompt important observations about learning that apply to the learning of grammatical options and skills as well as to any other kind of learning:

FIGURE 3–3. Use of apostrophes by a first grader

FIGURE 3-4. Use of
commas by a first
grader

Pink is my favorite color.
Pink is fengrnael polish' shirts'
swetrs' papr' dresis' crans'
harts' shorts' earsengs'

- Learners do not typically master something or do it correctly all
  at once. Indeed, learners may develop several hypotheses about
  how something is done before achieving adult or expert competence. (The drawings and the "pink" poem.)
- Something already learned may temporarily not be applied as
  the person is trying something else that's new. (The drawings.)
- New learning may be overgeneralized or overapplied. (The apostrophe in the simple plural *had's*.)

From such developmental patterns we can formulate some teaching
principles—observations and suggestions, really—for teaching grammatical constructions and skills:

- We need to teach something repeatedly, realizing that it may be
  better understood and more appropriately and completely applied with additional guidance and experience.
- We need to supply plenty of examples, since patterns may be
  deduced from the examples even if our explanations are not well
  understood.
- We not only need to show examples of a "new" grammatical
  construction or skill, we also need to contrast them with easily
  confused instances that are *not* examples.
- We need to applaud new learning, the trying out of new things
  grammatically, even when the learning is only partial or the
  understanding incomplete.
- We need to accept—even welcome—the new kinds of errors that
  come with experimentation and risk-taking, not to downgrade
  the writing or the writer. And when the time is appropriate, we
  need to guide students in learning to eliminate such errors.

The concept of "errors as signs of progress" comes from several
sources, initially Mina Shaughnessy's classic *Errors and Expectations*

(1977) and an article by Kroll and Schafer (1978), whose chart on different views of errors is included in Chapter 9. Connie's informal research led to the article "Welcoming Errors as Signs of Growth" (1982)—which includes "Errorwocky" (reprinted here), her poem about the dangers of having students attend to errors prematurely—and to a chapter in *Teaching Grammar in Context* that deals with developing a perspective on error.

Errorwocky

'Twas class time, and the eager youths
Did squirm and wriggle in their seats:
All ready were their fresh ideas,
And their paper was clean and neat.

"Beware the Error beast, my friends!
The jaws that bite, the claws that rend!
Beware the Run-on bird, and shun
The frumious Frag(a)ment."

They took their eraser tips in hand;
Long time the maxnome foe they sought—
Then rested they from the Error hunt,
And wrote awhile in thought.

And, as in uffish thought they wrote,
The Error beast, with eyes of flame,
Came whiffling through their ballpoint pens,
And burbled as it came!

One, two! One, two! And back and forth
The eraser tips went snicker-snack!
They left it dead, and to their teach,
They went galumphing back!

"And have you slain the Error beast?
You'll pass this year, victorious youths!
O frabjous day! Callooh! Callay!"
She chortled then, in truth.

'Twas class time, and the stunted youths
Did slouch and huddle in their seats:
All shortened were their sentences,
And their words had met defeat.

—*Connie Weaver*

11. Grammar instruction should be included during various phases of writing

Grammar taught in conjunction with writing will be most effective when reinforced through more than one phase of the process and with numerous writing situations and assignments.

It is obvious to anyone who has ever taught something—anything—that teaching it once and only once will not usually enable all students to master it completely, much less use it whenever appropriate.

This point has not been demonstrated by research, because of the complexity—or impossibility—of developing a design for researching it with solid experimental procedures and statistical analyses. However, it is obvious to anyone who has ever taught something—anything—that teaching it once and only once will not usually enable all students to master it completely, much less use it whenever appropriate. An example of teaching grammar throughout the process of writing a prequel or sequel to *The Paper Bag Princess* (Munsch, 1980) is offered in Weaver (2007), and a critique of that experience is included here in Chapter 5.

12. More research is needed on effective ways of teaching grammar to strengthen writing

There is a need for more research on differing approaches to teaching grammar when the primary goal is to strengthen students' writing.

Widely considered the most authoritative study of the effects of teaching grammar on students' writing is a three-year study involving 248 students (Elley et al., 1975/1976). The authors concluded "that English grammar, whether traditional or transformational, has virtually no influence on the language growth of typical secondary school students" (p. 18). This well-designed, well-conducted study is probably as definitive as we can get.

According to the authors of the York research summary (Andrews et al., 2004b):

> Despite a hundred years of concern about the issue of the teaching of grammar and thousands of research studies, the high quality research base for claiming the efficacy of syntax teaching is small. The first implication, then, is that there should be a conclusive, large-scale and well-designed randomized controlled trial to answer the question about whether syntax teaching does improve the writing quality and accuracy of 5- to 16-year-olds. Such a study should have a longitudinal dimension to test whether any significant effects are sustained. (p. 5)

But the difficulties in undertaking such a study would be staggering, and cost is only the beginning. It's not simple to design a "randomized controlled trial" that is "large scale," especially when the subjects of the study, the students, are taught in naturalistic situations—that is, ordinary class-rooms. (And if they aren't taught in ordinary classrooms, then what's the point of the study?) The time element is still more problematic: The longer the study, the more uncontrolled variables can enter the picture.

It's no accident that the only experimental study receiving a high rating in all four of the York researchers' criteria was an extraordinarily brief study by Fogel and Ehri (2000). In this study, a mere six features of main-stream English were taught to speakers of "Black English Vernacular" (BEV) in only a few minutes and with immediate testing afterward. While the teaching was successful, the one pretreatment session lasted about fifteen minutes; it was followed, about a week later, by an experimental treatment plus three posttest measures the students completed—all within a session that lasted no more than forty-five minutes. Both sessions in-volved translating sentences from BEV into mainstream English, but only the second session included a story-writing task. No wonder this study could be tightly controlled and thus rank high in quality!

While we agree with the York researchers that a highly controlled, lon-gitudinal experimental study might be helpful, we are not confident the variables could be controlled well enough in naturalistic settings, over several years, for the study to be both valid and reliable.

What kinds of research studies seem more realistic? Medium-length experimental studies, perhaps over one school year. And teacher-researcher studies, with rich descriptive data, including case studies and anecdotes—data that may be partially quantified but that is valuable particularly for the details of day-to-day teaching and learning.

What kind of research would be especially useful? As the York re-searchers suggest, since the direct teaching of grammar in isolation does-n't seem to have much effect on most students' writing, it's crucial that the effects of other ways of teaching grammar for writing be investigated. Our "wish list" includes research on:

- The effects of sentence imitation and expansion (sentence generating)
- The effects of sentence combining compared with sentence generating
- The effects of guiding students in revising to improve their own sentences
- The effects of teaching selected aspects of grammar before and/or while students are drafting, then helping them revise sentences and edit

We encourage you and your colleagues to undertake your own explo-ration of such topics—that is, to become teacher-researchers.

A better way

Most important, we believe that *conscious* use of grammar can enable writers to both enrich and enhance their writing. And we believe that grammar instruction in K–12 classrooms should focus on what works best for adding detail to writing, organizing ideas and connecting them effectively, suiting style and voice to content and audience, and using the conventions of language that are best suited to the author's purpose.

Regardless of the hopes of parents, politicians, administrators, and teachers, research does not show that teaching grammar in isolation has significant benefits for most students' writing. Another general belief, based on folklore, has been that novice writers need a thorough intellectual understanding of the language they are using in order to be fluent in it. This, too, is a myth, as demonstrated by the experience of many fluent published writers who don't "know" grammar consciously.

Thus the thesis of our text: that a minimum of grammar should be taught, in the context of and in conjunction with writing, for maximal effects on students' writing. Teaching writing and teaching grammar must be inseparably connected (like "peas and carrots," as Forrest Gump might say). Unlike some traditional views that consider grammar an issue of simple correctness, consisting of error hunts and drills on the "basics," we see grammar, selectively taught, as a resource for writers, necessarily tied to the writing process and inherently connected to issues of invention and drafting, revision and editing, proofreading and publication. We want to demystify grammar and empower novice writers not to fear grammar but to use it as another tool in their writing repertoire. It is the role of the teacher to understand those aspects of grammar—grammar that can enrich and enhance writing—and to guide their student writers in using grammar effectively.

Teaching writing and teaching grammar must be inseparably connected.

Teaching Grammar Throughout the Writing Process

4

In a high school classroom Jonathan visited recently, a teacher was explaining sentence combining. On the surface, the lesson was well developed and well organized. The teacher showed a series of simple sentences on an overhead transparency and asked for student reaction. After students offered such comments as "simple," "basic," "boring," or, in one case, "babyish," the teacher asked them how they would combine the sentences. He showed various techniques, ranging from taking out a word to make sentences connect to using coordinating and subordinating conjunctions. He even briefly taught the use of a semicolon. Then he challenged the students to revise the paragraph. They worked in pairs, arguing and developing ideas, until he asked for examples. As a class, they then revised the entire paragraph together.

Did the teacher integrate grammar into the writing process? Of course he did. Was the activity effective? Sadly, the answer is no, or at least not as effective as it could have been. Why not? Clearly, the activity itself was generally appropriate: Sentence combining has repeatedly been found effective for enriching writing (Andrews et al., 2004a), though there is also some evidence that imitating sentences or attending directly to students' own sentence structure may be at least as valuable. On the surface, the teacher was integrating grammar into the writing process—using minilessons to enrich and enhance student writing. Grammar was not being considered as "right" or "wrong"; there were opportunities to consider

Note: This chapter, except for the section on working with Max, previously appeared in "Grammar Intertwined Throughout the Writing Process: 'An Inch Wide and a Mile Deep,'" in the online journal *English Teaching: Practice and Critique* (Weaver, Bush, Anderson, & Bills, 2006).

53

not just grammar (what is possible) but rhetoric (what would be most effective); and the students were actively engaged in modifying text.

Yet there were serious flaws in the session. When the minilesson was over, the teacher passed out the students' "grammar" homework: a sheet containing twenty-five sets of sentences ready to be combined. He then said, "Okay, enough grammar. Open up your literature texts." As students dutifully put away their work and assignments and began another activity, one said to another, "What was that all about?" The response: "I dunno."

So close and yet so far! What went wrong? The teacher made grammar useful. He went beyond the idea of grammar as a list of rules to be memorized. But he missed the most important point: placing grammar in the context of real writing. He also forgot to talk about purposes, audiences, and possibilities. He taught the skill, much as he would teach any disconnected skill such as, say, tying a bowline knot. He gave examples. Then he gave an assignment. From his students' perspective, he taught sentence combining as an old sailor will teach youngsters about knots—because he knew the skill and he thought the students should know the skill as well. But the all-important notion of relevance was missing; there was little connection to how sentence combining can be useful in actual writing.

This grammar minilesson also appeared to be an isolated event. Students were not used to seeing grammar as meaningful and inherent to their writing. There were no follow-up lessons, no demonstrations of different ways that one sentence could be reduced to part of another, no writing workshops that made grammar or any other aspect of a writer's craft part of the students' daily work. Students seemed conditioned to think of grammar as a skill disconnected from their writing processes—and from literature. Jonathan had been invited into this classroom to see how the school was teaching "grammar in context," but this lesson seemed to be a dead end, destined to have little or no effect on students' own writing. The teacher didn't convince his students of the value of sentence combining, probably because he didn't guide them in combining sentences in their own writing, and they weren't able to make that connection for themselves.

Let's contrast the above lesson with the work of some teachers who understand and implement "best practice" in teaching grammar in conjunction with writing in their classrooms. Amanda Schripsema and Carol McNally are two middle school teachers in southwestern Michigan. For Carol and Amanda, grammar is not just an add-on, nor is it a chore or a sporadic activity. As Carol and Amanda demonstrate, teaching grammar can be an inherent, natural, and important part of teachers' support of their students' writing at all stages of the writing process.

Amanda offers a powerful analogy:

Do we force sixteen-year-olds to learn every gear and function
within a car's engine before we let them hit the road? No. Knowing how each gear will work will not improve the process of
driving. . . . What helped us to improve, our car manual, or hours
of driving practice? The same goes with writing. We need to let
our students practice, and it's through authentic practice that we
can explain why the gears grind when one does not shift properly.

For Amanda grammatical practice is part of the natural process of writing.
It is an inherent and useful part of learning to write. While students are
writing is an excellent time to introduce grammatical skills that they can
then practice in other pieces of writing, whether a paragraph or many
pages.

Amanda puts her analogy to work in a "grammatical rhythms in paragraphs" minilesson she teaches not as an isolated activity but as an everyday part of what her students do. Her students expect to participate in
activities that integrate grammar into their writing and are disposed to
understand why and how the grammar-generated content will enrich their
writing.

Amanda begins by showing several "professional" examples of sentence variation and sentence combining, including this one from *Make
Your Words Work,* by Gary Provost (2001):

This sentence has five words. This sentence has five words too.
Five word sentences are fine. But several together become monotonous. Listen to what is happening. The writing is getting boring. The sound of it drones. It's like a stuck record. The ear
demands some variety. Now listen. I vary the sentence length and
I create music. Music. The writing sings. It has a pleasant rhythm,
a lilt, a harmony. I use short sentences. And I use sentences of
medium length. And sometimes when I am certain the reader is
rested I engage him with a sentence of considerable length, a sentence that burns with energy and builds with all the impetus of a
crescendo, the roll of the drums, and crash of the cymbals, and
sounds that say listen to this, it is important. (p. 55)

She also shows literary examples, like this passage by Norman Mailer
(1975):

Foreman threw a wild left. Then a right, a left, a left, and a right.
Some to the head, some to the body, some got blocked, some

missed, one collided with Ali's floating ribs, brutal punches, jarring and imprecise as a collision at slow speed in a truck. (p. 181)

After showing these examples, Amanda asks students to make judgments about the writing, asking them, as fellow authors, which sentences and paragraphs they like, and how the authors convey meaning, voice, and emotion through sentence rhythm and variation. The students then practice varying their own sentences and add the skill to their repertoire, ready to be used again in their current and future writing projects.

Many teachers make the mistake of "covering" various grammatical skills and then assuming students know and can apply them. But in fact these skills need to be continually reinforced during the writing process, something Carol McNally does in her middle school classroom. Carol's target in this lesson is middle school writers' tendency to use a lot of short, choppy sentences, all of similar construction.

She begins by deconstructing a passage from Lois Lowry's *The Giver* (1993) into a paragraph of simple constructions, limited syntax, and minimal description (something "any middle school writer might have written"):

His training had not yet begun. He left the auditorium. He felt apartness. He made his way through the crowd. He was holding the folder she had given him. He was looking for his family unit. He was also looking for Asher. People moved aside for him. They watched him. He thought he could hear whispers.

The students give their opinions of this paragraph and, working together, fix the "choppy" sentences by combining, reworking, and rewriting them. Carol admits, "This class had previously studied the effects of beginning sentences with participial phrases . . . so, in addition to combining sentences, many students also integrated this previously learned stylistic grammar choice to enhance their re-creations of Lowry's passage" (Weaver et al., 2001, p. 23). Afterward, Carol shows the students Lowry's original, unaltered text and they discuss the grammatical choices Lowry made. On subsequent days, Carol prompts students to use these grammatical constructions and sentence-combining techniques in their own writing.

Amanda and Carol have made grammar real. It isn't just an exercise. Clearly grammar is being taught selectively as an important means of appreciating literature and enriching one's writing. Carol comments: "If I had started these lessons by telling my students we were going to be studying grammar, or more specifically, participial phrases and appositives, and doing sentence-combining, my guess is their attitude would have precluded the positive results that I see more and more often in their everyday writing" (p. 24).

Harry Noden offers another excellent example of grammar as enrichment in *Image Grammar* (1999). For Noden, grammar is a means of helping students develop their text much in the same way that painters use various brushstrokes to create an image on their canvas, or any artist or craftsman uses specialized skills:

> Traditionally, the study of grammar has dealt only with words, phrases, and clauses. However, when I began to see grammar as the process of creating art, it seemed unnatural—even impossible—not to view grammar as a continuous spectrum in a whole work. As I explored this view with my students, the connection seemed to bring grammar into a meaningful relationship with stories, novels, screenplays, poems, reports and songs—the ultimate products of the writer's art. (p. ix)

It takes a skilled artist to manifest and enhance the intricacies of an artistic notion. Our students are often like the novice artist who wants to replicate a beautiful scene but lacks the ability. With only rudimentary skills and tools at her disposal, she is unable to express those images in their full depth. The same applies to writing. It takes specific skills in crafting language to make writing interesting and sophisticated. As Noden demonstrates, it's most efficient and effective to teach grammatical options and stylistic techniques using students' own writing—even if what they write is one sentence imitating a master.

How can we teach grammatical options while students are working on a piece of writing?

The answers to this question are naturally varied. We teachers occasionally interrupt students while they are writing and teach a minilesson on mechanics when the need arises. But we are not as accustomed to teaching the use of effective language structures in the context of students' own writing.

Here's an example of how we might do so naturally and easily. Suppose your students are working on an assignment to write about a scary night. While you're walking around the room answering questions and offering praise you notice that one of the girls, after clustering ideas for her description and spontaneously producing some *-ing* modifiers, has incorporated two of them into a sentence: "I felt the wind going through the trees like ice cream melting in the summer." You write the sentence on the board and interject a brief minilesson showing the other writers in the class how they too can use similar action phrases in their description.

In the ebb and flow of the drafting process, there are many spontaneous opportunities like this to teach the use of modifying structures or parallelism or any other grammatical option. As students begin revising and editing, still more opportunities arise to teach effective ways of revising sentences and paragraphs and to teach editing skills like making verbs agree with their subjects or using punctuation conventionally. Sometimes teachers preplan a minilesson on a particular concept, then look for examples in the writing their students are doing that day.

But a teacher can often have the greatest long-term effect by presenting a preplanned lesson on using grammar effectively to express content and then teaching that same concept throughout the revising and editing processes. In Chapter 2 of *The Grammar Plan Book* (2007), Connie shares an extended example of teaching a single grammatical concept in several steps, beginning with a reading of *The Paper Bag Princess* (Munsch, 1980). Of course, time constraints make it impossible to do this sort of teaching with every piece of assigned or self-chosen writing, and even when we try our best, some aspect of the process may get shortchanged: usually revising or editing. When that happens, we need to make sure to emphasize the missing step next time.

Playing with grammar, becoming a writer

In the summer of 2004, Connie had the privilege of working on writing with a friend's son, Max Baird, who was then between his sophomore and junior years in high school. Because of Max's low self-esteem as a writer, Connie began by guiding Max in writing an "I am" poem that reflected his personality and character metaphorically.

Usually Connie would have shared written examples first, but since the tutoring sessions were casual and laidback, she helped Max focus on the concept by giving two examples orally: "I am a Bilbo's pizza" and "I am a whitewater raft." She deliberately left out modifying phrases, curious whether Max would add modifiers before or after the nouns in his initial metaphors. Mostly he didn't. But in one sentence he did: *I am an aged scared* [scarred] *blue whale.*

During the first round of revisions, Connie showed Max how the sentence would sound if the first two adjectives were put after the noun: *I am a blue whale, aged and scared.* She also pointed out that there would be a comma after the noun—*whale*—and before the adjectives. (She did not preteach the concept of noun, but simply used the term incidentally as she explained.) Liking the idea of modifiers after the noun, Max then went through his "I am" statements and added modifiers to many of the other things to which he had equated himself. Interestingly, in the whale analogy he left *aged and scared* before the noun, omitted *blue*, and added new postnoun modifiers: *I am the aged and scared whale, limitless in knowledge, ancient and gigantic, loving and peaceful, graceful and magnificent.* (Connie hadn't yet dealt with the correct spelling of *scarred;* she was focusing on content and style.)

When Max shared his next draft, Connie showed him how to add a present participial word or phrase (group of words) that would show what the thing in the "I am" statement was doing. Again using the technical term only in passing, Connie presented a number of examples of how words ending in *-ing* can add details after a noun as well as before. Together, they noticed that Max already had one *-ing* word (the phrase describing the whale as *loving and peaceful*). While *loving* in this context might be seen more as a state of mind than an action, it did illustrate grammatically the concept of an *-ing* word describing a noun. Max than added *-ing* modifiers to several of his nouns. Max's early drafts are shown in Figure 4–1.

Connie also talked about organization and the idea of leading up to those items that are most important, so they are the final images in the reader's mind. In the next draft, Max made the line about the whale the last image before the concluding "I am who I am" lines. At this point, Connie explained the difference in meaning between *scared* and *scarred,* and Max corrected his spelling.

With so many modifiers now following the metaphorical nouns, Connie also saw an opportunity to teach a useful editing concept, putting a colon after the basic "I am" statements. She explained that the colon is like a trumpet, announcing that something is coming—in this case, descriptive phrases modifying the previous noun.

Max liked the idea of using the colon this way. Ultimately, the original sentence *I am an aged scared blue whale* became:

I am the aged and scarred blue whale: limitless in knowledge, old
beyond years and larger than life, loving and peaceful, graceful
and magnificent, relating emotions of the life in wondrous songs,
living through all times both good, bad, and in between and triumphing in the end.

Would the sentence be better with a little more editing? Yes. Might the sentence be better without *all* those *-ing* phrases? Possibly. On the other hand, it illustrates what often happens when writers are learning a new skill: They tend to overuse it or apply it inappropriately or make a new kind of error in applying it (for example, adding a modifying construction after a noun but not including the comma needed before the modifier).

In any case, Connie felt it was time to stop editing. Writers can learn only a limited number of things at one time before their capacity to

FIGURE 4–1. Max's
early drafts

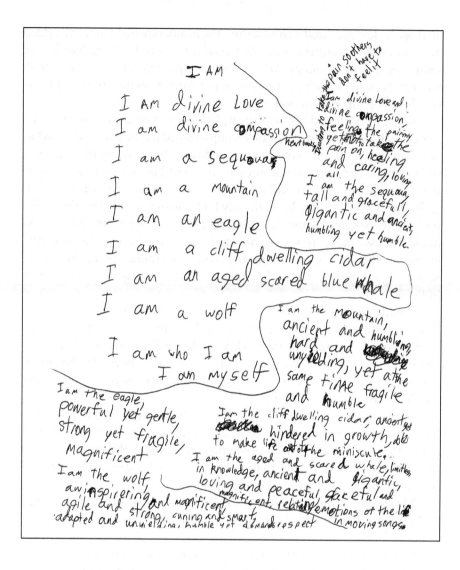

4: Teaching Grammar Throughout the Writing Process

remember them is exceeded. More important, we teachers need to learn to keep our hands off students' writing, lest their piece become our piece. When we take over the ownership of a piece by imposing our own revisions and edits, the only lesson they're likely to learn is that their own work is never good enough, so why try. At some point, idiosyncratic for each individual, we need to stop helping students revise and edit: Learning is our goal, not a perfect paper. Students need to consider the new things they have learned (or almost learned), bask in the glow of what they've accomplished, and publish the piece in some meaningful way.

Connie felt that Max and his poem were at that point. Together they reviewed the concepts Connie had taught and Max had applied. Then came publication. (Figure 4–2 is Max's final draft.) Max first shared it

FIGURE 4-2. Max's final draft

I am

I am divine love and compassion: feeling the pain and wanting to take the pain so others don't have to feel it, yet learning to not take the pain on; healing and caring, loving all.

I am the sequoia: tall and gorgeous, gigantic and ancient, humbling yet humble.

I am the mountain: old beyond comprehension and making one bow, hard and unyielding, yet fragile and bowing to others.

I am the eagle: powerful yet gentle, strong yet fragile—lordly.

I am the wolf: awe inspiring and magnificent, agile and strong, cunning and smart, perfected and unyielding, respectful to all yet demanding respect in return.

I am the cliff dwelling cedar: ancient yet hindered in growth, able to make life out of the miniscule yet flourishing beyond all expectations when given the right nutrient-rich environment.

I am the aged and scarred blue whale: limitless in knowledge, old beyond years and larger than life, loving and peaceful, graceful and magnificent, relating emotions of the life in wondrous songs, living through all times both good, bad, and in between and triumphing in the end.

I am the person that I am
I am who I am
I am myself
I am Max
I am me
I am

with everyone around who would look at it or listen to him read it; he then included it with his application for a much-sought-after international school, where it played a significant role in his being accepted; and he now has allowed the poem and the process leading up to it to be included in this book so teachers can see how a piece of writing can be guided from a sparse beginning to a rich and well-edited final draft.

Here's what Connie taught:

- The concept of putting modifiers after a noun
- The placement of a comma between the noun and the modifiers
- The use of *-ing* words and phrases as modifiers
- The rhetorical technique of leading up to one's strongest points or images by putting them at or near the end
- The use of a colon to introduce a list of modifying phrases

Did Max learn all these lessons then and there, once and for all? Of course not. That's why we emphasize that writers may need to be led through a set of steps again and again. In Max's case, we do know that he became more self-confident as a writer and, with some excellent classroom teaching, became a much stronger and joyful writer. In the fall of 2006, Max started his freshman year at Arizona State, and his strong writing helped him win a substantial scholarship!

A few concepts taught well and a few pieces done well can be much more important for a student writer's growth than many concepts and lessons taught superficially and many pieces of writing assigned without much guidance. Some students will make miles of progress with just one extended lesson, others won't. These others—many, perhaps most, of a class—can be brought along over time, as we teach and discuss beautifully written literature together and teach a few grammatical options and skills deeply on the way to producing a few final pieces done well.

A few concepts taught well and a few pieces done well can be much more important for a student writer's growth than many concepts and lessons taught superficially and many pieces of writing assigned without much guidance.

A framework for teaching grammar throughout the writing process

In planning to teach grammatical concepts over time, it helps to have a framework of steps you can use as reminders of what can make such teaching finally take hold and become part of students' own repertoire as writers. Here is one such idealized framework, often and necessarily modified in practice:

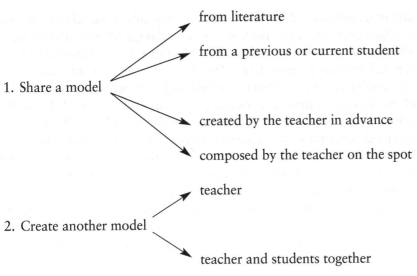

1. Share a model
   - from literature
   - from a previous or current student
   - created by the teacher in advance
   - composed by the teacher on the spot

2. Create another model
   - teacher
   - teacher and students together

3. Have students compose (or do a related preparatory activity) in small groups or pairs and share their work. Clarify as needed.

4. Have students compose a sentence or sentences individually and share their work. Check the work if desired and possible.

5. Ask students to apply the concept (that is, to use the grammatical element or writing skill) in their own writing.

6. Solicit peer feedback and/or provide feedback yourself. Read the students' papers to see what revision strategies should be taught.

7. Teach revision strategies (to the whole class, a small group, or an individual). Use examples from students' papers.

8. Consider supplying students with a checklist that includes the grammatical structure taught.

9. Have students prepare their "final" draft. Suggest particular strategies for individual papers, perhaps showing how one sentence could be restructured or expanded, or how two sentences could be combined. Follow up, if possible, by asking students to apply this strategy to at least one or two sentences in their paper. Check and respond.

10. If needed, go through the process again with a different piece of writing. At the very least, continue helping students draw on this concept again as they revise and/or edit other pieces of writing.

Again: this sequence is not set in stone but is simply a reminder of steps that can make the learning and application of the construction or skill more effective. What we actually do depends on our classes, no two of which ever seem to be the same. So we echo the oft-repeated advice of Theresa Reagan-Donk (Hudsonville, Michigan, Public Schools) to teach "an inch wide and a mile deep." Decide what aspects of grammar are really worth teaching and then teach them well—throughout the production of one piece of writing and over a period of weeks, as needed. It's also helpful to follow up the initial work over the rest of the school year as you guide students in revising their writing for greater effectiveness. The lessons take a while to prepare, but you can build a repertoire over time, share lesson plans among colleagues, and borrow appropriate literary examples and teaching ideas from elsewhere.

This framework is one way English teachers can plan the gradual release of responsibility as suggested by Pearson and Gallagher (1983). Although their final step is practice or application, our goal is independent and ultimately automatic application, so we have revised their figure slightly to make these final steps clearer as well as to indicate that the cycle may need to be repeated one or more times for a single grammatical concept (see Figure 4–3).

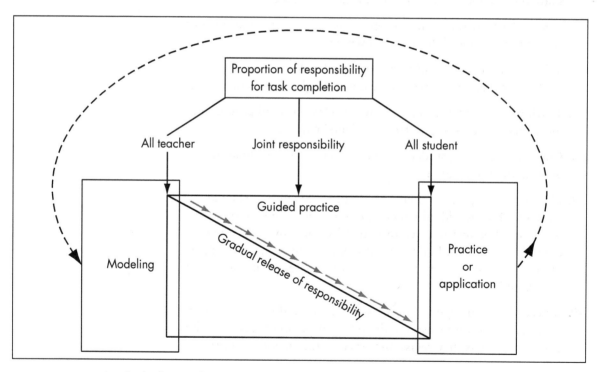

FIGURE 4–3. Gradual release of responsibility model (Pearson & Gallagher, 1983, after Campione, 1981). The dotted line to show recursive cycles has been added to Pearson & Gallagher's model.

What about writing workshop?

Writing process models typically reflect what we think of as a "writing event," from generating ideas to publishing. In middle school and high school classes especially, students often work on a writing project with a clearly defined beginning, middle, and end. While the process offers some flexibility, the end product is defined by the teacher (or the curriculum guide). Although this process is not strictly linear—students move back and forth as they draft, revise, re-envision, and draft again—teachers tend to consider in what "stages" of the writing process they can introduce this or that grammatical option or skill.

A second and very different approach to the writing process takes places within the writing workshop. While students sometimes all work on a specific genre or topic at the same time under the teacher's guidance, they more often work on different genres and/or topics of their own choosing. At any time they may be in any phase of writing, from idea development to publication. They may need very different aspects of grammar help to enrich and enhance their writing. Writing workshops depend on a teacher's sense of who needs what kind of support (with grammar or anything else) at any given time.

In *The Writing Workshop* (2001), Katie Wood Ray describes the differences between the "writing process" approach and her conceptions of the writing workshop:

> I have seen many classrooms where students "do the writing process," and the focus is on pieces of writing and how to take those pieces of writing through the writing process—prewriting, drafting, revision, editing and publication. . . . This down-the-line emphasis can be contrasted to writing workshop, where the focus is very much on the writers rather than the process that leads to finished pieces. Now, without a doubt, students in writing workshops utilize all the steps of the writing process—their teachers give them lots of instruction around the process so they can get ready for publication—but it's not like they really do the process. It's more like they use the writing process to get other things done. (p. 4)

Many secondary teachers are used to teaching writing as a single event, guided from beginning to end—a process whose value is unquestioned. While it may be more difficult to envision the concept of a writing workshop, we want to emphasize its immense value for all teachers, not just those in the elementary and middle grades, where writing workshops have been so successful. For a fuller description of writing workshop, we highly recommend Ray's *The Writing Workshop* (2001) and *Wondrous*

Words (1999), along with a number of publications by Nancie Atwell, including her book *Lessons That Change Writers* (2002).

How can grammar find a home in this very different and wonderfully student writer–centered version of the writing process, in which students may be writing at different levels in different genres and in need of different support, all at the same time? Specific answers derive from the knowledge all teachers have of their particular classrooms, students, and teaching goals, but some general principles and suggestions can help to guide us.

We asked our Western Michigan University colleague (and experienced fifth-grade writing workshop teacher) Patricia Bills to tell us how she integrates grammar into her writing workshops. There is considerable overlap between her processes and procedures and the general planning framework we presented earlier.

In the next sections, Patricia describes four components of writer's workshop—minilessons, focus lessons, teacher conferences, and demonstrations—followed by a note on conventions and editing.

Minilessons

Once administrative tasks such as a "status report" of student work are complete, a typical writing workshop begins with a minilesson (anywhere from five to no more than twenty-five minutes) on a specific grammar-related skill. The emphasis is on writing, not grammar. These minilessons are opportunities to enrich students' writing by teaching style-related grammatical skills or specific conventions. Many times the topics come from a teacher's own knowledge of universal (or close to universal) problems. Sometimes they relate to a "high needs" area: usually something a majority (more than 80 percent) of the class needs at the time. The key is to find an issue or skill that all students, no matter what they are currently writing, can then apply (with the understanding that the skill may be familiar to some but new to many).

Focus lessons

One of the problems with teaching the writing process in connection with a single writing event is that some students already have the skills being taught. In a writing workshop teachers can create a minilesson based on the needs of a smaller group of students. Sometimes all that's necessary is a general invitation: "I notice that some of our writers are interested in such-and-so. I'm going to teach more about this at our writers' table in about five minutes." Students who want to learn more about the specific grammatical point then come up. Other times, students who don't recognize their need may have to be specifically asked to join the group. In each case, it's a targeted audience.

Teacher conferences

One of the wonderful traits of the writing workshop and its working atmosphere is that the teacher can confer with students regularly. This is the perfect time to give individual grammar instruction based on the specific needs—enriching or enhancing—of that student. The trickiest thing about conferences is to pace them so that many students get meaningful feedback during each workshop. It's easy to fall into a conversation that takes too long. Talking with children is engaging, energizing, and exciting, but it's important to keep the meetings short and to the point (remind children that their next conference is not far off). Lucy Calkins (1994) recommends five minutes for each conference, which includes three stages:

1. Do research (listen to the student talk about or read the piece).
2. Compliment and decide (praise the student for what works in the piece and identify what the student needs most right now).
3. Teach (introduce a specific skill, with the understanding that you will check in with the student later in the workshop).

Conferences usually end with such directions as, "Give that idea a try, and I'll be back to find out how it went for you."

Demonstrations

It is important that teachers become writers along with their students. Teachers should not only talk about a particular grammatical issue and introduce a related skill; they should demonstrate that skill in their own writing. Sometimes these demonstrations happen as a part of the minilesson. With more difficult or complicated skills, they become part of longer lessons in which all students try to apply that skill in their own writing, then and there. An important part of a demonstration is allowing students to give feedback on teachers' own writing: It gives students a chance to conceptualize how the skill is being applied and includes the teacher in the writing community. This demonstrates that writing is for everyone, and everyone deals with grammar issues at every level. Grammar is not just for school writing, but all writing.

A note about conventions and editing

Conventions are the keys to communication. Students need a "writer's toolbox" of conventions and grammatical skills they can use at different points in their writing, especially when editing. When teachers read and respond to writing, they should identify specific conventions to teach to individual students. These conventions then become the focus of individual conferences, focus lessons, or—when a large number of students need it—a whole-class minilesson.

Editing: Every teacher's bugaboo

Now we come to the part of the writing process we fret about most—editing. Many others no doubt share our struggles. Why is teaching editing so hard? We contend it's because we as teachers no longer have control. It is up to our students to do the work: good, strong, intellectually challenging work as they clarify the expectations of their audience and engage with particular genres and texts, grammatical concepts, and stylistic elements—interrelated elements that all need to be addressed. We need to give students the tools to edit, but they have to use those tools themselves. Often, our students simply want us to be the experts and "fix" their grammar. And too often, perhaps out of frustration or a sense of obligation, we comply.

Nevertheless, a remark Connie made almost thirty years ago is still true: "There seems to be little value in marking students' papers with 'corrections,' little value in teaching the conventions of mechanics apart from actual writing, and even less value in teaching grammar in order to instill these conventions" (Weaver, 1979, p. 64).

In short, "fixing" papers doesn't teach much about using grammar. It just breeds dependence.

In short, "fixing" papers doesn't teach much about using grammar. It just breeds dependence. We need to take an opposite course: help our students seek independence, and help create our own irrelevance to their writing lives. One of our most important means of attaining irrelevance is to help students identify and understand their own convention and style errors and revise their writing independently. We want them to become their own mechanics—to be able to lift the metaphorical hood of their own prose, spot problems, and tinker with solutions. In some cases, they will be able to fix specific errors and address issues immediately and easily. In others, consultation and second opinions will be necessary. Most important, though, those opinions will be generated from the students' knowledge of their own writing and their ability to uncover and understand their own errors.

Chapters 13–15 (Part 3) illustrate various approaches to editing, with an emphasis on working with special students and populations.

Our "model" of grammar in the writing process

In this chapter we have presented an implicit model (the vignettes) and a somewhat more explicit model (the framework) of the writing process. Teaching writing is a fluid endeavor and depends, in part, on students' needs, developmental levels, and writing expertise.

If we were to create a visual representation of the writing process, it would be recursive rather than linear, and it would include more than the typical models do (as in Figure 1-1). Most writing process models contain the common phases of prewriting (planning or rehearsing), drafting (getting ideas down), revising (taking another look at one's work), proofreading, and publishing (sharing with the intended audience). We believe there should be more. Yes, writers need to reorganize, improve the flow, add interesting details, delete irrelevant ones—typical aspects of revision. In addition, however, they need another cycle—another pass through the text attending to such matters as combining some sentences into a longer, smoother sentence; rearranging syntactic elements; eliminating wordiness and redundancy; and choosing "just right" words. Editing is a crucial and still later step, in which subjects and verbs are made to agree; pronoun reference is clarified; and punctuation, usage, and spelling are refined. Over the school year, over all the years of their classroom education, student writers can learn to attend to more and more of these issues if teachers keep guiding them through the writing process and keep presenting needed writing skills and strategies.

The ebb and flow of waves is a useful metaphor, in effect a metaphorical model, for what goes on when writers write—especially when they compose on the computer and can readily make changes "back there" while drafting "here" and perhaps jotting down notes for the ending. The writing moves forward in swells, one swell cresting but not crashing, a larger swell crashing before ebbing again, and other nearby waves in various stages of swelling, cresting, crashing, and ebbing.

Photo courtesy of PD Photo.org

So it is with a piece of writing. We jot down ideas, start a draft, realize that the previous sentence didn't lead smoothly into this one, return to fix it, think some more, write a snippet that gets parked somewhere temporarily, move forward, reach back, plunk in an interesting tidbit that we later reject as "not fitting," and continue to reorganize, revise, and edit as we go along. The flitting back and forth is easier or harder, depending on the medium (computer or pen and paper) and one's skills and experience, but the ongoing process of writing a meaningful piece ebbs and flows rhythmically, if not always—or ever—smoothly or predictably.

The writing process is predictably unpredictable—the kind of phenomena addressed by chaos theory. But as students plan and draft and revise and edit and prepare their work for publication, there are many opportunities for knowledgeable and prepared teachers to intervene—not only to teach time-honored topics like lead sentences, smooth transitions, and using "standard" grammatical forms and punctuation, but also to teach the writing craft of using grammatical resources to add detail, create flow, foreground some sentence elements and background others, and in doing so write with a clear and appropriate voice. A conscious knowledge of certain aspects of grammar, along with the ability to use and manipulate them, has much to offer writers.

From Ice Cream to Dragons

Adjectival Modifiers at Work

5

"I want some ice cream!" claims Emily enthusiastically.

Hmmm. That shouldn't be part of my diet, but her craving could become my excuse, allowing me to rationalize a cone or dish of my own. "What kind?" I ask.

"Yummy," she replies, unhelpfully. "No, wait: I want frozen custard."

"Okay," I agree. "Culver's or Ritter's?" I'm hoping she chooses Culver's, which is closer, and she does. "They've got this build-your-own-sundae feature, so think about what you want."

"Two scoops!" Emily exclaims. "With hot fudge on one, and hot caramel on the other."

My own mouth begins to water: These are my favorite toppings too. "But," I caution, "I think they just pile one scoop on top of the other, so the toppings would run together."

Emily, of course, has a solution. "Ask for a banana split dish without the banana," she advises.

"Okay. Is there anything else you want on it?" I am beginning to picture the sundae.

"Yeah, a cherry on *each* scoop," she chortles, bouncing up and down as much as the car's seat belt will allow. "And nuts."

By now, I'm thinking that this sundae may exceed the three-toppings limit for a build-your-own sundae, but I don't say so—in part just to see what she'll say next. Sure enough, she chooses one kind of nut for one of the scoops and another kind for the other.

Note: Connie wrote the first part of this chapter. Teacher Emily Mihocko of the Round Elementary School in Hartland, Michigan, contributed the second. The ending returns to our joint voices.

"Peanuts on one scoop and cashews on the other."

My hunch confirmed, I go for broke: "Does it matter which scoop has the peanuts and which the cashews?"

"Yeah. I want the peanuts on top of the hot chocolate and the cashews on the hot caramel. And whipped cream, before they add the cherries."

I now see this sundae in its full splendor, even though so far it exists only in words.

Later, I have an inspiration: I can take Emily's sundae and describe it in writing, using grammatical options to demonstrate how details within details can be added to a single sentence instead of presented in short, choppy sentences that go clop-clop-clop, one after another, across a page. Or to put it the other way around, I can write a well-crafted paragraph— I hope—that not only conveys the value of specific details, but also employs some grammatical options for adding those details to sentences in a way that demonstrates syntactic variety and fluency. A paragraph, I think, that can demonstrate some of the popular "6 traits" of writing: ideas (details), sentence fluency, and maybe effective word choice and voice. So I begin.

Instead of writing a paragraph, though, I settle on a listing poem, with each stanza beginning "I want." I have found listing poems easy to write— for my students and for me—so this is a nonthreatening way to get started or even to end: The listing poem can be a worthy product in itself. Here is my quick draft:

> I want a B-I-G, yummy sundae,
>> with two scoops of frozen custard, vanilla
>> rounded and almost snow white,
>> their tops bald mountains waiting to be decorated.
> I want two toppings,
>> one hot caramel dripping down one mountain,
>> creamy, and golden to toffee brown;
>> the other luscious hot fudge, clinging momentarily to the other
>>> mountain, then sliding down like an accelerating avalanche.
> I want two kinds of nuts,
>> whole, roasted peanuts on the hot fudge mountain,
>> jumbo cashews on the other,
>> both cascading down their lava flows of melting snow.
> Finally, a mound of whipped cream shall top each mountain,
>> garnished
>> with a cherry that resembles Rudolph's nose.

I'm not sure it makes sense to refer to melting snow as lava or whether it's mixing a metaphor to suddenly imagine Rudolph's nose on top of each whipped cream mountain, but this is a first draft and I don't have any classmates or colleagues handy for critique. Concluding that this poem may in any case be good enough to illustrate grammatical options, I reread it.

I notice first that this is not an entirely static sketch but a moving portrait of a sundae, because things are happening: The hot caramel is *dripping* down one mountain, the hot fudge *clinging* momentarily to the other mountain, the nuts *cascading* down the lava flows of melting snow. These phrases that are headed by *-ing* words are called present participle (or participial) phrases: They convey present action, pulling readers into this moving portrait. Of course, I've had more than a little practice using such narrative descriptors, so the present participle phrases came without conscious bidding. I also have included some single-word adjectives that come after the noun they modify rather than before:

> I want two toppings,
>> one hot caramel dripping down one mountain,
>> <u>creamy</u>, and golden to toffee <u>brown</u>

Because I view *golden* and *toffee* as describing brown, I've indicated only *creamy* and *brown* as adjectives that occur after—but not immediately after—*caramel*, the noun they modify. In any case, labeling and analyzing is not the point: Rather, it's noticing opportunities for adding details and playing with grammatical options for doing so. Other postnoun modifying words are *rounded* and *white*, describing the scoops of custard (*rounded and snow white*).

In addition to the present participial phrases, there is a past participial phrase modifying the mound—or mounds—of whipped cream: *garnished with a cherry that resembles Rudolph's nose.* (The poem also includes appositives and absolutes, but I think we're getting in too deep for now.)

I also notice that each stanza of the poem goes from relatively general to more and more concrete. Take the second stanza as an example:

> I want two toppings,
>> one hot caramel dripping down one mountain,
>> creamy, and golden to toffee brown;
>> the other luscious hot fudge, clinging momentarily to the other
>>> mountain, then
>> sliding down like an accelerating avalanche.

We go first from the general concept of toppings to the more specific one of hot caramel, which is described more concretely as *dripping down one mountain* and then still more specifically as *creamy, and golden to toffee brown.* It's as if we were extending the zoom lens on a camera, visually bringing the object being photographed closer and closer. This kind of

Detail adds the content that is so often missing from student writing. The detail's the thing.

"zooming in" on detail is what our students need to learn to do in writing not only descriptive/narrative prose and poetry, but also expository (informative, explanatory) and persuasive (even argumentative) prose. Detail adds the content that is so often missing from student writing. The detail's the thing.

The possibilities of the "I am" poem are endless. Students can write about themselves—as Max did in Chapter 4—or another person, perhaps a literary character, or an animal or object, even a time or event ("I am Halloween," "I am the battle at Gettysburg"). See also the "I am from . . ." poems described in Chapter 15.

Even in writing courses for college freshman or for prospective teachers of writing, I start with descriptive/narrative poetry, because it can be rich and deep but is also brief. Students grasp the importance of specific details within one or two class periods and with guidance can quickly produce complete poems that enable them to feel like successful writers. After the poetry unit I can get students to write persuasive prose that is much more detailed in its examples and therefore much more convincing.

Adding modifiers via key grammatical options

In Francis Christensen's landmark collection of essays on writing well, *Notes Toward a New Rhetoric* (1967), he emphasizes teaching students to use grammatical options that will in effect force them to include details that are more and more specific. By focusing on adding modifiers by means of key grammatical options, we and our students are nudged to look more closely, perceive more deeply, and reflect more thoroughly on our lives and the communities and worlds in which we live. Christensen calls this "generative rhetoric," because the focus on grammar generates more precise observation and thought.

Generating sentences can result in the addition of various kinds of modifiers, both adverbial and adjectival. Since—according to Christensen and corroborated by personal observation—free modifying adjectivals (to be explained shortly) often require the most instructional coaxing, this chapter and the next deal with the four major kinds:

- Present participles and participial phrases
- Other single-word adjectives and adjectival phrases (including past participials)
- Appositives
- Absolutes

There is nothing sacred about this order, but present participials are easy to teach at a wide range of grade levels. Also, since I've already introduced them in Max's poem in Chapter 4 and in the ice cream sundae poem, I'll continue with a few more examples. Chapter 6 deals with adjectives and diverse adjectivals "out of order" (Noden, 1999), then with appositives and absolutes.

Understanding present participials

By definition, a *participle* is a single word, while the term *participial* also encompasses phrases. *Present participials* include both the single-word participles ending in *-ing* and the phrases having an *-ing* participle as the "head," or fundamental, word.

Some participles occur before the noun they modify, just as many other single-word adjectivals do; technically, that is, they may occur between a word like *a*, *an*, or *the* and the noun:

Laura's eyes were riveted on the <u>sparkling</u> water as the pinpoints of light danced invitingly.

A <u>screaming</u> infant finally got on Bill's nerves, so he was glad to leave.

The <u>careening</u> sled smashed into our giant walnut tree.

Such modifiers are *bound* to their noun.

While the use of such prenoun adjectivals is worth teaching, especially when we emphasize choosing the "just right" *-ing* word, the focus of this chapter is not on modifiers that occur right before the noun they modify, but rather on modifiers in three other places: right after the noun, separated from it by a comma; at the very beginning of the sentence, separated by a comma from the subject nominal they modify; or at the very end of the sentence, with a comma before. These set-off modifiers are called *free modifiers* (Christensen's term) because they may sometimes be moved to some other position in the sentence.

If we revise the preceding sentences, we can create some options that have freely modifying *-ing* words and phrases instead of bound ones:

Laura's eyes were riveted on the water, *sparkling with pinpoints of light that danced invitingly.*

Sparkling with pinpoints of light that danced invitingly, the water caught Laura's eye.

Sparkling, the water caught Laura's eye as pinpoints of light danced invitingly.

The water, *sparkling*, caught Laura's attention with its pinpoints of light that danced invitingly.

Screaming loudly, an infant finally got on Bill's nerves.

An infant, *screaming* loudly, finally got on Bill's nerves.

Careening every which way, the sled smashed into our giant walnut tree.

The sled, *careening every which way*, smashed into our giant walnut tree.

In the last examples with the infant and the sled, we would not want to put the free modifiers at the very end of the sentence because that would contradict the natural order of events: The infant screamed loudly *before* getting on Bill's nerves, and the sled careened down the hillside *before* crashing into the walnut tree. Our sentence structure chronologically and logically reflects that order.

You may have noticed a couple of other things too. First, in free modifying positions, the *-ing* word is not preceded by a word like *a*, *an*, or *the*. Most important, in free modifying positions the *-ing* words are expandable into phrases, which in turn provide more detail. Figure 5–1 includes more examples of free modifiers of the present participial kind, taken from a thought-provoking and award-winning novel by Dia Calhoun (1999), *Firegold*, which features an adolescent boy caught between two cultures and belonging to neither—until the very end.

Another Emily teaches present participials

In this section Emily Mihocko, who teaches at the Round Elementary School, in Hartland, Michigan, gives a first-person account of teaching the "I am" poem to her students.

. . .

Throughout the school year, I laid the foundation for the following lesson through our language arts experiences. I introduced, reviewed, and discussed parts of speech during shared reading and writing. I also highlighted the importance of being aware of and using different sentence structures while writing.

At the end of April we had just completed a unit on nonfiction writing. In that unit we focused on one animal or thing, and students, pulling from what they previously knew and what they had learned, wrote an "all about" book. The poetry unit that followed began with studying a num-

Smiling, Karena walked over to the shed. (p. 78)

Scowling, he attacked a clump of spiked dremweed. (p. 88)

She leaned forward with her lips parted, concentrating. (p. 170)

Jonathon backed away, feeling as though he had swallowed coals from the fire pit. (p. 23)

His mother laughed and a breeze lifted her purple cloak, rippling the cobalt-blue lining. (p. 33)

Frantic, Jonathon stuffed the rock back into his pocket, wondering how long had his father been riding toward him. (p. 61)

His mother spun around, looking toward the hills below the sagebrush flat, where a score of Dalriades rode swiftly toward them. (p. 80)

He stiffened, staring upward, thinking of the hooded man; last night the nightmare had been worse than ever before. (p. 67)

Moving slowly this time, Jonathon slipped out of bed and began to raise the lid; the hinges creaked. (p. 131)

Shining across the wall, from cliff to cliff and top to bottom, was a great golden tree laden with apples. (p. 196)

The colt nodded, tearing at the snow with his left foreleg, then backed up and bolted down the pasture like a flaming star. (pp. 77–78)

One peak, glittering like red glass, soared higher than all the others. (p. 197)

The look pierced Jonathan's mind, burning, shooting through layer upon layer into a realm that was not dream or memory or vision, but a combination of them all. He was riding a stallion along high cliffs and meadows, riding lost through peaks with shapes almost familiar: a bear with wings; a deer with a man's head; a skull tipped on one side, *listening*. Drums echoed, pounding with his heart in fear and exhilaration. (p. 60)

As he looked over the work he had done, the magic of the Valley—planting and growing—surged in his blood, calling to him from all his ancestors who had worked this land, waking both joy and pain. (p. 102)

For three days and three nights, a smoky haze crept through Stonewater Vale, gathering, thickening, grinding like a heel into the hearts of the besieged. (p. 111)

FIGURE 5–1. Present participials from *Firegold*, by Dia Calhoun (1999)

ber of poets and discussing the meanings of *poem* and *poet*. We discovered and discussed that poetry is generally writing that is focused, using as few words as possible to get across meaning, and that it may or may not rhyme.

When my students the year before had written "I am" poems about an animal, I had first shown them models written by students three grade levels above them. [See the animal "I am" poems in *The Grammar Plan Book* (Weaver, 2007, p. 52).] This year I couldn't relocate those models, so we began by discussing how important it is as writers to use different sentence structures in our writing so that it engages the reader. Then I had all the students focus on the same animal, a cat, and we all become that animal for a few minutes. As a class we generated a list of all the things we would do in a day as this animal—making sure to include the present participle form of the word. I mentioned the term, but then said, "These words tell what the animal is doing—we will call them *-ing* words and phrases." Here's the list we came up with:

- Hissing
- Meowing
- Scratching
- Pawing
- Purring
- Lapping
- Chasing
- Laying

I then showed the class how we could plug the words from the list into the template below to create our poem:

I am a _____,
_____ing
_____ing
_____ing
_____ing
_____ing
_____ing

I explained that if necessary we could always revise our poem and move phrases around while constructing it. (I added that this is what good writers do all the time.) We knew we needed to add more to each of the *-ing* words as we wrote, to help the poem make sense. We also knew that we might not have to use all the words from the list and that while writing, we might think of a word not on the list. This is the first poem that we created together:

I am a cat,
>   Meowing at my owner
>   Laying on the end of the sofa
>   Purring as I am softly being stroked
>   Meowing when the dog comes in the room
>   Scurrying away from the barking dog
>   Hissing to scare the dog away
>   Relaxing as the dog is shooed out of the room
>   Making my way back to my spot on the sofa

Having modeled the process, I now asked my students to become the animal or thing they had just researched in the previous nonfiction writing unit. As they began listing present participles about their topic, I walked around to see if anyone needed help. I suggested to students having trouble that they retrieve their "all about" books from our classroom library to help them along. I also suggested getting out the books they had used to research their topic and looking for *-ing* words.

The following day, I modeled the process again, using a different topic. The students provided more help with this poem and seemed eager to write their own. I asked them to take out their list from the day before and gave each student a paper copy of the "I am" poem template.

The students were able to complete their *-ing* poem successfully, about 90 percent of them with little or no one-on-one assistance. Much to my delight, my students' poems were as strong in word choice and content as those of the students three grade levels above mine! In the days to follow, over half of the children used the structure when writing other poetry and during their content-area work. Their immersion in rich vocabulary related to their topic in the nonfiction writing unit may have contributed to their success.

.   .   .

Have you guessed what grade these students were in? Perhaps the "all about" book assignment was a clue, or maybe the topic of the collaboratively created poem gave it away. They were first graders. First graders in a middle- to upper-middle-class school district, we grant you, but first graders nevertheless. Emily employed several steps of the idealized framework in Chapter 4, brainstorming with the students, creating models with them—not once but twice—and giving them a frame or template to scaffold their learning. She also provided individual help—conducted miniconferences—as needed, suggesting resources to some students and collaborating with others on part of the task to get them started (more scaffolding). Teachers like Emily are models for us all. As college professors, Jonathan and I find too that some of the teachers and prospective teachers in our classes need substantial scaffolding with some of the grammatical options we teach in our Grammar in Teaching Writing course.

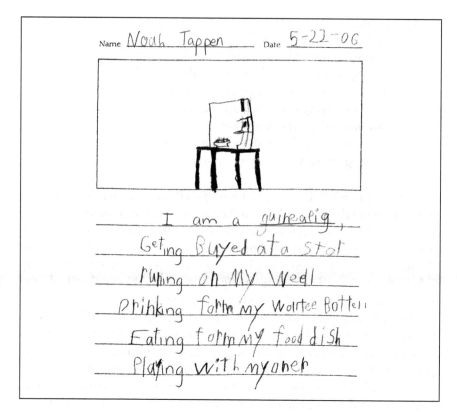

FIGURE 5–2. "I am a guinea pig," by Noah Tappen

I am a guinea pig,
   Getting buyed at a
      store
   Running on my wheel
   Drinking from my
      water bottle
   Eating from my food
      dish
   Playing with my
      owner

Of course, having "spilled the beans" about the students' grade level, we want to include examples of what these first graders wrote (see Figures 5–2, 5–3, and 5–4). As you can see, Emily encourages her first graders to spell as best they can in order to get their ideas down and to use the sophisticated words they know but can't yet spell conventionally. Constructed spellings of sophisticated words are a good example of "errors" as signs of progress. (Figure 5–5 includes more of the students' poems, with conventional spelling.)

Errors as signs of progress

Our point? That our reach—ours and our students'—should exceed our grasp. That writers of all ages can make best use of their vocabulary if they just get the words down in early drafts. More broadly, that whenever writers of any age experiment with "new" words or grammatical features, they may make errors that reflect their progress. And that if we encourage and respond positively to such experimentation and then help students see how to edit—at least sometimes—to eradicate their new kinds of errors, they will grow as writers.

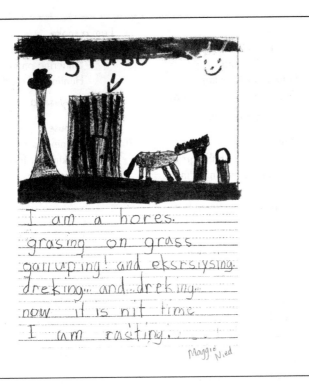

FIGURE 5-3. "I am a horse," by Margaret Nied

I am a horse,
   Grazing on grass
   Galloping and
     exercising
   Drinking and drinking
   Now it is night time
   I am resting

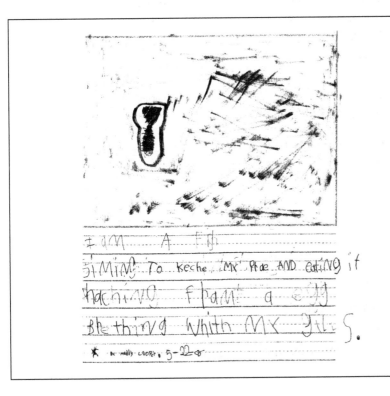

FIGURE 5-4. "I am a fish," by Madeline Cooper

I am a fish,
   Swimming to catch
    my prey and eating
    it
   Hatching from an egg
   Breathing with my
    gills

I am a horse,
>Running and being a horse
>Having fun and
>Eating too After this
>Going to play with friends

>>—Caitlin Forhan

I am a horse,
>Running through the grass
>Winning to the finish line
>Eating the grass
>Skipping to my horse barn

>>—Matthea

I am a monkey,
>Swinging on a branch
>Being cute
>Eating bananas
>Sleeping on leaves

>>—Ben Glasco

I am a fish,
>Hatching out of an egg
>Growing into a bass
>Jumping out of the water
>Flipping into the water

>>—Joe

I am horse,
>Racing to win
>Running just for fun
>Eating because the grass is good
>Galloping because it is fun
>Making sounds because I want to

>>—M. J. Page

I am a dog,
>Eating and someone is feeding me
>Drinking my water
>Running across the yard
I'm done eating.
I'm done drinking.

>>—Morgan Seguin

I am a snake,
>Hissing at a lizard
>Slithering on the ground
>Hunting for food

>>—Jessica

I am a mouse,
>Running fast
>Looking for food
>Eating cheese

>>—Richard

I am a mouse,
>Nibbling my cheese,
>Hiding from a cat,
>Talking to the mice,
>Screeching to my friends
>Working all day

>>—Kenneth Redner

I am a dog,
>Running at a cat
>Peeing at it
>Barking at it
>Jumping at it

>>—Collin

I am a frog,
>Swimming in a pond
>Jumping in the grass
>Swimming fast so no one
> can catch me

>>—Justin Wallace

FIGURE 5–5. More -ing animal poems from Emily's first graders

An extended lesson with sixth graders

If you're thinking that students in middle school and high school don't need much scaffolding, you may be right—or not. In *The Grammar Plan Book*, Connie describes how she and sixth-grade teacher Jeff Henderson, at Baldwin Middle School in Hudsonville, Michigan, taught an extended lesson on free modifying present participial phrases, the end product being students' own prequel or sequel to *The Paper Bag Princess* (Munsch, 1980). Figure 5–6 is Julia's prequel about the princess, and Figure 5–7 is Caleb's prequel about the dragon. Both students included several *-ing* phrases, but not all of them function as adjectives—as present participial phrases—which is what Connie was teaching. Caleb's paper, in fact, includes only one of these. We have underlined the adjectival *-ing* phrases that occur after the noun they modify or before it at the very beginning of the sentence.

Here are the preplanned steps Connie and Jeff carried out:

1. Read the book to students and show the pages on a transparency, so students can both hear the story and see the illustrations. [It turned out that most of these sixth graders had been read this story by a previous teacher.]

2. Introduce examples of sentences with *-ing* participial phrases from a sequel to the story that Connie has already written. Discuss these sentences, including whether certain participial phrases can be moved to the front of their sentence.

3. Conduct guided practice in pairs. Give the students bare-bones sentences about a prince and about a dragon, with instructions to add—either at the beginning of the sentence or the end—a participial phrase that modifies the subject. Start off as a class by composing some modifiers that can be added to one of the sentences.

4. Provide individual help. Walk around the room, helping students who are having difficulty with the participial phrase concept—or simply with ideas of what the prince or dragon might do.

5. Share a model of a prequel or sequel. [Connie shared the prequel she had written and pointed out more things about the *-ing* participial phrases she had used.]

6. Give the assignment: Write a prequel or sequel to *The Paper Bag Princess*, using at least two present participial phrases.

After reviewing students' first drafts, Jeff, on a subsequent day, clarified that he wanted participial *phrases* (not just single words) that gave extra details and would therefore be separated from the rest of the sentence

Prequel
Princess Elizabeth: A Hero

"What shall we name her?" the Queen asked. She had just given birth to the famous Princess Elizabeth. Looking deeply into her daughter's eyes, the Queen decided upon a name. "Elizabeth", she said. "Elizabeth", the King agreed. He smiled warmly, <u>wondering what lay ahead in the future</u>. The Queen, too, was thinking deep thoughts, <u>dreaming about her daughter becoming a hero</u>. Little did she know how soon her dreams would come true.

Little Elizabeth grew up fast, <u>seeming always to ask "Why this?" or "Why that?"</u> But she soon learned that many things unknown to her were happening beyond the safety of the castle wall. She learned that a terrible dragon came to the nearby village, <u>threatening to harm the royal family unless given daily provisions</u>. The village's supply was running low, but the cunning and clever dragon could not be stopped.

One day, as Elizabeth was riding through the village, she heard a concerned whisper. She listened for awhile, but turned to go, <u>realizing that she had been eavesdropping</u>. "But the village's supply has run out", came the voice. "And unless we do something, the dragon will devour the castle, <u>leaving nothing behind</u>. Elizabeth hesitated, then decided to stay and listen. "But what can we do?" the other voice asked. "You know that the guards won't let us in for a minute. They won't believe us, and there's no other way to warn them. "We'll find a way." came the reply although Elizabeth knew that he, too, was unsure of himself. Eliabeth had heard enough. She turned and galloped toward the palace, <u>beginning to form a plan in her mind</u>.

"Mother!" Elizabeth cried. "Mother! Father! An awful thing has happened!" She explained to her parents everything that she had overheard. The Queen, <u>doubting that anything could be done</u>, wanted to stay and hope nothing happened. Elizabeth, however, had other ideas. Remember that old, abandoned castle you always talk about?" Elizabeth asked. "We can go there until it's safe here! And didn't you say something about some Prince Ronald guy that lives nearby?"

Well, that pretty much settled it, <u>seeing that there were no other options</u>. Everyone packed up as fast as they could and left, and not a moment too soon. They had just reached the gate when they heard a loud, crackling noise behind them. They turned to see the castle going up in flames. Nobody could have survived it. "Elizabeth, you're a hero!" everyone cried.

They moved into the old castle and lived there peacefully for a time. But before too long, another catastrophe struck and Elizabeth once again was a hero, although not everyone thought so. But if you want to read about Princess Elizabeth's further adventures, you have to read <u>The Paper Bag Princess</u>.

FIGURE 5–6. Julia's prequel, "Princess Elizabeth: A Hero"

Spook the Dragon

Spook, a horrifying dragon always seemed liked he was always lonely. He was a dragon that was always eating, but Spook was always busy. Spook wasn't a typical dragon, but was very unique, he was black, and had violet eyes. Spook always wanted to have a friend.

<u>Walking to town</u>, on a gloomy day he passed a little girl named Reida. Once Reida saw the dragon she screamed so loud that you could hear her all the way in a far away castle, which a beautiful princess lived, but as she screamed the dragon couldn't figure out what to do. Spook was so sad that day that nobody wanted to be a gracious friend, so he started to cry. The girl stopped screaming, and she ran as fast as she could to her grandma geane's. Then, as she ran the dragon didn't notice.

As spook was crying, the meanest girl in the town of charlotte came up to him and started laughing at him because she thought that he got hurt. Spook then told her what happened and she started laughing even harder than she was before. After a while, she stopped and asked him what he said again, and he replied "i'll tell you if you don't laugh. Ok the girl said. Spook, then went on and told her, but this time she did more than laugh, she laughed so hard that she started to cry. Then spook, finally told her to be quiet and then she ran off.

Later, spook kept walking until he met the nicest girl in the town of charlotte. Spook, then noticed that somebody said hi for once in a life time. He felt so odd, and he seemed like he was, going to go crazy, although spook was very shy, but he had to say something. Finally, he said something very unusual, HOLA! Mary, then didn't know what to say, infact mary didn't even know what language the dragon was speaking. So, mary decided that spook was such an confusing that she left him all alone and he did more than cry this time, he cried such a bi puddle, that if you walked past the puddle you could easily drown.

So, then the dragon felt so bad by, penetrating everybody's hearts, making everybody so afraid of him, but so mad at them for not trying, so now his name is THE APPRENTICE!

FIGURE 5–7. Caleb's prequel, "Spook the Dragon"

by a comma or commas. He tried to distinguish the participial phrases that function like adjectives from *-ing* words used in other ways, but many students were still confused, perhaps even more confused than before. After receiving the students' final drafts, Jeff estimated that about 40 percent of his students grasped the concept adequately during this first extended sequence of lessons. Any teacher can feel encouraged by that rate of success, yet Connie and Jeff couldn't help wondering how the teaching could have been better the first time around.

Looking at the sequence of steps, can you identify where more teaching should probably have occurred before the students were asked to write the prequel or sequel? In retrospect, Connie thinks there are at least two other things that should have been done. First, she and the class should have together composed more participial phrases in sentences—an expansion of step 3. Second, she should have had the students write a short paragraph about one of the three characters—not a story, necessarily, but a description and/or part of a story—for Jeff to check before assigning the prequel or sequel. (This could have occurred between steps 4 and 5 but would have required that the basic lesson be extended over two class periods.) Another option would have been to include fewer concepts in one lesson—for example, concentrating only on *-ing* phrases occurring at the end of the sentence and modifying the subject.

In addition, we believe it would have helped if Jeff had displayed some sentences from students' first drafts on an overhead transparency and had the class work together to add participial phrases at the end. Then he could have challenged students to do the same with two sentences from their own stories. He might even have had the students write down their two expanded sentences on a piece of paper and hand them in for his approval or help. In other words, we suggest adding these steps:

- Model how to restructure, combine, and/or expand sentences from students' own papers by adding an *-ing* participial phrase.
- Have students try this on a new sheet of paper with two of their own sentences and submit these for teacher feedback.
- Reteach to those who still need help.

For example, with Caleb's permission, we might have taken example sentences from his paper to demonstrate expansion or restructuring:

Expansion

Original: Then spook, finally told her to be quiet and then she ran off.

How about adding an action to describe Spook? Here's one possibility, with the capitalization and punctuation corrected too:

Then Spook, <u>feeling defeated</u>, finally told her to be quiet and then she ran off.

Of course, someone might suggest reducing the participial phrase to just the word *defeated*, which would be even better! Here's another participial expansion for the same sentence:

Then Spook finally told her to be quiet and then she ran off, <u>cracking up with laughter.</u>

With the Jeff's help, students could have offered different alternatives and Caleb could have chosen one—or come up with still another himself.

Restructuring

Original: Mary, then didn't know what to say, infact mary didn't even know what language the dragon was speaking.

Revised: Not even knowing what language the dragon was speaking, Mary didn't know what to say.

This revision is more logically ordered, with the participial phrase giving the cause and the main clause expressing the effect. While most sixth graders may not be able to accomplish such a revision on their own, an example like this can make the general point that a sentence opener often sets the scene for the main part of the sentence.

Most of the sentences in Caleb's paper are rather long, so we aren't suggesting a sentence-combining lesson be drawn from it. In fact, we wouldn't draw all these examples from any one student's paper: the intent here is simply to demonstrate how these techniques—sentence revising, sentence expanding, and sentence combining—can be taught during the revision process. Such teaching would have been an invaluable addition to the lesson Connie and Jeff taught.

Such work during revision helps students see how to add details to their writing and how to subordinate details to a main statement. With the suggested detail added to Caleb's paper, we don't yet have details within details—that is, layers of details, as in Connie's ice cream sundae poem—but it's a start. By working with student sentences like Caleb's, we can help students learn to add depth and texture to their writing.

Figure 5–8 is an expanded plan for Connie and Jeff's lesson. If you compare this with the idealized lesson framework in Chapter 4, you'll find them very similar. In fact, the Chapter 4 framework was developed after Connie and Jeff taught these lessons! Isn't hindsight wonderful?

Still another step—or set of steps—could involve editing for the comma or commas that set off these free modifying participial phrases

Repeatedly emphasizing the point that we are adding *specific, interesting details*, we might revise our original lesson plan as follows:

1. Read the book to students and show the pages on a transparency, so students can both hear the story and see the illustrations.

2. Introduce examples of sentences with *-ing* participial phrases from a sequel to the story that Connie has already written. Discuss these sentences, including whether certain participial phrases can be moved to the front of their sentence.

3. Conduct guided practice in pairs. Give the students bare-bones sentences about a prince and about a dragon, with instructions to add—either at the beginning of the sentence or the end—a participial phrase that modifies the subject. As a class, start off by composing some modifiers that can be added to one of the sentences. Discuss these, then compose and discuss a few more examples.

4. Provide individual help. Walk around the room, helping students who are having difficulty with the participial phrase concept—or simply with ideas of what the prince or dragon might do.

5. Provide more individual composing practice, plus follow-up response and teaching. Have students write just a paragraph—not yet a plotted story—about one of the three characters, the princess, the prince, or the dragon. Ask the students to include an *-ing* phrase in—or add it to—two of the sentences in their paragraph. Have them be sure they've set off each participial phrase with one or two commas, as needed, before handing in the paragraphs.

6. Check the students' work on these paragraphs; then determine and provide whatever additional teaching might be needed before assigning the prequel or sequel to *The Paper Bag Princess*.

7. Share a model of a prequel or sequel. Call attention to the present participial phrases or have students locate them.

8. Give the assignment: Write a prequel or sequel to *The Paper Bag Princess*, using at least two present participial phrases.

9. Help with revision. Model how to expand sentences from students' own papers by adding an *-ing* participial phrase.

10. Have students try this on a new sheet of paper with two of their own sentences, including the needed comma or commas, then submit these for teacher feedback.

11. Reteach concepts to those who still need help, and have students do final revisions.

12. Collect students' final drafts, and publish and celebrate their work!

FIGURE 5–8. Expanding Connie and Jeff's lesson on *-ing* phrases (described in Weaver, 2007, pp. 17–22)

from the rest of their sentence—but that could launch a whole new set of editing lessons!

Basic approaches to teaching modifiers and helping students revise

In *The Grammar Plan Book* (pp. 48–49), Connie suggests three common ways to teach grammatical constructions for writing:

1. *Sentence imitating.* Share one or more model sentences, discuss the grammar of the modifier with the students, and ask them (in groups, pairs, or individually) to create their own sentence or sentences following the pattern used in the model. This is generally easy for students to do; it's also relatively motivating, because they are creating their own sentences, not combining someone else's.

2. *Sentence expanding.* After sharing and discussing model sentences, ask students to expand a sentence with a modifier that follows the pattern used in the model. The basic sentence may be one you suggest, one the class has brainstormed, or one the student has written.

3. *Sentence combining.* Have students combine two or more sentences to create a longer, more effective sentence. This requires the least independent thought and creativity on the part of the students and is therefore likely to be the least motivating. However, teachers sometimes use this technique in preparation for sentence expanding or sentence imitating, especially when working with the class as a whole. This technique is most successful when teachers draw the sentences from their students' own writing—particularly if they are still in the process of revising.

Two or all three of these techniques might be used during the process of producing one piece of writing. To these, we now add a fourth:

4. *Sentence restructuring.* Revise an existing sentence to make one or more parts grammatically subordinate to the main part. Or rearrange elements as needed for the best effect.

Sentence revision can include all of these techniques.

Looking back at our examples, we see that Connie showed Max how to expand his sentences with participial phrases and did this herself in her "I am" poem about the ice cream sundae. Emily Mihocko taught these modifiers to her first graders by first helping them expand a sentence as a class ("I am a _____"), then asking them to imitate the cat poem model and providing a template as an additional scaffold. We showed Jeff's sixth graders models that they discussed, gave them other sentences to expand, and asked them to create sentences with participial phrases independently in their prequel or sequel. We think the teaching would have been still more successful if Jeff or Connie had helped the students combine or expand sentences in their own stories, in order to include participial phrases and reduce the sameness of their sentences.

Modifiers in nonfiction

By nonfiction we mean not just biography and autobiography, not just creative nonfiction as a self-proclaimed genre, but mainstream articles in magazines or journals and books designed to be explanatory, informative, and persuasive. Of the four kinds of adjectival free modifiers, the two that occur most often in such prose are participial phrases and appositives. We offer an example here in order to:

- Demonstrate that participial phrases occur in nonfiction
- Show how the use of a participial phrase might be combined with other free modifiers to create sentence fluency within a paragraph
- Illustrate that participial phrases may occur in a grammatically parallel series

Francis Christensen (1967, p. 20) quotes a sentence from the anthropologist and naturalist Loren Eiseley that illustrates all three points. We reproduce the sentence as Christensen presented it, with indenting and numbering to show the layers of the sentence as the modifiers go deeper and deeper into the topic:

1 It is with the coming of man that a vast hole seems to open in nature,
2 a vast black whirlpool spinning faster and faster,
  3 consuming flesh, stones, soil, minerals,
  3 sucking down the lightning,
  3 wrenching power from the atom,
    4 until the ancient sounds of nature are drowned out in the cacophony of something which is no longer nature,
      5 something instead which is loose and knocking at the world's heart,
      5 something demonic and no longer planned—

    6 escaped, it may be—
    6 spewed out of nature,
    6 contending in a final giant's game against its master.

There are four set-off participial phrases in this sentence, as you can see. The second line, *a vast black whirlpool spinning faster and faster*, is an appositive modifying *hole* in the first line. Within this appositive is a participial phrase that is bound to *whirlpool*, the word it modifies. And so forth.

As writers push themselves to add adjectival modifiers, they force themselves to become deeper observers, deeper thinkers, and better conveyers of the detail that makes their writing memorable and their explanations and arguments persuasive. Again, this is why Christensen claimed that his focus on deepening the layers of grammatical constructions constituted a *generative* rhetoric.

Remembering our purpose

It's easy to lose sight of the forest for the trees when we're focusing specifically on some grammatical construction we want to add to students' repertoire. We can get so caught up in this limited intention that we forget we are merely and mainly trying to help students add details to their writing. We may get so focused that we ignore the other ways that students themselves have found for adding detail. We may mark things "wrong" when what we might better do is show appreciation for what the student did or tried to do, explain why what the student has done isn't what we were trying to teach or isn't done quite right, and then demonstrate with another example or two what we were trying to teach.

If you have read Connie's *Grammar Plan Book*, this advice may sound "old hat." But it's important nonetheless. We need to have a playful attitude about our teaching, a playful attitude toward students' learning. Playful when it comes to trying new things, and playful about new kinds of errors.

After the York summary of research on the teaching of grammar was released (Andrews et al., 2004b), Philip Pullman, author of award-winning fantasy novels for young adults and adults, wrote an essay titled "It's Time English Teachers Got Back to Basics—Less Grammar, More Play" (2005). Pullman talks about the attitudes with which teachers can approach students and their learning:

We need to have a playful attitude about our teaching, a playful attitude toward students' learning.

> The most valuable attitude we can help children adopt—the one that, among other things, helps them to write and read with most fluency and effectiveness and enjoyment—I can best characterise by the word *playful*.

It begins with nursery rhymes and nonsense poems, with clapping games and finger play and simple songs and picture books. It goes on to consist of fooling around with the stuff the world is made of: with sounds, and with shapes and colours, and with clay and paper and wood and metal, and with language. Fooling about, playing with it, pushing it this way and that, turning it sideways, painting it different colours, looking at it from the back, putting one thing on top of another, asking silly questions, mixing things up, making absurd comparisons, discovering unexpected similarities, making pretty patterns, and all the time saying "Supposing . . . I wonder . . . What if . . . ?"

Let's help our students—often more inhibited than the children of whom Pullman speaks—rediscover this playfulness, this attitude that language and grammar are to be played with, toyed with, bent, expanded, crafted, enjoyed. Let's free our students from their fears about "being wrong," releasing and guiding them to become the writers they are capable of being.

Bringing in the Rest of the Gang
More Adjectival Modifiers

A t the end of the last chapter we emphasized Philip Pullman's point that being playful with language is the best way to stimulate students' growth as readers and writers. You might never have thought of experimenting with color and design as part of grammar study, but as a prelude to teaching our remaining categories of free modifying adjectivals, we'll offer one way to do just that. Many students are amazing artists, something we English teachers are often unaware of. It makes sense to take advantage of students' strengths and interests in helping them learn about grammatical structures.

As she began her last semester of teaching, Connie was suddenly inspired to have students "diagram" the major chunks of sentences artistically. She had already handed out a list of about fifty sentences from Robert Ludlum's *The Sigma Protocol* (2001), divided more or less evenly between the categories of modifiers to be discussed. At the end of class, Connie parceled out the groups of sentences to different groups of students and made an optional homework assignment: *Choose one of the sentences from your group's set, divide the sentence into major chunks of meaning/structure, and draw a picture to illustrate how the chunks relate to one another—ideally a picture that somehow reflects the content of the sentence.* Since the assignment was optional, few students accepted the invitation, but those who did invariably divided the sentences into the same chunks we would have.

Connie calls this "sentence chunking." It differs from traditional sentence diagramming in that it focuses on determining *major* "chunks" of grammar and meaning in a sentence and expressing how they relate to one another, instead of reducing the sentence to single words, indicating how each word relates to another, and (typically) identifying each word's "part of speech." Chunking a sentence into its major units does not necessarily involve naming those units, though it may.

Connecting sentence chunking to art: Some examples

In Figure 6–1, Eda (Liesbeth) Koning illustrates a sentence with two present participial phrases: *Fog had settled over the gray streets of this port town, blanketing it, closing it in* (Ludlum, 2001, p. 18). The phrase *blan-*

FIGURE 6–1.
Sentence chunking
by Eda Koning

keting it is depicted as part of a blanket; the other participial phrase, *closing it in*, closes off the blanket at the foot of the bed.

In Figure 6–2, Kim Jay illustrates a sentence with two adjectives "out of order": *He could taste liquid, brackish and metallic, and he touched his lips* (pp. 21–22). Cleverly, she shows chemical symbols for metals dripping from the person's lips.

Michelle Jackson-Long's illustration of a sentence with an appositive— *Then a second car passed Ben's Opal: a gray sedan with two men inside* (p. 77)—shows all three cars: the tail end of the first car that passed Ben's Opal, the gray sedan with two men inside, and then Ben in his Opal (see Figure 6–3).

In Figure 6–4 Kim Jay illustrates a sentence containing two absolute constructions: *His mouth was caved in, the baggy skin of the face pallid, the eyes gray and watery* (p. 18). The phrase *his eyes gray and watery* is written over the eyes; *the baggy skin of the face pallid* is written below the eyes (as if the skin below the eyes is baggy and pallid).

FIGURE 6–2. Sentence chunking by Kim Jay

FIGURE 6–3. Sentence chunking by Michelle Jackson-Long

FIGURE 6–4.
Sentence chunking
by Kim Jay

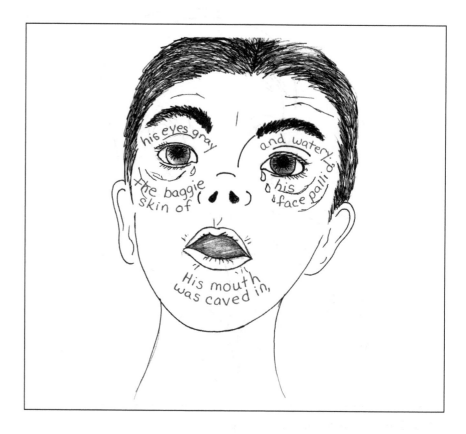

Playing with adjectivals out of order

In Chapter 5 we saw that present participials can occur out of the normal prenoun position and that they are especially likely to do so if they are phrases rather than single words. Another way of adding detail that writers of all ages especially enjoy playing with is positioning adjectivals, either single words or phrases, sometimes paired or tripled. In the following examples of single or paired adjectives, which are from Dia Calhoun's *Firegold* (1999), notice that:

- Adjectives modifying the subject of the sentence (or clause) may occur before it, after it, or at the end of the sentence.
- Wherever these extra-detail, free modifying adjectives occur, they are separated from the rest of the sentence by a comma (by two commas if they occur right after the subject). Such adjectives don't always modify the grammatical subject, but often they do.
- Sometimes the out-of-order adjective or adjectives can be moved to another position in the sentence and still sound good—or even better.

<u>Taut</u>, <u>arched,</u> the bow shimmered, freed from its linen covering; someone had strung it. (p. 131)

He saw himself shackled to a post, <u>wild-haired</u>, <u>slavering</u>. (p. 41) [Yes, the second underlined modifier is specifically a present participle.]

<u>Tall</u> and <u>rangy</u>, she was among the best runners in their bristol and hoped to be a Master Hunter someday. (p. 256)

<u>Keen-eyed</u>, <u>long-limbed</u>, they wore leather and carried gleaming bows. (p. 202)

Someone, something, called Jonathon's name. He looked at his father, then at Uncle Wilford, who were both staring at him, <u>bewildered</u>. (p. 74)

<u>Unconvinced</u>, Jonathon dug his heel in the snow. (p. 79)

<u>Dazzled</u>, Jonathon squinted: he was half-blinded, but unable to look away. (p. 196)

The knife's shadow reared up, <u>huge</u>, <u>grotesque</u>, cast on the house behind him. (p. 145)

Rosamund looked, <u>unperturbed</u>, at the brown stains. (p. 98)

Sometimes the chronological order of events or a cause-effect sequence makes one free modifying position preferable to any others. Do you find that true in any of the sentences above?

Out-of-order adjectival phrases: The motley crew

An *adjectival phrase* is a group of words that together function like a single adjective. Some specific kinds of free modifying phrases are present participial phrases, appositives, and absolutes. Here, "out-of-order adjectival phrases" is a catch-all category for the other kinds of free modifying adjectival phrases, some of which have an adjective as a "head" word. (Some of the preceding sentences also include free modifying adjectival phrases, but we didn't underline them there.) In the following examples, again from *Firegold*, notice that the placement, punctuation, and movability of such modifiers follows the pattern of single adjectives.

> Red as blood, the rock stood out from all the others on the stony bank. (p. 5)
>
> "My son," she said. Her eyes, nutmeg brown, looked straight at him. (p. 10)
>
> It looked like the kind of place that would always have a pie, piping hot, just out of the oven. (p. 165)
>
> Jonathon twisted the quilt, bitter that Uncle Wilford had brought him inside instead of his father. (p. 67)
>
> Then he remembered how happy his father had looked when he first came home, happier than Jonathon had ever seen him, his face bright and alive. (p. 69)
>
> Jonathon relaxed, certain now that she had not seen the rock, and glanced up at her. (p. 95)
>
> A woman stared at him; her dark hair, peppered with white, was coiled in a braid on her head. (p. 165)
>
> The trees, stitched in fantastic shades of red violet, orange, and turquoise, bowed under their bounty of golden fruit (p. 171)
>
> He thought of how the colt had come to him at last, drawn by the rock's glowing magic. (p. 66)

In the last three examples, the "head" of the adjectival phrase seems to have more of a verb sense than an adjectival sense. Transformational linguists would point out that *drawn* is the past participle form of the verb *draw*, which simply means it's the form we'd use after the auxiliary verb *have*, *has*, or *had*: *the rock's glowing magic had <u>drawn</u> the colt*, which transformationalists would consider the underlying structure. The words *peppered* and *stitched* also may be said to come from past participial forms, though that's not so obvious because the simple past verbs also end in *-ed*. These past participial free modifiers may be more common—certainly in some writings—than many other adjectivals, except for the even more frequent present participial *-ing* forms. Here are some examples from a photo/text "art" book, *Bridges: A History of the World's Most Famous and Important Spans* (Dupré, 1997):

> <u>Constructed</u> with an economy of materials and means, the innovative Natchez Trace Parkway Arches treads lightly indeed. (p. 101)

> <u>Faced</u> with brick, granite and textured concrete, the bridges have been designed to reflect the city's greatest treasure, the three centuries of architecture that surrounds them. (p. 103)

> The bridge, <u>*completed* just two months before the handover at midnight, June 30</u>, is a big, if not elegant, signal of the changes in store for Hong Kong. (p. 111)

Rebecca teaches adjectives out of order to ninth graders

Fascinated with out-of-order adjectives when first explicitly introduced to them, Rebecca Schipper, a teacher in the Hudsonville, Michigan, school system, decided immediately to teach these modifying phrases to her ninth graders. The class was reading about the Holocaust, through such accounts as Elie Wiesel's *Night* (1969), Gerda Weissmann Klein's *All But My Life* (1957/1995), Carrie Ten Boom and John Scherrill's *The Hiding Place* (1971), Edith Hahn Beer's *The Nazi Officer's Wife: How One Jewish Woman Survived the Holocaust* (1999), and Primo Levi's *Survival in Auschwitz* (1996). All are first-person accounts by survivors of Nazi concentration camps. To introduce the concept of out-of-order adjectives, Rebecca prepared a handout with examples from each of these books. She included not only adjectives themselves, but phrases headed by an adjective or, in any case, functioning adjectivally:

> They said he was a charming man—<u>calm</u>, <u>likable</u>, <u>polite</u>, and <u>sympathetic</u>. (*Night*, p. 7)

> On the Saturday before Pentecost, in the spring sunshine, people strolled, <u>carefree</u> and <u>unheeding</u>, through the swarming streets. (*Night*, p. 10)

> <u>Busy with getting our packs ready, with baking bread and cakes,</u> we no longer thought of anything. (*Night*, p. 16)

Past participial modifiers

In all these examples, the head word derives from an underlying verb: SOMEONE <u>*completed* the bridge</u>, from which derives *the bridge was completed by someone*, from which derives the adjectival phrase headed by *completed*: *completed just two months before the handover at midnight, June 30*. While this is more information than you may want, we're including it because we've found that students often look at a sentence like the original examples and consider the head adjectivals to be verbs. Students of language are often more sensitive to the "underlying" structures postulated by transformational linguists than to the surface structure on which structural linguists and traditional schoolroom grammar books focus. If these be errors—though we don't think they are—they are errors born of deeper understanding.

They put me to bed, where I cried into the pillow until, <u>exhausted</u>, I fell asleep. (*All But My Life*, p. 9)

Usually it was fog in January in Holland, <u>dank</u>, <u>chill</u>, and <u>gray</u>. (*The Hiding Place*, p. 1)

They were a slave population, <u>conquered</u> and <u>helpless</u>; transported away from their parents, wives, and children; longing for home. (*The Nazi Officer's Wife*, pp. 4–5) [There are two adjectival *phrases* here, too: *transported away from their parents, wives, and children* and *longing for home*.]

The different emotions that overcame us, <u>of resignation</u>, <u>of futile rebellion</u>, <u>of religious abandon</u>, <u>of fear</u>, <u>of despair</u>, now joined together after a sleepless night in a collective, uncontrolled panic. (*Survival in Auschwitz*, p. 16) [The prepositional phrases function adjectivally, to clarify and modify the noun *emotions*.]

After discussing these out-of-order adjectivals with the students, Rebecca handed out and explained their assignment (see Figure 6–5). It included more examples, a question about the location of the adjectives, and a question about punctuation (comma use). The students were then to write sentences using adjectives out of order: first a sentence on the topic of school, and then one on the topic of Thanksgiving dinner. The follow-up assignment was to use out-of-order adjectivals in a paragraph describing the main character in the Holocaust book that each person had chosen to read.

Almost all of the students successfully included at least one out-of-order adjective in their character descriptions—often, a pair of adjectives, as in many of the examples. Sometimes the required comma or commas were used, and sometimes not—another example of new kinds of errors accompanying new learning. Here is a range of examples from the class.

Carrie Ten Boom, <u>middle aged</u> and <u>compassionate</u>, lives in the middle of Harlem, Holland.

Primero Levi, <u>fatigued</u> and <u>dehydrated</u>, lost not only his hair, but also his dignity.

Primero Levi is a hopeful man, <u>determined</u>, and <u>self-motivated</u>.

The guard men, <u>cruel</u> and <u>ruthless</u>, treat the prisoners as if they were dirt.

Now he knew; the people, <u>stubborn</u> and <u>ignorant</u>, didn't even listen to a word he said!

She and her family spent a night in the basement, <u>damp</u> and <u>chilly</u>.

"Out-of-Order" Adjectives

Improving word choice in writing can add a lot to your work. It can take a paper from being a "typical" to being a "wow" paper. After looking at some samples of student work and evaluating those using the rubric, it is now your turn to work on word choice. One way to improve word choice (and, along the way, detail in your writing) is through the use of something called "out-of-order" adjectives. Basically, what this means is using adjectives in your sentences in different places than you normally would. Great writers (including Shakespeare!) have used these and have proven their use to be a great addition to writing. Here are some examples, taken from Harry Noden's *Image Grammar* (1999):

The woman, <u>old and wrinkled</u>, smiled upon her newborn great-grandson with pride.
    —Stephanie Schwallie

The boxer, <u>twisted and tormented</u>, felt no compassion for his contender.
    —Chris Hloros

The cheetah, <u>tired and hungry</u>, stared at the gazelle, which would soon become his dinner.
    —Zach Vesoulis

What do you notice about the location of these phrases in the sentence?

How are these phrases punctuated?

Using the topic of **school**, write your own new sentence using this method of "out-of-order" adjectives.

Trying this again, using the topic of **Thanksgiving dinner**, write another new sentence using this same method.

Your assignment: Write a paragraph describing the main character in your novel. Use the "out-of-order" adjectives to add detail and improve word choice in your paragraph. You should write this paragraph on the back of this paper. Keep in mind the following things:

- no first/second person
- no outlawed words
- spelling
- punctuation
- include at least two "out-of-order" adjectives (underline them, please!)
- at least five sentences in your paragraph

FIGURE 6–5. Rebecca Schipper's assignment sheet on "out-of-order" adjectives

Primo Levi, <u>full of confusion and sarcasm</u>, tells his story for all to hear.

<u>Hopeful</u> and <u>grateful</u>, Gerda is different from any other 15 year old girl.

<u>Walking in the steaming house</u> she hears the tick tock of the clocks. <u>Calm</u> and <u>steady</u>, she starts supper. <u>Hearing her precise dad</u>, she decides to make more hardy supper.

She quickly ran into her father's restaurant, <u>panting for air</u>, she scanned for anyone she knew that was close by. [To fix the final run-on sentence, the writer could change either of the commas to a period and modify the capitalization accordingly.]

My Thanksgiving, <u>fun</u> and <u>full of food</u> is going to be fun. [Comma missing.]

Carrie Ten Boom, <u>gracious</u> and <u>giving</u>. [Fragment.]

Gerda, <u>strong willing</u> and <u>frightened</u>, <u>that her brother may not make it back from war OK</u>.

[This writer got lost in the sentence, ending up with a sentence fragment, two commas missing, and a misplaced comma that should have come after *OK* if the sentence had been completed. But look at what he or she attempted!]

Rebecca simply celebrated her students' success in employing adjectives—and adjectival phrases—out of order. Months after Rebecca had taught out-of-order adjectives, she noted in her journal:

> Well, it is February now, and the kids are using the "out of order" adjectives, appositives, and parallel constructions on their own! I am amazed that something has actually stuck with them. . . . Consider me sold on the idea of intertwining grammar with writing!

Renaming or categorizing with appositives

An *appositive* is a strange animal: a noun or pronoun in structure but an adjectival in function. The appositive usually categorizes, renames more specifically, or expands on something—it's some other noun (or pronoun) that designates someone or something. Examples are underlined in the following sentences from *Firegold* (Calhoun, 1999):

> With one eye on the girl, he heaved the fish, <u>an elger</u>, into the air and backed away from the river's edge. (p. 2) [Specifies what kind of fish.]

> Fear filled his throat until he couldn't swallow or even breathe—the girl was a barbarian, <u>a Dalriada from the Red Mountains</u>. (p. 2) [Categorizes the girl.]

> <u>A fabulous cook</u>, his mother never used recipes, but everything tasted wonderful and nothing ever tasted the same twice. (p. 11) [Places *his mother* in the category of fabulous cooks.]

> "I've had another lead on the Firegolds, <u>a serious lead</u>, from Endless Falls." (p. 151) [Expands on the first instance of *lead*.]

> He waited, breathing as Tlell had taught him, until a song seemed to come over him, <u>a song of the lake, of blue water and sky</u>. (p. 257) [Expands on the first instance of *song*.]

Teaching appositives to sixth graders

As Connie was planning her teaching demonstrations for the Greenwich (Connecticut) Country Day School, she hit on the idea of having students write appositives describing objects in Chris Van Allsburg's *Just a Dream* (1990). The book begins by introducing a boy named Walter who has no concern for the environment, as his actions demonstrate. That night he has a dream—a nightmare, really—in which he sees his home and neighborhood as they might appear in the future if others, too, do not protect the environment. The rest of the book contains illustrations of how his surroundings might look—neglected junk heaps nearly as high as the houses, trees cut for lumber, smokestacks belching poisons into the environment, and so forth—as Walter and his cat travel by means of his bed through the neighborhood and far beyond, even to Mount Everest.

Knowing that the forty-five minutes allotted would not allow enough time to prepare the students for writing, Connie asked the teacher, Betty Roberts, if she would not only teach in advance a reminder lesson on metaphors, but also read the book aloud, showing students the illustrations and discussing the book with them.

When Connie reread the book to the students, she projected transparencies of the illustrations. In order to encourage metaphorical appositives, she also projected two example sentences to go with the picture of Walter and his bed floating on clouds of pollution that obscure the earth. Each sentence began with a literal "I am" statement about an object in the illustration, which was followed by a metaphorical appositive:

> I am a white cloud,
>> a fluffy cushion for your bed.

> I am a bed,
>> a spaceship carrying you through the night sky.

Asking the students to work in pairs, Betty and Connie then walked around the room giving help.

Not all of the resulting poems included an appositive, let alone a metaphorical appositive, but some did include metaphors. The following poem was written in response to the illustration that showed tree stumps in a yard of barren grass, with Walter and his cat on his bed in a big tree on his street and two men with a crosscut saw looking up at Walter, ready to cut down the tree in which his bed rests:

> I am a forest, a graveyard of stumps.
> I am a shadow a sticky marshmallow, never letting go.
> I am the leaves, a roof over the bed.
> I am a saw, a mouth of sharp teeth devouring the tender trunk of
>> the tree.

> —*Lucy Williams and Annaliesa Routh*

The following poem was prompted by a double-page spread showing smokestacks emerging from clouds of their own smoke, everything portrayed in orange with orange-black shadows:

I am smog, a wall preventing sight.
I am a smokestack, the creator of clouds.
I am a lizard an orange Komodo dragon.
The horizon was a mystery enfolding in front of there eyes.

—*Thomas Galluccio and Robert Said*

Here are some lines from other poems in which the appositive—not always set off by commas, as you can see—is metaphorical:

I am trash bags, a field of glumpy milk. (Terra Arguimbau and Anna-Sophia Haub)

I am a cat, a stone soldier awaiting my next battle. (James Graham and Colin Bernard)

Of course, Connie and Betty knew it was too much to expect that on a first try all the sixth graders would create appositives, much less appositives that were metaphorical—but nothing ventured, nothing gained. Overall, the results were exciting, as even those students who hardly created any appositives used some other free modifying constructions: One poem included participial phrases modifying most of the objects specified, while James Graham and Colin Bernard included an absolute: *I am a fish, a wet scaly blanket wrapped around me*. We can tell this is an absolute and not an appositive because the fish is not being equated with a blanket but rather wrapped in it. Almost a complete sentence, the absolute would actually be a sentence if we inserted "was" before *wrapped*. (Absolutes are discussed in the next section.)

Adjectives out of order and appositives

It is quite common for students to confuse appositives with other kinds of adjectivals. For example:

Carlos, weary from the work, stood up slowly.
Carlos, a weary worker, stood up slowly.

In the first sentence, the head of the modifying phrase is the adjective *weary*. In the second, the head of the modifier is *worker*, a noun functioning adjectivally to categorize Carlos. But it's easy to lose track of the distinction, since both function adjectivally to modify another noun, in this case *Carlos*. Notice that both kinds of modifiers are also potentially movable to the beginning or end of their sentence. While we may teach these two kinds of adjectivals separately, and maybe even contrast them explicitly, do writers really need to be conscious of the distinction? We think not: Writers only need to be able to use either kind when appropriate, not label them.

Absolutes, absolutely!

Connie admits that until she'd read Francis Christensen's *Notes Toward a New Rhetoric* (1967), she'd never heard of an absolute construction. On the other hand, she later discovered three of the constructions in "A War Death," a poem her fifteen-year-old son had written (see Figure 6–6):

I found myself in a ditch, <u>the foul smell of rotting corpses groping at my nostrils</u>.

I heard the screams of others as they fell beside me, <u>blood oozing from their mouths</u>.

I could smell the explosive powder in the air, <u>hand grenades whizzing overhead</u>.

FIGURE 6–6. "A War Death" by John Weaver

A War Death

Shrapnel pounded into the dirt around me.
My buddies fell as the murderous pieces of metal embedded into their skin.
I ran. I tripped. I fell. I found myself in a ditch, the foul smell of rotting corpses groping at my nostrils.

I could smell the explosive powder in the air, hand grenades whizzing overhead.
Bombshells dropped like hailstones.
Men dropped to their knees and then to their deaths.
The death gases were now stinging my lungs.
I was dying.

A cold shiver shook my soul. I looked on as a hand grenade landed at my feet.
It exploded. I screamed. Blood more than trickled out of my legs, for they were only half attached. A numbness overswept my legs.
My eyelids let themselves slowly shut as a sense of peace overcame me.
I was dead.

  —John Weaver

Connie was curious how her son happened to use the constructions, since there were none in the poem his class was imitating—William Stafford's "I Am Fifteen"—and absolutes were not included in his class's grammar book. "Oh," said John nonchalantly, "all writers know how to use those." Or course he had no idea what "those" really were; he had just used them naturally, having picked up their structure from his reading.

What's so special about such constructions? After all, absolutes are only one more way to use our zoom lens as artists and writers, homing in on details—usually details associated with an object or, more often, a person or persons. Structurally, though, what's interesting is they contain the *essence* of a sentence. Typically they could be restored to a full sentence by adding *was* or *were* (if the writing occurred in the past tense) or *is* or *are* (for present tense). John could have written the following complete sentences instead:

I found myself in a ditch. The foul smell of rotting corpses *was* groping at my nostrils.

I heard the screams of others as they fell beside me. Blood *was* oozing from their mouths.

I could smell the explosive powder in the air. Hand grenades *were* whizzing overhead.

However, the separate sentences make the poem choppier and contain a weak use of a form of *to be*. Perhaps most important, with these details presented in separate sentences, readers may not have such a strong sense of viewing them through the eyes of the first person "I."

Here are more examples of absolutes, from Dia Calhoun's *Firegold* (1999). Three categories are illustrated under four headings, the third being a combination of examples:

- Absolutes that include an *-ing* word and express action, typically the action of a part of the entity specified (the noun modified)
- Absolutes that provide descriptive details, not action details
- Absolutes not modifying anything in the main clause

Action absolutes, with the noun followed by an -ing phrase

She bounded from stone to stone, her feet hardly pausing on one before she was soaring through the air again, her strange red hair streaming behind her. (pp. 3–4)

Jonathon woke sweating, his heart slicing through his chest, and pulled the quilt over his head. (p. 15)

His heart pounding, Jonathon remembered the hooded man in his nightmare. (p. 28)

Descriptive absolutes (no -ing word)

His knuckles white, he traced the green squares that crisscrossed the blue circles on his quilt, trying to see them instead of the arrow. (p. 66)

She bent down, her face hidden, and rearranged the arrows in his quiver. (p. 32)

Action and descriptive absolutes together

Jonathon stared up at his mother's portrait. She seemed to sail out from the canvas, her brown hair loose, blown by the wind. She clutched her baby, his face hidden against her shoulder. Eyes glittering, chin defiant, she looked into the distance, but her head tilted toward his; one strand of hair fell across his shoulder. A gold velvet dress buttoned tightly around her throat. (p. 127)

Absolutes not modifying anything in the main clause

Jonathon walked up the canyon, the leaves from the wild-rose bushes crunching beneath his feet. (p. 132)

After school on Monday, Jonathon slammed the kitchen door behind him and waited for his mother's voice to scold, an angry answer ready on his lips. (p. 27)

The Red Mountains spread across the northern horizon, the tallest peak a cone of scarlet in the sunset. (p. 135) [*Peak* relates to *Red Mountains*, of course, but not grammatically.]

The first two examples in the last group do include *his* as a reference to Jonathon, but they do not describe any aspect of him. The third example has no grammatical link at all to the main clause. What they have in common with the other absolutes, though, is their internal structure: They could be restored to a full sentence by adding *was* or *were*.

Absolutes seem to be used much less often in nonfiction prose than in fiction (see examples later in this chapter, though). When they occur, they may manifest as one of these two main types: absolutes that are grammatically related to the sentence, whether they show action or mere description, and absolutes that add details with little or no grammatical relationship to the main clause.

However, absolutes with *being*, not usually mentioned in grammar books (we all too often see fragments with *being* punctuated as if they were complete sentences), seem more frequent in nonfiction prose than in fiction:

The sky being blue when we left on our hike, we never anticipated an afternoon deluge in the mountains. [Narrative nonfiction.]

The situation being uncontrollable, we should bail out—fast. [Persuasive nonfiction.]

The authorities can't tell us exactly what happened, the truth being that they simply don't know. [Explanatory nonfiction.]

Standardized tests being inevitable, we still don't have to buy into the notion that they are an adequate measure of students' knowledge or progress. [Persuasive nonfiction.]

I rush home to the Blue Haven at the end of the day, pull down the blinds for privacy, strip off my uniform in the kitchen—the bathroom being too small for both a person and her discarded clothes—and stand in the shower for a good ten minutes, thinking all this water is *mine*. (Barbara Ehrenreich, *Nickel and Dimed*, p. 85) [Narrative nonfiction.]

How shall we teach absolutes? One way is by doing sentence combining, as Connie illustrated in *The Grammar Plan Book* (2007). For instance, we might take some of the preceding examples from *Firegold*, break them down into constituent sentences, and show students how to combine them to create an absolute in each case:

The original:

His heart pounding, Jonathon remembered the hooded man in his nightmare. (p. 28)

Deconstructed sentences:

Jonathon remembered the hooded man in his nightmare.
His heart was pounding.

Another original:

She bent down, her face hidden, and rearranged the arrows in his quiver. (p. 32)

Deconstructed sentences:

She bent down and rearranged the arrows in his quiver.
Her face was hidden.

Recombining these constituent sentences, we could create the originals. One advantage of a sentence-combining approach is that it nudges us to consider the best placement of an absolute within a sentence. Would it be best to write:

> Jonathan, his heart pounding, remembered the hooded man in his nightmare.

Or:

> His heart pounding, Jonathan remembered the hooded man in his nightmare.

And why wouldn't we choose:

> Jonathan remembered the hooded man in his nightmare, his heart pounding?

And do any of the following options seem clearly better than the others?

> Her face hidden, she bent down and rearranged the arrows in his quiver.

> She bent down, her face hidden, and rearranged the arrows in his quiver.

> She bent down and rearranged the arrows in his quiver, her face hidden.

When there is clearly more than one option, students may be eager to find out whether their first choice is the one the original author used.

Imitating sentences may be an even better way to introduce absolutes than combining them. Expanding sentences is also helpful, as is restructuring sentences—subordinating one to another—in students' own papers to create an absolute (or any other modifying construction). See the discussion of these techniques in Chapter 5.

Teaching absolutes with the novel Good Night, Mr. Tom

Sometimes we get lucky and see an unusual way to link teaching a grammatical construction with having students express their understanding of a novel. That happened when Connie was reading *Good Night, Mr. Tom*, by Michelle Magorian (1981). In this novel, families in London at the brink of World War II send their children off to the countryside for their safety. Among them is a boy named William Beech, who until now has

Imitating sentences may be an even better way to introduce absolutes than combining them.

lived in squalor with his abusive mother. The novel chronicles the changes in Willie as he learns to live with "Mr. Tom" in the country and becomes accepted by other kids—with an intervening period of relapse when he is forced to return to his mother.

Here is a greatly condensed sequence of lesson plans that would prompt students to use absolute constructions to express their understanding of Willie/Will/William's growth as a character:

- On a transparency, share some examples of absolutes describing Willie near the beginning of the novel, when he is still timid, afraid of being "bad," and bruised both physically and emotionally:

Willie watched him [Tom] silently, his bony elbows and knees jutting out angularly beneath his thin gray jersey and shorts. (p. 4)

Willie walked shakily towards the cottage, his head lowered. (p. 10)

Willie stared in amazement at the fields, his thin woolen socks heaped around his ankles. (p. 19)

Willie stood in the hallway shivering helplessly, his teeth rattling inside his clamped jaw. (p. 22)

Willie stood to face the fire, his head bowed over the stove. (p. 23)

Willie sat on the stool holding the fork in front of the fire, his long socks trailing across the floor. (p. 25)

- Brainstorm with students a short list of basic sentences (independent clauses) that the writer might have written about Willie/Will, first as he is getting to know Zack and then other kids, then as he is starting school and coming out of his shell. (You will probably want to discuss the differences in Willie/Will's appearance and actions in this section first.) Here are some possible sentences:

Willie looked up at Zack in amazement.

Willie followed George.

Willie answered Mrs. Hartley in a whisper.

- Next have students brainstorm for details by creating and sharing absolutes that focus on Will as he is relaxing into his new surroundings and experiencing support from the people he encounters—especially Mr. Tom.
- Repeat these steps at additional points in the novel, such as when Will has been forced to return to his mother and later when he comes back to Mr. Tom's.

Of course, there are other kinds of constructions that could be taught, such as infinitives. (See the section on parallelism in Chapter 12 for examples of infinitives.) Of the modifying constructions that remain, the ones we consider most useful are adverbial phrases—and the ordering of them for greatest effectiveness—plus adjectival and adverbial clauses. For convenience, we leave these constructions to Chapter 11, while taking to heart here what we have observed and Francis Christensen (1967) noted in an inductive study he conducted: "Our faith in the subordinate clause and the complex sentence is misplaced . . . we should concentrate instead on the sentence modifiers, or free modifiers" (p. xiii). This is particularly true for narrative/descriptive writing, which we contend is a foundation for all prose.

Free modifying adjectivals in poetry

We hardly know where to begin citing examples from poetry, since so many poets use these free modifying constructions to add details to their writing. We'll offer just one and then move on to nonfiction.

An all-time favorite poem of Connie's is "Between the World and Me," by Richard Wright (see Figure 6–7), about the frequent hanging of black Americans in the South, a practice that remained commonplace for all too long in the twentieth century. The participial phrases in this poem

---

Between the World and Me

And one morning while in the woods I stumbled
  suddenly upon the thing,
Stumbled upon it in a grassy clearing guarded by scaly
  oaks and elms
And the sooty details of the scene rose, thrusting
  themselves between the world and me. . . .

There was a design of white bones slumbering forgottenly
  upon a cushion of ashes.
There was a charred stump of a sapling pointing a blunt
  finger accusingly at the sky.
There were torn tree limbs, tiny veins of burnt leaves, and
  a scorched coil of greasy hemp;
A vacant shoe, an empty tie, a ripped shirt, a lonely hat,
  and a pair of trousers stiff with black blood.
And upon the trampled grass were buttons, dead matches,
  butt-ends of cigars and cigarettes, peanut shells, a
  drained gin-flask, and a whore's lipstick;
Scattered traces of tar, restless arrays of feathers, and the
  lingering smell of gasoline.
And through the morning air the sun poured yellow
  surprise into the eye sockets of the stony skull. . . .

FIGURE 6–7. Richard Wright, "Between the World and Me" (Wright, 1978, 246–247)

And while I stood my mind was frozen within cold pity
   for the life that was gone.
The ground gripped my feet and my heart was circled by
   icy walls of fear—
The sun died in the sky; a night wind muttered in the
   grass and fumbled the leaves in the trees; the woods
   poured forth the hungry yelping of hounds; the
   darkness screamed with thirsty voices; and the witnesses rose and
   lived:
The dry bones stirred, rattled, lifted, melting themselves
   into my bones.
The grey ashes formed flesh firm and black, entering into
   my flesh.

The gin-flask passed from mouth to mouth, cigars and
   cigarettes glowed, the whore smeared lipstick red
   upon her lips,
And a thousand faces swirled around me, clamoring that
   my life be burned. . . .

And then they had me, stripped me, battering my teeth
   into my throat till I swallowed my own blood.
My voice was drowned in the roar of their voices, and my
   black wet body slipped and rolled in their hands as
   they bound me to the sapling.
And my skin clung to the bubbling hot tar, falling from
   me in limp patches.
And the down and quills of the white feathers sank into
   my raw flesh, and I moaned in my agony.
Then my blood was cooled mercifully, cooled by a
   baptism of gasoline.
And in a blaze of red I leaped to the sky as pain rose like water, boiling
   my limbs.
Panting, begging I clutched childlike, clutched to the hot
   sides of death.
Now I am dry bones and my face a stony skull staring in
   yellow surprise at the sun. . . .

FIGURE 6–7. Continued

are used to create heartrending rhetorical effects, and the poem can be related to novels that may be taught in secondary English classrooms. Here are the relevant sentences, from the narrator's perspective—someone who has come upon the scene of a recent hanging and is now identifying with the hanged:

> And then they had me, stripped me, battering my teeth
>   into my throat till I swallowed my own blood.
> My voice was drowned in the roar of their voices, and my
>   black wet body slipped and rolled in their hands as
>   they bound me to the sapling.
> And my skin clung to the bubbling hot tar, falling from
>   me in limp patches.
> And the down and quills of the white feathers sank into
>   my raw flesh, and I moaned in my agony.
> Then my blood was cooled mercifully, cooled by a
>   baptism of gasoline.
> And in a blaze of red I leaped to the sky as pain rose like water,
>   boiling my limbs.
> Panting, begging I clutched childlike, clutched to the hot
>   sides of death.
> Now I am dry bones and my face a stony skull staring in
>   yellow surprise at the sun. . . .

With amazing skill the poet combines past-tense narration with present participial phrases to convey a sense of immediacy. Here are the most obvious examples, but there are others:

> And then they had me, stripped me, battering my
>   teeth into my throat till I swallowed my own blood.

> And my skin clung to the bubbling hot tar, falling
>   from me in limp patches.

> And in a blaze of red I leaped to the sky as pain
>   rose like water, boiling into my limbs.

Furthermore, even though not strictly sequential, these lines create a grammatical parallelism of sorts: a sentence with past-tense verbs, ending in a present participial phrase. This structure—used, but not overdone—also contributes to the feeling that we are *there*, to our inclination to identify now with the narrator of the poem.

Both grammatical parallelism and the use of free modifying constructions are common in poetry, which is an excellent vehicle for introducing these structures and emphasizing the importance of detail and grammatical flow in writing.

Free modifying adjectivals in nonfiction prose

While recognizing that free modifying constructions occur in a lot of poetry, many teachers still wonder whether they occur in nonfiction. The answer is yes, definitely—though certain topics and genres call for such constructions more often than others. Present participial and other adjectival words and phrases, for instance, are especially likely to occur in any genre that has a narrative sense, such as biography and autobiography; writing that seeks to recreate historical events; environmental and nature writing, which often deals with process; and informational writing that explains any other kind of process. Appositives are found in any writing where persons, places, or events need to be briefly characterized, not just named. Absolutes are found less commonly—we might even say rarely—though they are useful for a deeper level of description, regardless of the genre. We occasionally use them ourselves in the informative or persuasive books and articles we write for teachers.

To illustrate the use of these free modifying adjectivals in nonfiction, we first raided Connie's collection of nonfiction for middle schoolers/secondary students/adults for texts we ourselves find interesting and informative. These are the books we chose, listed in order from the shortest or simplest texts to the most complex. (Picture books are excellent for introducing writing techniques at all levels.)

- *Dinosaur Ghosts: The Mystery of Coelophysis*, by J. Lynett Gillette, illustrated by Douglas Henderson. The author explains the discoveries of bones of a small species of dinosaurs, particularly a large find at Ghost Ranch, north of Albuquerque, New Mexico. After describing the *coelophysis* as a species, the author turns her attention to theories about why the dinosaurs, all dinosaurs, disappeared from the earth. Structurally, her subsequent pages consist of a question like "Stuck in the mud?" to represent one of these theories, a narrative/descriptive paragraph or paragraphs describing the dinosaurs in the condition specified by the question, and a discussion of the plausibility of the theory—each opposite a full-page illustration.
- *The Librarian Who Measured the Earth*, by Kathryn Lasky, illustrated by Kevin Hawkes. This informational picture book describes the intellectual curiosity and life of Eratosthenes, a

Grammatical structure and good literature

Sharing and discussing well-written literature—whether poetry or prose—is one of the best ways to promote students' use of effective grammar in their writing. The Chapter 3 vignette featuring a student in Judy Miller's class shows this carryover taking place and reminds us that examining the language and language structures of literature can become an important bridge to writing.

Greek who lived more than two thousand years ago. Beginning with his birth and ending with his death, this biography is chronologically ordered and illustrated with informative and intriguing art that complements and helps explain the text.

- *Lewis and Clark: Explorers of the American West*, by Steven Kroll, illustrated by Richard Williams. This historical picture book describes these explorers' journey to map the Louisiana Territory from above St. Louis to the West Coast, traveling up from one river to another. The illustrations complement the text, conveying a sense of the historical journey and the time period more effectively than words alone could do. This text is also valuable for introducing adverbial phrases (often prepositional in structure) that set the scene at the beginning of sentences.
- *A Grand Canyon Journey: Tracing Time in Stone,* by Peter Anderson, illustrated with Grand Canyon pictures by several photographers. This book is structured both spatially and chronologically, as the author leads us on an imaginary walk down into the canyon.
- *The Nuclear Disaster at Chernobyl*, by Robin Cruise. This little book, chronically organized, has only two illustrations—two photos—and perhaps the topic suggests why: if any photos were taken at the time, they may not have been released to the public.
- *The Wright Brothers: How They Invented the Airplane,* by Russell Freedman, with original and numerous photographs by Wilbur and Orville Wright. This nonfiction text, a Newbery Honor Book, goes beyond biography, chronicling as well the early history of flight.

These books include all the genres we suggested as especially likely to include participial phrases and other free modifying adjectivals. The previously quoted *Bridges* (Dupré, 1997)—for adults and young adults— also falls in this range, for it is a fact-filled informational book with a narrative/descriptive structure and marvelous photos of the major bridges in the world (the book is three feet wide when opened). The following examples of different kinds of free modifying adjectivals are taken from these books.

Present participials

Present participials occur frequently in narrative/descriptive prose, including nonfiction:

Looking closely at the skeletons, paleontologists could see that none of the bones of any of the dinosaurs or the other animals seemed to be cracked from drying a long time in the sun. (*Dinosaur Ghosts*, p. 15)

<u>Balancing on their small front legs</u>, they crouch down and drink, unaware that the water is poisoned. (*Dinosaur Ghosts*, p. 22)

When paleontologists began looking at the rocks around the bones of these dinosaurs, they sometimes found mud cracks, <u>suggesting that some of the animals died on sun-baked mud</u>. (*Dinosaur Ghosts*, p. 26)

Lewis frequently walked onshore, <u>taking notes on plants and animals</u>. Clark stayed with the boats, <u>mapping their course</u>. (*Lewis and Clark*, p. 10)

<u>Pressing on</u>, the men began to see animals they had never even imagined: antelope and prairie dogs, a white pelican, a jackrabbit, coyotes. (*Lewis and Clark*, p. 13)

<u>Traveling upstream</u>, the Corps had to lug the canoes around the larger rapids and tow them up the smaller ones. (*Lewis and Clark*, p. 27)

<u>Looking back up at the meeting place of the Hermit and Coconino layers</u>, we can see how different they are. (*A Grand Canyon Journey*, p. 24)

Then they began to manufacture them [bicycles], <u>turning out two custom-built models</u>, the Van Cleve and the less-expensive St. Clair. The brothers made many of the parts themselves, <u>using simple tools like a turret lathe, a drill press, and tube-cutting equipment</u>. (*The Wright Brothers*, p. 13)

That morning, a brave young engineer named Charles Manly, <u>wearing a cork-lined life jacket and automobile goggles</u>, climbed into the fabric-sided pilot's car suspended beneath the airplane. (*The Wright Brothers*, p. 22)

For a few thrilling moments, he [Wilbur Wright] lay motionless between the great white wings, <u>sailing down the slope</u>, <u>picking up speed as he rode sea-scented breezes above the dunes</u>. (*The Wright Brothers*, p. 38)

To accommodate the public rail lines running over the bridge, the bascule also operates quickly, <u>taking a total of four minutes to open and close</u>. (*Bridges*, p. 105)

Ferry service, <u>operating since 1917</u>, ended the day before the bridge opened. (*Bridges*, p. 109)

An older-style deep truss was used to stabilize the deck, giving it a heavier profile than the slender, aerodynamic decks of most recent spans. (*Bridges*, p. 115)

Other adjectivals out of order

Exceedingly few examples caught our eye in these books. Few of the following examples are single-word adjectives, and most are, or begin with, an adjectival ending in -*ed*. In most cases, these reflect a sense of some action received by—or done to—the noun they modify. Something—the snow—*forced* Lewis and Clark to turn around. The splashing fish *attracted* the dinosaurs; the lack of food *exhausted* them. The big picture *fascinated* Wilbur Wright; the water *drenched* Manly. Linguists in the transformational tradition would say that in the underlying structure, these adjectivals are verbs.

Dapper and tidy, he [Orville Wright] was by far the most clothes conscious of the two. (*The Wright Brothers*, p. 5)

Weak and exhausted, the dinosaurs fall, one by one, and do not get up. (*Dinosaur Ghosts*, p. 21)

Forced to turn around because the snow was so deep, they set out again on June 24 with three Nez Percé guides. (*Lewis and Clark*, p. 27)

Other dinosaurs gather, also attracted by the splashing fish, but they too are caught in the treacherous ground. (*Dinosaur Ghosts*, p. 16)

Wilbur was more of a visionary, fascinated by the big picture rather than its individual parts. (*The Wright Brothers*, p. 5)

Drenched but unhurt, Manly was rescued, while the Aerodrome was fished out of the Potomac. (*The Wright Brothers*, p. 22)

These examples consist of, or are headed by, simple adjectivals:

The completed island, *visible* at the base of the tower, protects the tower against collision by ships. (*Bridges*, p. 111)

Eleven acres of riverfront parks, now *alive* with people, are dotted with places for music and theater. (*Bridges*, p. 103)

Appositives

David Barnard Steinman (1886–1960) grew up in a poor neighborhood under the Brooklyn Bridge, a lifelong inspiration. (*Bridges*, p. 88)

The Macinack Bridge is my crowning achievement—the consummation of a lifetime dedicated to my chosen profession of bridge building. (David B. Steinman, *Miracle Bridge at Mackinac*, 1957, quoted in *Bridges*, p. 88)

Here are some additional examples from two adult books suitable for interested high school students. In *Nickel and Dimed: On (Not) Getting By in America* (2001), journalist Barbara Ehrenreich researches the lives of the working poor by temporarily living and working among them, "Serving in Florida, "Scrubbing in Maine," and "Selling in Minnesota" (her major chapter titles). In this sociologically important and absorbing book, Ehrenreich persuades us to be concerned for the working poor, doing so through *pathos*, the emotions, rather than through *logos*, logic. Our other choice, *The Secret House: The Extraordinary Science of an Ordinary Day* (1986), by David Bodanis, describes the physics involved in our everyday activities, from morning to night. Bodanis seems fascinated, also, by the activities of mites, bacteria, fungi, amoebae, and pseudomonads with tails that act as propellers. We are also treated to an exposé of corporate America, as we read—both fascinated and horrified—about the harmful ingredients in the foods we eat and the everyday chemicals we encounter in personal care products—just for starters. Both books contain a variety of free modifying adjectivals in addition to these appositives:

> Linda, my supervisor—a kindly-looking woman of about thirty— even takes time to brief me about my rights: I don't have to put up with any sexual harassment, particularly from Robert, even though he's the owner's son. (*Nickel and Dimed*, p. 62). [*My supervisor* is an appositive modifying *Linda* and further clarifying who she is, while *a kindly-looking woman of about thirty* is an appositive referring to *my supervisor*. The material after the colon works as an appositive, too, specifying rights.]

> There's also a nice dose of insecticide and bactericide in the mixture [of deodorants], chemicals that are near-identical to poisons in your garden shed, and which here are murder on any soft, unshelled creatures in their way. (*The Secret House*, p. 121). [This long phrase, headed by the noun *chemicals*, is an appositive describing *mixture*.]

What we noticed particularly in the examples from these two books is that the sentences with appositives are often long and complexly structured, yet flowing and easy to comprehend because everything builds off of something previous to it. Such sentences are called right-branching or *cumulative* sentences because the details accumulate, one after another, each adding to what came before.

Absolutes

We noticed few appositives and almost no absolutes in our informative picture or illustrated books for young people, though informational texts often include them. For absolutes, then, we turn entirely to *Bridges* and the adult books from which we just quoted:

> Through gaps in the urban fabric, the [Erasmus Bridge] slides unexpectedly into view, <u>the hooked pylon grey-blue against the sky</u>, <u>the ultra-thin parapet sweeping towards terra firma</u>. (Raymond Ryan, quoted in *Bridges*, p. 104)

> Indeed, it is at night, when the massive bridge is transformed into an ethereal silhouette, <u>its bundled cables now long strands of light</u>, that one becomes most aware of the bridge's structure and the vital connecting role played by its daytime self. (*Bridges*, p. 105)

> As I search for the exit, I notice a skinny, misshapen fellow standing on one foot with the other tucked behind his knee, staring at me balefully, <u>his hands making swimming motions above his head</u>, either for balance or to ward me off. (*Nickel and Dimed*, p. 58)

> There are a few genuine adepts present who throw themselves rapturously into the music, <u>eyes shut</u>, <u>arms upraised</u>, waiting, no doubt, for the onset of glossolalia. (*Nickel and Dimed*, p. 67)

In the next passage, from *The Secret House*, Bodanis is describing the Doppler effect with a specific example:

> Speeding towards you in a souped-up car, <u>head leaning out of the window</u> and <u>passionate Italian opera emerging from his throat</u>, even the deepest baritone of a lover would come out squeaking like Donald Duck. (p. 81)

You may have noticed that the two absolutes are preceded by a present participial phrase. In fact, some writers—of nonfiction as well as fiction—employ more than one kind of adjectival within a short stretch of text, as seen in various sentences previously quoted. Here is another example, part of three paragraphs in which Bodanis discusses mites:

> The spiders went on to be great multi-eyed hunting carnivores; the mites went a different way, and many have ended up as peaceful

grazers, munching whatever is left over from the larger creatures they shelter near.

In the house these leftover nibbles are skin: tiny rafts of human skin flakes. There's plenty of it around. It's rubbed off when you move in bed, and it's brushed off when you dress. It falls off the body at a stupendous rate whenever you walk—tens off thousands of skin flakes per minute—and it tears off at only slower rates [sic] when you stand perfectly still. For us the skin flakes are insignificant, noticeable only when they build up as dust, but for the waiting mites they are manna.

Hidden down at the base of the carpets these mites only have to wait, mouth up, for this perpetual haze of skin flakes to rain down on them—the ultimate in parachuted food rations. (pp. 8–9)

We see *mouth up* as an absolute, a reduction of an underlying sentence— *the mouth is up*, in which a form of *to be* is the verb. What other free modifying adjectivals do you notice? We notice a present participial phrase, an appositive introduced by a colon, a adjective-headed phrase "out of order," an introductory adjectival phrase that seems to need a comma after it, the previously mentioned absolute, and a final appositive, separated by dashes.

To keep in mind

Remember, our purpose is more to illustrate than to analyze. Indeed, one semester long ago when Connie was using literary examples to illustrate interesting grammatical phenomena, one student burst out, "This is why I don't like literature. Teachers analyze it to death." This is a warning to be held constantly in mind as we discuss how literary models work: appreciate and reflect on how parts of sentences go together and what makes them effective, but don't overanalyze. If we overanalyze, we will kill the literature, or at least our students' interest in reading it, and possibly also their interest in writing.

This is a warning to be held constantly in mind as we discuss how literary models work: appreciate and reflect . . . but don't overanalyze.

Revision to the Rescue

7

hy didn't they get it? teachers sometimes wail, after doing an excellent job of teaching a particular grammatical option or skill. *What use is it to try to teach them new things?* Of course this doesn't apply to all students: Some not only get it—whatever "it" is—when it's taught, but also apply it in their writing, at least in the assignments where they're explicitly told to. But what of the other students?

When the two of us have taught grammatical options—alternative ways of structuring sentences—to teachers, we've found that even they aren't always able to apply the teaching to their own writing. They need help, one small step after another, just as we need lots of patient, respectful help, one step at a time, in learning other things—new software programs, for instance, or aerobics or Pilates routines or how to fix the plumbing. (Connie, for instance, had four private lessons, with certain routines taught repeatedly, before joining a Pilates class, and Jonathan started fixing his home plumbing by following the simplest "idiot's guide" directions for replacing a section of pipe—not for replacing a toilet or kitchen sink.) When learning something new, all of us need help that acknowledges where we are and seeks to move us forward a little at a time.

So it is with guidance in writing. When writers aren't initially able to apply newly taught—even newly learned—skills to their own writing, we further help them see how their writing can be improved. Given time constraints, we may first have to teach a minilesson to the whole class or a large group within it, but this sets the stage for additional follow-up. And yes, we admit that sometimes we conclude there's not much that can be done with a particular piece of writing except start over, so we resolve to give more help next time prior to and during drafting. In the big picture, though, we're convinced that sentence revision is crucial—as suggested in the idealized lesson framework in Chapter 4. As Lucy Calkins (1983) found in working with young students, what's first learned in revision may later be applied while drafting. This is our goal.

To accomplish this goal, we obviously have to assign fewer papers while spending more time with those few. In Chapter 5, we mentioned *sentence imitating* as good preparation for writing more effective sentences, and *sentence restructuring*, *combining*, and *expanding* as important revision strategies. Though restructuring sentences by adding the kinds of modifiers discussed in Chapters 5 and 6 can be important, it's not easy to generalize: The strategy depends a lot on the particular sentence. On the other hand, as teachers we can be alert for golden opportunities to teach students to combine or expand sentences—that is, we can take instructional advantage of whole pieces of writing that lend themselves to such revision. Minilessons for the whole class or a group can be derived from such drafts.

Noticing when sentences can be combined

Let's start with an example that Harry Noden uses in *Image Grammar* (1999), an example Connie has previously discussed in an article in *Voices from the Middle* (Weaver, McNally, & Moerman, 2001). Noden borrows a revision scenario described in Olson's *Envisioning Writing* (1992). The teacher had asked the students to write a brief character sketch. One of the sixth graders wrote:

The Big Guy

James weighs 240 pouonds and use to be the champ. He beat Mohamad Ali for the crown. He's 38 know and he had drugs and pot. He's been in jail for 5 years and that ended his carrear. He's had a though time finding a job. His face is scared. He wears a ripped T shirt with knee pants. He's trying to make a come back in the boxing world.

It's tempting to wield the red pen and go straight for the jugular of the Error Beast (see "Errorwocky" in Chapter 3). Instead, however, the teacher had students draw the character they were describing, then revise the writing to include details from the drawing: In other words, she asked the student to zoom in on the physical details of the boxer instead of summarizing. Here is the student's final edited version:

The Big Guy

The lonely man stood in a ring holding tight to the ropes. His head was bald. His chest was hairy and sweaty. His legs looked like they were planted to the ground like stumps. His muscles were relaxed in the dark ring. His mouth looked mean and tough the way it was formed. He was solid looking. His boxing gloves had blood stains on them. His still body structure glowed in the darkness. He braced himself against the ropes. His white pants had red stripes, the hair on his chin prickled out like thorns.

In terms of detail, this paragraph is *much* better than the original—and with this particular writing and this writer, it might be time to stop and celebrate what he has accomplished. Still, we're struck by the monotonous structure of the grammatical sentences, almost all of which begin with *his*. The details all have equal grammatical status, since they all are presented in independent clauses rather than subordinate grammatical constructions. This creates a boring, clumpety-clump rhythm within the paragraph.

What can we do to help the writer make the sentence structures themselves more interesting, and how can we develop a minilesson (or several minilessons) using this piece of writing? What details will we subordinate? Indeed, what details will we group together before even trying to combine sentences and thereby subordinate some details? Below we've italicized one combinable pair of sentences and another independent clause, and underlined still another pair of combinable sentences:

The lonely man stood in a ring holding tight to the ropes. *His head was bald. His chest was hairy and sweaty.* His legs looked like they were planted to the ground like stumps. His muscles were relaxed in the dark ring. His mouth looked mean and tough the way it was formed. He was solid looking. His boxing gloves had blood stains on them. His still body structure glowed in the darkness. He braced himself against the ropes. His white pants had red stripes, *the hair on his chin prickled out like thorns.*

Next we restructure one sentence and group together sentences that relate in terms of content or contain details that can be subordinated (doubtless this reordering is influenced by our already having some idea how we want to restructure the sentences):

The lonely man stood in a ring holding tight to the ropes.

His head was bald.
The hair on his chin was prickling out like thorns.
His chest was hairy and sweaty.

His muscles were relaxed in the dark ring.

He was solid looking.
His legs were planted to the ground like stumps.
His mouth was formed mean and tough.

His boxing gloves had stains on them.
His still body glowed in the darkness.

He braced himself against the ropes.

Then we create a revised draft:

The Big Guy

The lonely man stood in a ring holding tight to the ropes. His head was bald, the hair on his chin prickling out like thorns, his chest hairy and sweaty. His muscles were relaxed in the dark ring, but he was solid looking, his legs planted to the ground like stumps, his mouth formed mean and tough. His boxing gloves had blood stains on them and his still body glowed in the darkness as he braced himself against the ropes.

In this revision we've created four new absolute constructions. While this may be overkill, at least the paragraph flows better and may seem more interesting, just because ideas have been combined into only four sentences. When we've done this activity with teachers, their results have been similarly condensed and more effective—though always different from this version! Such revisions, ours and the teachers', always reflect Loban's "tighter coiling of thought" (1976), described in Chapter 3.

Seven of the eleven simple sentences in the original character sketch begin with *his*, and two begin with *he*. Evaluating these sentences against an analytical guide we present in Chapter 12, we find that the original exhibits a low level of grammatical development:

Low: Many sentences follow the basic subject + verb + object pattern, often with the same subject, such as *I* or *he* or *she*.

In our four-sentence revision, no sentences begin with *he*, though three begin with *his*. Our version nevertheless jumps past the guide's middle-level characteristics and achieves a level-three, or high, rating:

High: Generous use of various grammatical and stylistic tools for flow or other effect, such as—but not confined to—participial phrases, appositives, and absolutes.

Of course, we might want to simplify this revision process in the classroom. For example, we might first help students see ways of combining only two or three of the sentences, not multiple groups of sentences. We might teach a minilesson to the whole class, then follow with small-group or individual help. But whatever our strategies, helping students revise by combining *their own* sentences needs to be part of *our repertoire* as teachers and *students' repertoire* as writers.

Noticing when sentences can be expanded

It takes determined practice to notice automatically when some sentences in a student's writing can be combined or be expanded by adding details, perhaps using one of the grammatical structures discussed in Chapters 5 or 6. Sometimes we see the possibility of adding or moving an adverbial to the beginning or end of a sentence (more often the beginning, where they set the scene). Usually, adjectival modifiers of one kind or another can easily be added after some nouns to provide clarifying details. And it's easiest to notice the potential for such modifiers, and help students insert details in effective constructions, when the sentence ends with a noun.

Let's examine a portion of a paper written by seventh grader Julie Nickelson. She titled the paper "Uniform 411," and almost any teacher reading it would chortle with delight at the structure of her paper and the strength of her argument, perhaps even giving Julie an A. But papers like this can still be made much more enticing, more compelling, and thus more strongly persuasive. Here is Julie's second paragraph:

> If we students at MRMS had uniforms, it would be possible for us
> to be able to learn more. By having uniforms, we would not be
> distracted by the "showy" clothes that many students currently
> wear to school, despite the rules we have. If we had uniforms, it
> would help us keep focus in class, for we wouldn't have to worry
> about fashion. Also, if we had uniforms we would have more time
> for schoolwork, since since we wouldn't need to spend so much
> time on clothes. Think of what high scores we could get on
> statewide tests if we had more time to study by having uniforms.
> Our school could even be the highest scoring in the state.

Not bad, but we could help her make some of her ideas more specific—mostly by attaching modifiers, many of them at the end of a sentence. So with her permission and her help with the details, let's use this paragraph as the basis for a minilesson that we imagine beginning something like this:

Teacher: Obviously, Julie's argument for school uniforms is
    amusing. But in the interest of seeing how we can all make

In Chapter 12, there's a chart (Figure 12–1) to help you decide what to teach next in terms of grammar that will enhance not only sentence variety and fluency, but also details, voice/style, organization, word choice, and conventions. One factor is grammatical options for creating a tighter coiling of thought: that is, saying more in fewer words and more sophisticated and varied grammatical constructions.

our writing more detailed and compelling, let's work with Julie to add some details. Julie, maybe we should specify a particular class, so we can be more specific with the details. Okay? What class do you want to put us in, as readers?

Julie: English class. [*She giggles—this is English class.*]

Teacher: Okay, so let's add *in English class* at the end of your first sentence. [*Does so on an overhead transparency.*] What are you learning in English class?

Various students:

We're reading *Siddhartha.*

Yeah, and we just read *Touching Spirit Bear.*

I read *Bless Me, Ultima.*

We're learning to write better.

Yeah, and you're showing us how to add details to our writing.

Teacher: Good points. Let's see, we can add some of those details like this. [*Demonstrates by adding to the first sentence:* If we students at MRMS had uniforms, it would be possible for us to learn more in English class—more about *Siddhartha,* more about *Touching Spirit Bear and Bless Me, Ultima,* and more about how to make our own sentences interesting!]

As the lesson progresses, we might suggest adding *you see* to the next sentence to make the voice more intimate and adding *whether preppy or sloppy* to describe *students*, resulting in: "By having uniforms, you see, we would not be distracted by the "showy" clothes that many students, whether preppy or sloppy, wear to school every day, despite the rules we have." Okay, we've added *every day*, too. By now, however, the students should be catching the drift, and *they* can specify what kinds of clothing the rules forbid.

Together with Julie and her classmates, we might come up with something like the following version, changes underlined, including some designed to bring a smile to the English teacher's lips and a voice to the piece of writing:

If we students at MRMS had uniforms, it would be possible for us to learn more in English class—more about *Siddhartha,* more about *Touching Spirit Bear* and *Bless Me, Ultima,* and more about how to make our own sentences interesting! By having uniforms, you see, we would not be distracted by the "showy" clothes that many students, whether preppy or sloppy, wear to school every day, despite the rules we have against low-slung pants, revealing necklines, hole-infested jeans, and the like. If we had uniforms, it would help us keep focus in class, boring as it sometimes might be, for we wouldn't have to worry about fashion—what earrings Joanie is wearing today, whether Barbie's neckline offers a view of her bra, or whether Lionel's jeans are not only low-slung but so loose they're in danger of falling off. Also, if we had uniforms—maybe navy and white—we would have more time for reading novels and writing persuasive essays, since we wouldn't need to spend so much time outside of school on clothes: buying just the right sexy sweater, snatching our sister's favorite Calvin Kleins while hanging on to our heart necklace, and keeping our clothes ready to be changed into at a moment's notice. Think of what amazingly high scores we could get on the statewide MEAP assessments in reading and writing if we had more time to study by having uniforms, plain and uninspiring so we won't be distracted. Our school could even be the highest scoring in the state, triumphing over Grosse Point and other ritzy districts.

Obviously we've done a lot to increase sentence variety and flow in the piece (and we've relocated Julie to Michigan, too!). As revised, this piece shows the previously mentioned high-level sentence development—by means of appositives, participial phrases, and adjectives out of order. We have even—quite accidentally!—added not only some effective words, but some organizational, cohesive devices: the repetition of *low-slung* jeans and *distracted*. Most important, we've added the kinds of details that make writing come alive instead of lying formulaic and voiceless on the page.

By using grammatical options for adding detail, we have, in fact, enhanced all six of the commonly accepted traits of good writing—even the conventions, with use of a colon to introduce some phrases, and dashes to emphasize the possible colors for their potential school uniforms.

But hold on, you say, seventh graders wouldn't write like that unaided. We agree: That's why we showed the beginning of a dialogue in which the teacher would structure some of the additions and offer details. Most college students wouldn't write like that unaided, either, so with older students, too, the teacher would have to not only elicit but also make a lot of the contributions. But notice: Now the piece has a clear audience—Julie's English teacher and her classmates. Julie has a clear purpose: not only to persuade but to entertain while doing so (by employing pathos, or emotional appeal, and ethos, her credibility as a fashion-conscious student). This piece of writing has a voice. And the sentences are not only more varied, but also more engaging and compelling because of the details, added mostly via those adjectivally functioning constructions. By revising collaboratively with Julie, we've produced a model that can be used later as a reminder. After all, isn't our goal for writers the ability to write pieces like this that others genuinely enjoy—and find persuasive when appropriate? And can't we show our students how to accomplish this by interactive modeling?

By using grammatical options for adding detail, we have, in fact, enhanced all six of the commonly accepted traits of good writing.

Editing Begins with Observation

Adverbial Clauses and the AAAWWUBBIS

8

JEFF ANDERSON
RAYBURN MIDDLE SCHOOL AND TRINITY UNIVERSITY,
SAN ANTONIO, TEXAS

D o you ever think about how we teach editing in our schools? In the past? Today? Is it really that different? In the past we thought marking every error on an essay somehow enabled a young writer to write correctly. Later, when we realized this wasn't working, we tried a more systematic approach: writing sentences on the board that students corrected orally—at least in theory. With the teacher still focusing on correcting the errors in each paper, the students would then use those conventions correctly the next time they wrote—or so we hoped, often in vain. That's the past. But is it really that different in most classrooms today, when it comes to teaching students about editing? Or is it all about the error?

In my classroom, I project a powerful (and correct) sentence on the overhead for students to admire. "Tell me what you notice," I say. In the beginning, all my students can do is find something wrong with the sentence. They home in on apostrophes, capitalization, and commas. They know the drill: *If a teacher puts a sentence up on the board, he wants us to find something wrong with it.* Students have come, over time, to see editing as electric shock therapy. Get ready. Zap! Their hands shoot up and they begin the process of telling me where we should use a capital or add or delete a comma. The problem is that the sentence is completely correct.

One teacher told me she used to make photocopies of error-ridden sentences that her students would then correct using standard proofreading marks (an activity sometimes called daily oral language—even if it's rarely daily or oral or about language). One week she accidentally handed

---

Note: Some of the general comments on editing were previously included in Jeff's sections of Weaver 2007 and in Weaver et al. 2006.

out the corrected daily oral language sentences rather than the sentences with errors. Dutifully, her students marked up the correct sentences to kingdom come—just like they had done every week with the sentences with errors. She abandoned the activity after that, realizing what was really happening. The activity had appeared to "work" until that day.

I am not defiling any one particular product so much as saying there are many editing programs that present students with a sentence or sentences full of errors, which they correct. Is that working? Is it transferring into students' writing? Is it giving young writers a sense that punctuation and capitalization are ways to shape meaning and voice?

Often the teaching of writing, especially editing, is done from the deficit stance. Teachers and students just look for what they think is wrong. All the writing gurus tell us to reward students for what is there, to highlight their strengths, and we do a good job of this—until it comes to editing instruction.

Though the red pen has been put away by many teachers, red-pen thinking still marks the approach in most English classrooms, as do grammar and test preparation materials. The error is it's all about the error—that's the focus, with students' writings beaten like a dead horse. Error. Error. Error.

All the writing gurus tell us to reward students for what is there, to highlight their strengths, and we do a good job of this—until it comes to editing instruction.

Facing the error of our ways

Most editing instruction remains stuck in the "error hunt" (Weaver, 1982; 1996). We teach students only to look for errors, without also helping them consider how punctuation can create special effects for the reader. We, and consequently they, forget things like using commas to separate major chunks of grammar or meaning, or choosing between a pair of commas and a pair of dashes, and just try to "get it right," with no thought to rhythm or visual effect or meaning.

Teachers, parents, and the public often get all worked up if student writers are careless enough not to edit their work. Professional writers have copy editors to catch final errors, but woe to the student whose final draft has even one or two mistakes. To head off this tongue clicking, we teachers may try to teach kids to get all worked up about errors as well. Then students—as well as their teachers—end up in one big tizzy over error. The students are afraid they will make a mistake, and they freeze up. The teachers are afraid if they don't mark up papers or sentences, their students won't succeed on standardized tests, or they themselves will be criticized for not teaching grammar in isolation—as if that would have made a difference.

No wonder our students feel pulled under by the constant undertow of errors, or by our attention to them—kids internalize our message that there is probably something wrong with their writing, and maybe a lot of somethings! Sometimes they give up and err with abandon; other times, they guess. For example, we may teach the use of the comma, but if students haven't gotten it yet—especially when we've taught one textbook lesson and then moved on—they may simply guess. Sometimes they get it right. You either use a comma or you don't, so you have a fifty-fifty chance to get it right—or wrong. It's easy to get student writers to the point where they know they should worry about commas, but that's where our "teaching" often stops. It's not about the process or writing or meaning or effect. Students' mantra becomes, "Yeah, I know this is where I mess up." But they just put something down to get on with it.

Worse yet, students all too often don't know *what* is wrong or *how* to fix it. It's not far from there to a negative, unproductive identity: *I can't write.*

As I see it, effective editing instruction is more about teaching students the patterns and concepts of the English language that readers expect courteous writers to use and follow than it is about rules, mechanics, or grammar. Happily, I have found more fruitful ways to teach language patterns and editing concepts and relate them to students' own writing (Anderson, 2005, 2006, 2007a, 2007b).

In math, students are not expected to practice something until it is modeled correctly for them—the thought processes behind it and what it looks like, not just a do-as-I-do example. In math, they usually focus on a few new things at a time, not a wide array of all the errors a student can make. With revision and editing skills, too, we need to focus on fewer concepts than the typical grammar books offer but teach those skills well and with attention to the effects on a reader.

With revision and editing skills, too, we need to focus on fewer concepts than the typical grammar books offer but teach those skills well and with attention to the effects on a reader.

Working editing into the writing process: The AAAWWUBBIS comes alive!

Editing is partly a visual skill, so I use that to advantage. But instead of correcting error-ridden sentences on the overhead, I can show students powerful examples from their writing, my writing, and literature. It makes sense to stare at and discuss effective writing. That way kids are learning about writing at many layers simultaneously—meaning, beauty, and effect.

However, I can't stop at showing great sentences to kids and asking what they notice. That will only begin to help them with editing. I need to build on the knowledge that they're gleaning not only by helping students edit their own and others' writing for important basic concepts (like using commas to set off introductory elements), but also by having the kids write sentences to show how the comma helps shape how we read a sentence and how we make meaning from it. Writing must be seen as "a creational facility rather than a correctional facility" (Anderson, 2006).

Introductory elements can help students make connections between their ideas within and across sentences and paragraphs as well as give students options when we want them to write varied sentences. They need more advice than, "Make some sentences long and some short." To write with a variety of sentence patterns, writers need options, and in the end knowing these options will develop their editing eyes.

I start my lesson on complex sentences by introducing the AAAWWUBBIS (Anderson, 2005). I can't teach all the types of complex sentences at once. That won't help with editing. I begin with one of the most common errors that students are expected to correct on editing tests: omitting the comma after an introductory element. For some time before I tell them what an AAAWWUBBIS is, I start talking about it, and whenever the students are ready, I write the acronym on the board.

"Hey, what's that?" they ask.

"Wouldn't you like to know?" I am shameless. I will do anything to build interest in my class—especially if it is the grammar and mechanics concepts they need in order to be successful editors. Aren't you just dying of anticipation? First, though, the theoretical stance from which the AAAWWUBBIS springs.

In *Teaching Grammar in Context*, Connie Weaver taught me to look at complex sentences and fragments in a new light. Oftentimes students attain a certain level of fluency in writing "correct" sentences in third grade. Then, during the next few years, they seemingly veer off. All of a sudden, a fifth grader like Chevelle starts writing fragments all over the place: *When my sister turned five. We took her to the Teddy Bear Factory. After we she finally picked out the clothes. We went to eat at the Cheese Cake Factory*. It's easy to notice that *When my sister turned five* and *After we she finally picked out the clothes* are sentence fragments. Yet I see these errors as something to celebrate, to love and nurture. You see, Chevelle is showing complex sentence readiness. Her thinking is becoming more complex and growing beyond the simple sentences she once mastered. Now her skills aren't able to keep up with the speed and complexity of her thinking.

Look at all she knows. She knows to pause after the subordinate clauses. She just happened to use a period rather than a comma. She is ready for a writer's secret (Spandel, 2003). "Chevelle, you're doing something so sophisticated. You're using an AAAWWUBBIS."

"An a-woo-what?"

"Wow! You're so brilliant you can use it before you know what it is. I will be telling you all about it soon. You are showing me that you're ready." Looking in her eyes, I tell her with as much sincere reverence as I can muster, "You are ready for a writer's secret. May I share a writer's secret with you?"

I haven't been turned down yet. This is the perfect way for me to be invited into her writer's world and to share a piece from mine. "You did such a good job with these sentences." I have her read the sentences back to me and note how she knows exactly where to pause, and then I explain, "When I write sentences like these, I do one thing a little different. Let me show you." On a sticky note I write, *When my brother went to kindergarten, I was jealous. After he came home and told me about his teacher, I knew I had to figure a way to stow away in his* Adam 12 *lunch kit.* "My sentences are just like yours," I say, "but on these parts I used a comma. What did you use?" I explain that using a comma after we start sentences with *when* and *after* is very common—and that she would learn more when we discussed the AAAWWUBBIS.

Have you figured out the AAAWWUBBIS yet? Cathy Bird, at Rudder Middle School, shared this term with me (thanks, Cathy). It stands for several common subordinating conjunctions: *After, As, Although, When, While, Until, Because, Before, If, Since.* If I tell my class we're going to discuss subordinating conjunctions and how they will help us form complex sentences and avoid fragments, all the air is sucked out of the room. If I say we're going to learn about the AAAWWUBBIS today—and I really whoop up the *woo* part—I have my kids' undivided attention.

As with any mnemonic, some time must be spent going over it. But before we delve too deeply, I explain that when an AAAWWUBBIS is the first word of a sentence it is more often than not a "comma causer" (Anderson, 2005). As Harry Noden (1999) taught us: simplify, simplify, simplify. Of course, there are exceptions, but we are looking to teach our students patterns that are useful. We don't start off with a list of exceptions. That shuts everything down. "If a sentence starts with *if* . . ."—I pause and stare blankly for a moment—"I have left you hanging, haven't I? You know there is more to come when you start a sentence with an *if* or any of the other AAAWWUBBIS words." I write it on the board: *If a sentence starts with an AAAWWUBBIS, you will probably need a comma in the sentence.* I ask the students to start reading the sentence together and to pause when the first part is complete. The students and I stick with that concept for a while, saying sentences back and forth to each other and pausing after the introductory part.

Jacob finally offers, "When everybody keeps talking in AAAWWUBBIS sentences, I get irritated."

"Absolutely, Jacob. Might I say, if it bothers you, then *you* should stop." Then I sit down at the overhead and start scratching out an

AAAWWUBBIS-ridden stream of consciousness: "When I said that, did you know I was using an AAAWWUBBIS? After doing it so long, I can't seem to stop. If I don't stop doing this soon, I might forget to let you go to lunch."

They all start yelling, "No way!" but they remember the AAAWWUBBIS. The next day I show them that when a sentence starts with an AAAWWUBBIS and doesn't have a comma, it is often a sentence fragment. In fact, on our state test, many of the fragments students have to identify start with AAAWWUBBIS words and leave you hanging: *Since you forgot to give me my allowance.* We discuss how taking off the AAAWWUBBIS, the word *since*, would affect the sentence and its "conditional-ness." Real editing is all about meaning and patterns, not errors.

Real editing is all about meaning and patterns, not errors.

Making the AAAWWUBBIS stick

To help this pattern stick, I start pulling sentences from literature that use the pattern. Then I post examples like this one from *The Adventures of Captain Underpants,* by Dav Pilkey (1997):

> George and Harold were usually responsible kids. <u>Whenever something bad happened</u>, George and Harold were usually responsible. (p. 2)

I ask the kids what they notice. Sometimes I might leave the comma out and ask where it goes or read just the subordinate clause to help them hear how it leaves you hanging, waiting for the other shoe, in the form of a sentence, to drop. To stay true to my tenet that grammar and mechanics should be a creational facility rather than a correctional facility, I have to find ways to help my young writers see concepts and patterns in the context of effective print—student and professional.

Once I find a passage or story rich with AAAWWUBBIS words in the first position of a sentence, I have students look at the text in groups of three. I want them to discuss the sentences in the passage I have selected and decide which sentences to highlight or record on chart paper. I want them to see how these sentences work in whole texts but also pull them out to zoom in on them up close (Anderson, 2006). Once some time has passed we discuss which ones we found and talk about whether each needed a comma or not; then I start helping them see how these sentences are used to connect ideas from sentence to sentence and paragraph to paragraph.

Next the groups find two or three examples of the AAAWWUBBIS at the beginning of sentences, or they simply create some of their own. This lets me know students' level of understanding so that I can target these problems in further sessions where we notice things in our reading and writing.

I also ask students to write one sentence about a read-aloud or any reading. They can write the sentence in their notebook or on a tiny strip of paper they give to me as they leave the classroom (Yoshida, 1985). Of course, as the need arises, discussions should be held around the meaning of each of the AAAWWUBBIS words. Later, students can go back and search for more. I type up these "found" AAAWWUBBIS sentences and have students cut them up and categorize them. This way students have a ready supply of examples to refer to. For many students, visuals and examples are more powerful teachers than rules.

I cue students to write sentences as soon as possible after we've imitated, hunted, categorized, discussed, and clarified, so they can see how we use complex sentences as writers. Isn't it better for students to master concepts before we start asking them to edit for these concepts? Of course, at any point, I could post one of the sentences they have found, take the comma out, and ask them to help me add it. "How did you know?" Or maybe take the Captain Underpants sentence and put a period in place of the comma. They can see what's wrong and help me correct it. They immediately start using the sentence patterns we discuss— because I require them to use a few—and then we do quick edits of our own writing rather than fixing someone else's. It's all about creating meaning, not hunting errors. It's about teaching first and later helping students apply the concepts, editing for style as well as correctness. Simply practicing is not going to develop young writers' independent editing skills.

For many students, visuals and examples are more powerful teachers than rules.

Enhancing meaning with the AAAWWUBBIS: What condition are your transitions in?

If we leave editing to a discussion of sentences or even lessons in which we highlight patterns in reading and writing, we still will leave out an important connection—the crucial one, in fact. Students need to reenter their own writing and try to improve it with their new knowledge of AAAWWUBBIS words (or whatever pattern we're teaching). This is the most meaningful practice. Now that students have the concept, they can cement their learning by applying it directly to a piece of their own writing. And wouldn't that be the perfect place for them to polish their editing skills?

I like to connect any editing issue I can with other craft issues. With my packed curriculum and lost instructional days in the name of testing and accountability, I have to combine things. But this activity really helps editing stick and have meaning. It shows the special effects student writers can create for the reader.

A natural connection can be made between AAAWWUBBIS words in students' writing and revising for transitions. Paragraph hooks are a great strategy for achieving the ever-elusive paragraph-to-paragraph progression (Anderson, 2006). The first time I saw the phrase "paragraph-to-paragraph progression" on the state rubric, I froze. How could I teach that? Then I found Lucille Vaughn Payne's book *The Art of Lively Writing* (1975): "You want your reader to be pleasantly aware that your paragraphs are firmly linked, but you don't want him to see the chains too clearly or hear them clank too audibly into place" (p. 87). Payne suggests students can go beyond more obvious transition words and phrases like *consequently* and *as a result* and create deeper hooks. She also suggests we can create these deep paragraph-to-paragraph hooks by echoing or simply repeating an important word from the last sentence of the paragraph and inserting that word in the first sentence of the next paragraph. (See also the discussion of cohesion in Chapter 10.)

Sixth grader Samantha played with paragraph hooks in her essay, "The Drama":

> Drama always starts on Monday. Everybody had all weekend to be bored and make up things about this person or that. Somebody decides they want to start some stuff by talking <u>smack</u>.
>
> *As soon as someone talks <u>smack</u>*, the drama begins. This girl is pointing at that one and standing real close. Too close. Her voice gets loud. Too Loud. Then someone pulls some hair or slaps a face and then everyone makes a big <u>circle</u> around them.
>
> *When a big <u>circle</u> forms*, that means the teachers will be there soon, telling everyone to back off, blowing whistles and making a big scene.

By repeating an important word, *smack*, from the last sentence of paragraph one in the first sentence of the next paragraph, which begins with an AAAWWUBBIS, Samantha glues the two paragraphs together. To link the third paragraph to the second, Samantha starts the sentence with *when* and repeats *circle*.

AAAWWUBBIS words give writers some more options for how to connect paragraphs. Showing students the mechanics of the paragraph hook will give them a concrete way to practice using a comma after an introductory element in a meaningful way, connecting ideas and paragraphs.

Making editing a positive experience

Here are my personal guidelines for making editing a positive experience instead of painful drudgery:

1. Make editing more of a creational facility than a correctional facility.

2. Spend more time highlighting what is right and beautiful than hunting for errors.

3. Make grammar about meaning. There is a purpose for the punctuation marks and other editing conventions we use, and writers are responsible for knowing why they do what they do. This empowers us to sometimes break the rules.

4. Constantly write and collect examples and refer back to literature and students' own writing.

5. Teach concepts and patterns deeply.

Moving away from red-pen thinking and error hunting takes time. I constantly have to temper my desire to show children all their errors when they share the writing they are so very proud of. Correction of all their errors is not what they need, but I have also learned that they are not helped by my ignoring errors, either. I think of the song "Cruel to Be Kind" by Nick Lowe. Some members of our profession think that marking up a student's draft is the medicine they need to become good writers: tough love, if you will. I am cruel now, they think, but this will translate into kind later. But if I am only kind—"Domingo, this is so good"—and I never help him refine or hone his grammar and mechanics, I am cruel in his future.

So instead of either wielding the red pen or ignoring grammar and mechanics completely, I make my class about discovery, models, beauty, categorization, visuals; about writers using grammar and mechanics to shape text and create meaning. Teaching before practicing. Trying, writing, playing, then editing. My students edit their writing—not me. I instruct and guide: My students are writers and editors. I blur the lines on purpose. Because editing is designed to help create powerful writing, not avoid error.

Editing

Approaching the Bugaboo in Diverse Classrooms

9 ❧

Why did we say, in Chapter 4, that editing is every teacher's bugaboo—and what did we mean? This photo of the Bugaboo Extensions, a region of the Purcell Mountains in British Columbia, offers a hint: Some of the mountains would be difficult if not impossible to climb, and sometimes it feels as if editing is almost impossible to teach—at least to some of our students, at least to the point of application. The word *bugaboo* has an interesting history, though: The *Oxford Universal Dictionary* cites 1740 as its earliest reference, noting that *bugaboo* comes from *bugbear*, an imaginary being invoked to frighten children (or in this case, teachers?). The *Oxford* and other dictionaries point out that, more broadly, a bugaboo is an object

The Bugaboo Extensions, Bugaboo Glacier Provincial Park
Photo © Russ Heinl

of unnecessary dread. How appropriate for us as we consider how to teach editing skills and how to get students to apply them! After all, we can employ minilessons, focus lessons created for small groups, individual conferences, and editing checklists, all offered with lots and lots of patience—and the strategies and inspiration of teachers like Jeff Anderson (Chapter 8), Sharon Moerman (Chapter 13), Rebecca Wheeler (Chapter 14), and Jason Roche and Yadira Gonzalez (Chapter 15). In this chapter, though, we focus on what to teach as much or more than on how to teach.

As Connie wrote in *The Grammar Plan Book* (2007), today's smart teachers have learned that red-inking (or blue-inking or green-inking) students' papers with corrections is not an effective way to teach editing skills. But the swing of the pendulum back toward teaching grammar has brought with it increased pressure to teach numerous skills of the editing kind, often in isolation from writing. We teachers must resist. We do not have to repeat either of the devastating learning experiences of this un-named teacher:

> My own research has convinced me that red-inking errors in students' papers does no good and causes a great many students to hate and fear writing more than anything else they do in school. I gave a long series of tests covering 580 of the most common and persistent errors in usage, diction, and punctuation and 1,000 spelling errors to students in grades 9–12 in many schools, and the average rate of improvement in ability to detect these errors turned out to be 2 percent per year. The dropout rate is more than enough to account for this much improvement in ability to detect these errors if the teachers had not even been there. . . .
>
> When I consider how many hours of my life I have wasted in trying to root out these errors by a method that clearly did not work, I want to kick myself. Any rat that persisted in pressing the wrong lever 10,000 times would be regarded as stupid. I must have gone on pressing it at least 20,000 times without visible effect. (Farrell, 1971, p. 141)

We now know that we'll be more successful teaching a modest number of editing skills in conjunction with the writing process, and teaching them an inch wide and a mile deep. But how do we decide what skills to focus on?

Deciding what editing skills to teach

The short answer is to teach what our students' writing suggests they need most. All too often, though, we haven't analyzed our students' writing to see what they need but instead have taught our pet peeves, whether they are major issues or not. Connie's pet peeves in the writing of upper-level college and graduate students are using the wrong spelling for homophones like *its/it's* and *their/there/they're*; spellings like *would of* for *would have* and *should of* for *should have*; confusion about the uses of *affect* versus *effect*; using the apostrophe in nonpossessive nouns and even in verbs (*he run's*); comma splices in long sentences; and lack of parallelism. The first three kinds of errors are distracting, but do they warrant much teaching time and effort? No. On the other hand, avoiding comma splices and using parallelism (and avoiding unparallel constructions in a series) both warrant more instructional time.

So perhaps we can include some of our pet peeves in our list of what to teach, but we have to be careful. After conducting a massive study of teachers' marking of student errors, Connors and Lunsford (1988) found:

> Teachers' ideas about error definition and classification have always been absolute products of their times and cultures. . . . Teachers have always marked different phenomena as errors, called them different things, given them differing weights. Error-pattern study is essentially the examination of an ever-shifting pattern of skills judged by an ever-shifting pattern of prejudices. (p. 399)

Wow. Do you as an English teacher (or perhaps even as an intern teacher) feel justifiably indicted? We certainly do.

Are there any research studies or other factors that can help us draw on more than our own pet peeves in making decisions about what editing skills to teach? Yes, up to a point—though of course, examining our own students' editing needs is the best strategy of all. (See Chapter 12.)

So what editing issues might we be well advised to address? The Connors and Lunsford study (1988) revealed which "errors" college teachers of writing marked most often. Below we've divided these twenty errors into categories (much to our surprise, many of them deal with the use of commas):

Punctuation

- Missing comma after an introductory element
- Missing comma in a compound sentence
- Comma splice
- Missing comma in a series
- Missing comma(s) with a nonrestrictive element
- Unnecessary comma(s) with a restrictive element
- Sentence fragment
- Fused sentence
- Missing or misplaced possessive apostrophe

Verb and Pronoun Issues

- Lack of agreement between subject and verb
- Lack of agreement between pronoun and antecedent
- Wrong tense or verb form

- Wrong or missing verb ending
- Unnecessary shift in tense
- Unnecessary shift in pronoun
- Vague pronoun reference

Other

- Wrong word
- Wrong or missing preposition
- Misplaced or dangling modifier
- *Its/it's* confusion

If these features are rampant in your classroom, then it makes sense to prioritize the ones that are most annoying to readers and teach them first and most intensively.

Using appropriate connecting words and the associated punctuation is another crucial issue, especially for teaching informational and persuasive writing. Why didn't any of these factors show up on the Connors and Lunsford list? It's our hunch—and theirs too—that the items marked most often by college teachers were simply the items they found easiest to mark!

A more recent study by Kantz and Yates (1994) used methodology much more likely to produce an accurate picture of college teachers' reactions to various kinds of errors than the Connors and Lunsford study. Kantz and Yates presented college teachers with a well-designed survey that covered 29 different kinds of errors, including 11 errors involving homophones like *its/it's*, *their/there/they're*, and *affect/effect* or commonly misspelled words. The errors in the sentences (78 items, 6 containing no errors) were not specified, but respondents were asked to mark on a 6-point scale their response to whatever error they identified (or thought they did). A rating of 6 equaled "highly irritating," while 0 equaled "no irritation." The survey was returned and completed correctly by 141 faculty members from various disciplines.

While there were significant differences among individuals and certain groups in the responses (e.g., women identified the errors much more accurately than men), there was a definite hierarchy of errors. Certain ones were consistently among the more irritating: The top five were nonstandard verb forms, confusion between *you're* and *your*, confusion between *their* and *there*, ineffective sentence fragments, and subject-verb agreement. (As you can see, the more irritating items do not necessarily warrant the most instructional time.)

The survey included four facets of comma use: the comma splice (which ranked 18 in severity), failure to use commas with parenthetical or nonrestrictive elements (ranked 27), no comma in a compound sentence (ranked 29), and no comma after an introductory element (ranked 33).

(The latter two issues were rated less irritating than two of the error-free sentences that were misperceived as having errors!)

Kantz and Yates conclude not only that there is "cross-disciplinary agreement about a hierarchy of error" but also that the individual differences in identifying—and misidentifying—errors suggest that "the lack of accuracy in doing the survey means that we [teachers] should perhaps express our judgments about correctness with a bit of humility."

Maxine Hairston's earlier landmark study (1981), mentioned in Chapter 3, sought to determine what kinds of writing errors were responded to most negatively by businesspeople responsible for hiring company employees. Though her methodology was less than ideal, no one questions that certain kinds of errors are "status marking": that is, they tend to suggest that the person is uneducated, whether or not this is true. Here, again, is Hairston's list of status-marking errors, based on her selective questionnaire:

- Nonstandard verb forms in a past or past participle: *brung* instead of *brought*; *had went* instead of *had gone*.
- Lack of subject-verb agreement: *we was* instead of *we were*; *Jones don't think it's acceptable* instead of *Jones doesn't think it's acceptable*.
- Double negatives: *There has never been no one here*; *state employees can't hardly expect a raise*.
- Objective pronoun as subject: *Him and Richard were the last ones hired.*

Clearly these grammatical constructions would suggest to middle-class America that the writer is uneducated or undereducated.

Dealing with such features, however, is greatly complicated by the fact that they are common in different dialects and language communities, particularly urban or rural; in African American English; and in communities in which English is not the students' native language and may or may not be spoken in the home. Speakers of a nonmainstream dialect, or even these who use just a few nonmainstream features, are understandably reluctant to accept the idea that their language variety may not be acceptable in all life situations; indeed, they may resent the school's apparent rejection of their home or peer language and resist attempts to help them code-switch to standard features. Teaching such code-switching as part of editing is perhaps the least threatening, least resistance-generating way to approach it: After all, everybody needs to edit.

The situation with English language learners (ELLs) is different: They may simply be incapable of incorporating, at whatever phase in their acquisition of English, the grammatical features of standard English that we happen to be teaching. Therefore, we teachers need to be very familiar

Teaching such code-switching as part of editing is perhaps the least threatening, least resistance-generating way to approach it: After all, everybody needs to edit.

with native and nonnative English language acquisition and be aware that ELLs use well-defined, as well as idiosyncratic, "interlanguage" features (discussed later in this chapter and in Chapter 15)—some that defy explanation—in both their speech and their writing. With ELLs, then, we need to address switching these features or patterns to standard English during the editing process, but with the understanding that the acquisition of the corresponding standard forms will be gradual and also idiosyncratic, no matter how, or how well, we teach.

Teaching writers to code-switch from African American English to standard

Like other dialects of English, including ones with little or no prestige in mainstream society, African American English is a viable and vibrant language. Though not accepted in all speaking and writing situations, it works in many home, peer, and community contexts for those who employ it. From the late 1960s through the 1970s, considerable research into the nature of African American English (AAE) uncovered its most common features—the patterns that differentiate this dialect from mainstream English though somewhat overlapping with other social dialects and with Southern speech more generally. Most of the patterns that Rebecca Wheeler has recently found most common in the writings of many urban African American students were predominant in that earlier research as well. Figure 9–1, which also appears in Wheeler's chapter on code-switching (Chapter 14), is her "Code-Switching Shopping List for Student Editing": a list of the most dominant AAE features that can easily be contrasted with the features of standard English—or "formal" English, as Wheeler and others diplomatically call it.

Among the points we and Wheeler consider important are these:

- AAE—and other nonmainstream dialects—are complete language *systems*, with language patterns that differ from the patterns of mainstream English.
- One's language, one's dialect, is intimately tied to one's sense of identity, and teachers need to respect, and demonstrate their respect for, these other language varieties—perhaps by sharing literature that reflects them, as Wheeler suggests.
- Contrasting the features and patterns of students' home dialect or language with the features used in most public writing is a respectful way of approaching the editing issues—and can, of course, ultimately influence the students' more formal and general speech as well.

Code-Switching Shopping List for Student Editing

Name: _____

Do any of the top informal English patterns appear in your paper? If so, put a check in the corresponding box and then *code-switch* to formal English! Put a smiley face ☺ to show when you use formal patterns in your writing. "Flip the Switch!"

Informal v. Formal English Patterns	Paper 1	Paper 2	Paper 3	Paper 4
Verb Patterns				
1. Subject-verb agreement she walk v. she walk<u>s</u>				
2. Showing past time (1) I finish v. I finish<u>ed</u>				
3. Showing past time (2) she <u>seen</u> v. she <u>saw/had seen</u>				
4. A form of the *BE* verb understood (such as *is, are, was, were*) he cool with me v. he'<u>s</u> cool with me				
5. Making negatives she <u>won't never</u> v. she won't <u>ever</u>				
Noun Patterns				
6. Plurality: "Showing more than one" three cat v. three cat<u>s</u>				
7. Possessive the dog tail v. the dog'<u>s</u> tail				
8. *A* versus *an* an rapper v. a rapper a elephant v. an elephant				
9. Other pattern: _____				
10. Other pattern: _____				

FIGURE 9–1. Code-switching shopping list for student editing. Modified from Wheeler and Swords (2006). *Code-Switching: Teaching Standard English in Urban Classrooms.* Urbana, IL: NCTE. Used with permission.

- The concept of code-switching is one that students can readily understand and accept: after all, we change our clothes depending on where we're going and what we're going to do, and the concept of appropriateness can be addressed in this familiar context.

In Chapter 14, Wheeler shows how code-switching can work for you and your students, with practical sections on seeing student writing as data and using that data for minilessons, teaching grammar early in the writing process, code-switching during editing, and more.

Promoting the acquisition of English: Editing in language-rich and literacy-rich classrooms

In their book *ESL/EFL Teaching: Principles for Success* (1998), Yvonne and David Freeman write:

> Traditional methods have not worked well for English language learners. For example, in the United States, even among those who complete high school, only a small number go on to four-year colleges. In many foreign settings, students study English for years but never progress beyond a basic knowledge of English grammar. To reverse this trend of failure, a new approach is required. For many teachers, the answer is to base their practices on a new set of principles. (p. xv)

Why do we need to replace traditional teaching practices? "At the beginning of the semester, I could read only three or four pages at a time in English and write just a few sentences, but by the end I could read a hundred pages and write several pages," writes an Asian student in her evaluation of a graduate course in a program for learning to teach English to speakers of other languages (TESOL). In her home country, instruction in English focused exclusively on studying grammar, learning vocabulary by memorizing definitions, and translating texts word for word. She and classmates with similar backgrounds had scored high enough on the TOEFL (Test of English as a Foreign Language) to be admitted to Western Michigan University's TESOL graduate program, but most had not really learned to read or write in English—or to speak more than a few halting sentences. Steven Krashen (1981) calls this a distinction between *learning* English by studying it in a classroom—which we prefer to think of as "studying" English—and *acquiring* it through use. Though we may make limited use of grammatical knowledge we have "learned," part of the difference between learning and acquiring a nonnative language is the difference between having grammatical knowledge—*knowing about* the grammar of the target language—and *using* its grammar automatically and effortlessly.

We worry that students in some intensive English programs here in the United States, nonnative speakers of English who are being taught the grammar and vocabulary of the language, may not be acquiring it so much as studying it (see, for example, Fu, 1995). They may be learning to pass tests on English grammar—as Connie's graduate students in the TESOL program had done in their home countries—but not learning to read and write in English, or even to become comfortable speaking it, at least in classroom settings. However, the purpose of this discussion is not to argue that issue—you know if the shoe fits—but to offer an alternative learning and teaching perspective within which students not only learn to read and write English, but also learn the conventions needed to do well on standardized and state tests.

Historically, native speakers of another language who are learning English have often been referred to as ESL—English as a second language—students. A term currently popular in the United States is English language learners (ELLs). This term is more broadly applicable than ESL, since some of our students may already be multilingual before learning English. Still, the term English language learner is less than satisfactory. First, even native speakers are English language learners. Second, and more important, when we teachers use such terms, there is the danger of thinking of these students only in terms of their English proficiency (or lack thereof): a danger of mentally reducing these students to one aspect of their total being, as learners and as humans. When we label students—ESL, ELL, ADD, SLD, EMI, or whatever—we wrongly imply that the only important thing for teachers to know about these students as learners is that particular attribute—and most labels suggest a deficiency. As adults who do not like to be simplistically labeled in any way, we need to keep that in mind as we teach and develop plans and programs for teaching. Thus, although we use the term English language learner here, we must always keep in mind the dangers associated with it and similar terms.

Our perspective on teaching English grammar to students who do not speak English natively derives from research on various topics—most notably on nonnative language acquisition and interlanguage, but also on acquiring grammar in language-rich and literacy-rich classrooms (briefly discussed in Chapter 3, described more thoroughly in Krashen [2004], and exemplified in the classrooms of the California teachers who wrote Chapter 15).

Second language acquisition

Since the 1970s, there has been substantive observational research on the acquisition of a second language. The basic assumption is that "learners create a language system, known as an interlanguage" (Gass & Selinker, 2001, p. 12), a concept discussed more fully later in this chapter.

Stephen Krashen (1981, 1982, 1985), a pioneer in the field of second language acquisition, offers a broad perspective that we find useful. First, as we've already noted, he emphasized the difference between "learning" a language—that is, studying its features—and "acquiring" such a language. Foreign language study in school emphasizes, or at least used to emphasize, learning "correct" English grammar and avoiding "errors." However, when we emphasize acquiring a language in the context of using it to speak, read, and write, we necessarily must realize not only that language acquisition is a gradual process but that it involves increasingly sophisticated phases of use, in the process of mastering key features of the target language. Another early researcher, Terrell (1991), found that adults acquiring a second language will acquire the basic grammatical markers of that language in a fairly predictable order, even if the grammar has been explicitly taught to them in a different order (p. 55).

Initially, the acquisition of English as an additional language reveals many of the same patterns young native speakers exhibit as they begin speaking English.

Initially, the acquisition of English as an additional language reveals many of the same patterns young native speakers exhibit as they begin speaking English. For example, at the earliest stages of acquiring English, young native speakers do not include the kinds of noun and verb endings mentioned earlier; or prepositions (like *to, in, from, for*); or verb forms that end in *-ing* (*walking, eating*, and so forth); or the articles *a, an,* and *the.* All these patterns are common also among those who are at the early stages of acquiring English as an additional language. Samway and McKeon (1999) phrase it succinctly: "Learners who are acquiring a second language typically 'try out' the language with equal creative fervor as children learning their first language" (p. 18). They focus first on communicating meaning and only gradually on form.

While Krashen uses the term *acquisition* to refer to an individual psychological process of learning a language, Gee (1992) offers an expanded definition that includes a social component:

> Acquisition is a process of acquiring something subconsciously by exposure to models, a process of trial and error, and practice within social groups, without formal teaching. It happens in natural settings that are meaningful and functional in the sense that the acquirers know that they need to acquire the thing they are exposed to in order to function and that they in fact want to so function. (p. 113)

Gee's points need to be considered when creating classrooms where English language learners can succeed (as exemplified in this book in Chapter 15).

Behavioral versus constructivist approaches to teaching and learning

Though obviously we are convinced that *some* instruction in features of the English language can be valuable for ELL students when they are ready, overall we reject the behavioral approach—which emphasizes the desired product rather than the processes of getting there—in favor of a constructivist approach that honors the gradual process of language acquisition.

Behaviorism—that is, behavioral psychology, originally popularized in the 1920s—spawned the teach-practice-test model of instruction that still haunts us today. Basically behaviorism advises us to reduce a concept or strategy to its smallest constituent parts and then teach, have students practice, and test the mastery of each skill separately, in isolation from one another and from their intended or hoped-for use. The assumption is that learners will or should be able to combine the parts into a coherent and usable whole and apply the knowledge or strategy when needed. Unfortunately, such teaching procedures all too often fail to produce the desired outcome—as Greene (1950) noted long ago with respect to teaching grammar skills. From a behavioral point of view, the learner—or sometimes the teacher—is deemed to be at fault.

In the last several decades, cognitive psychology has given rise to vastly different principles of teaching and learning, according to which learners must inevitably construct strategies and skills for themselves—this is simply the nature of human learning, regardless of our teaching. The observation that behavioral teaching practices do not facilitate the learning of concepts and strategies to the point of application—as so often they don't—confirms for those steeped in cognitive psychology that the behavioral learning theory is inevitably at fault, not the learner or the teacher. From a cognitive, constructivist point of view, behavioral teaching practices reflect a faulty theory about how people learn concepts and strategies—in this case, about how they acquire a language.

Within a constructivist view of learning and a process approach to reading, writing, and acquiring language, explicit instruction does have a definite but limited role. Even Krashen, who offers research evidence that the most important thing we can do to promote ELLs' acquisition of the language is expose them to a lot of comprehensible input, makes the point that a limited amount of explicit grammatical assistance can be helpful at the right time (2003, p. 8). However, the study of native and nonnative language acquisition itself—in natural settings and in classrooms—reflects a cognitive, constructivist perspective—and has since the early 1970s.

Another important difference between behavioral and constructivist approaches is the different way behaviorists and constructivists view language learners' "errors." Kroll and Schafer (1978) contrasted these key differences in a chart (reproduced in Figure 9–2). Especially important are the final two points attributed to the constructivist view:

- Errors are a natural part of learning a language; they arise from learners' active strategies: overgeneralization, ignorance of rule restrictions, incomplete rule application, hypothesizing false concepts.
- We need to assist the learner in approximating the target language by supporting active learning strategies, while recognizing that not all errors will disappear.

When we come to appreciate the processes involved in native and nonnative language acquisition and the developmental nature of the "interlanguage" created by those learning an additional language, we see why it might be better to reject the concept of "error" altogether and speak of the "features" and "patterns" in our English language learners' use of English.

Understanding interlanguage

Within the overall perspective of second language acquisition lies the phenomenon of "interlanguage," as Larry Selinker (1972) chose to call the developmental features of a second language acquired through use, rather than studied with the goal of avoiding "errors." (See also Gass & Selinker, 2001.) An *interlanguage* is an emerging language system created by someone acquiring another language: It contains some of the grammatical features of the language being acquired, but not all. It may include some words, language patterns, and ways of expressing grammatical meanings from, or influenced by, the person's native language. These interlanguage features are commonly termed *language transfer features*, although that phrase is not really broad enough. Learning strategies reflected in an individual's interlanguage include simplification, overgeneralization, and creative experimentation as the learner strives to make himself or herself understood in the new language. Creative, idiosyncratic innovations are common.

Research in child language acquisition and the interlanguage systems created by nonnative language learners began with Brown's studies (1973) in the patterns of development in young children who were learning English as their first language. He focused on children's learning of grammatical morphemes. (A morpheme is the smallest possible unit of meaning in a language. For example, *boys* contains two morphemes, *boy* and the

Issue	Product [Behavioral] Approach	Process [Constructivist] Approach
Why should one study errors?	To produce a linguistic taxonomy of *what* errors learners make.	To produce a psycho-linguistic explanation of *why* a learner makes an error.
What is the attitude toward error?	Errors are "bad." (Interesting only to the linguistic theorist.)	Errors are "good." (Interesting to the theorist and teacher, and useful to the learner as active tests of his hypotheses.)
What can we hope to discover from learners' errors?	Those items on which the learner or the program failed.	The strategies which led the learner into the error.
How can we account for the fact that a learner makes an error?	It is primarily a failure to learn the correct form (perhaps a case of language inference).	Errors are a natural part of learning a language; they arise from learners' active strategies: overgeneralization, ignorance of rule restrictions, incomplete rule application, hypothesizing false concepts.
What are the emphases and goals of instruction?	A *teaching* perspective: eliminate all errors by establishing correct, automatic habits; mastery of the target language is the goal.	A *learning* perspective: assist the learner in approximating the target language; support active learning strategies and recognize that not all errors will disappear.

FIGURE 9–2. Contrast between behavioral and constructivist approaches to learners' errors (Kroll & Schafer, 1978). The fourth paragraph in the process column is credited to Richards (1971).

bound -s signaling plural; *walked* contains two morphemes, *walk* and the bound -ed indicating past tense; and the past tense *went* includes the morpheme (meaning) of *go* plus the past tense.) Early research in acquiring English as a second language (e.g., Dulay & Burt 1974a, 1974b, 1975) focused especially on the similarities between native and nonnative speakers' appropriation of such grammatical morphemes as noun plural and possessive markers, past tense markers, and the -s or -es on verb forms that occur in mainstream English with a single noun or pronoun: *Charlie agrees, she thinks, it works, he fixes everything.* (This -s or -es ending on a verb is called a *third singular* ending, as many students of a foreign language have learned).

We should emphasize that students from vastly different language backgrounds—Chinese and Spanish, for example—are likely to exhibit some of the same interlanguage features. Chinese has no noun endings for plural and no tense endings for verbs. Spanish, in contrast, has plenty of endings: noun endings for plural and possessive and grammatical gender; verb endings for present and past tense; and even adjective endings that must match the endings on nouns. One might think that speakers of Spanish—or other languages with similar grammatical endings, like French—might not only use but overuse these kinds of grammatical endings in English. This is not the case, however: Whatever the native language, it seems, speakers of English as an added language seem at first to leave off such endings. They simply go first for the basic words, and second for word order that makes their meaning clear—just as children learning English as their first language do.

Are there developmental phases in the acquisition of English?

The short answer to this is yes—and no. As we've noted, English language learners acquire certain grammatical morphemes in an order not unlike that of those acquiring English as a first language. The important point, though, is that these morphemes are to a substantial degree mastered before some of the other interlanguage patterns we see, especially in the writings of older students.

Figure 9–3 reproduces a paper that an eleventh grader wrote for the Michigan Educational Assessment Program's (1997) timed essay. Surely this student must be an English language learner, for her writing shows the omission and nonmainstream use of prepositions and articles. These patterns show up in the initial phases of acquiring English as a second language, but are not readily relinquished in favor of the standard variants. Why? Because the choice of a preposition is typically idiomatic, something that not even native speakers can ordinarily explain. The same difficulty arises with articles: Though patterned and rule-governed rather than idio-

Students from vastly different language backgrounds—Chinese and Spanish, for example—are likely to exhibit some of the same interlanguage features.

One day my Gym teacher told us about if ~~I~~ you don't want to do anything at in the Gym class, then don't come Gym class, go home or stay another classroom, so I went home. Then teacher call me and parents.

This choice was ~~bad~~ not bad, I think, because ~~th~~ techar told me about I can go home. I learned don't believe that teacher any more.

I learned about what is bad choice from my parents. They always toll me ~~th~~ what is bad choice before I do something, but if I choosed bad choice, then my parents ~~te~~ teach me that's bad.

If I made choice, but still feel bad, then I will keep doing, because I made it, ~~but~~ and I don't care about my feel, but I care about another people feels, because I can't do anything with myself. The exxample is company, study, business, and train. These things need many people to work, so I care about other persons feel.

The good choice make happy but bad choice make unhappy. The exsample are election of president. ~~everyone going to vote, then one guy will be~~

If [?] everyone choose own choice, then one guy ~~g~~ will be president, but other guy can't be president.

FIGURE 9-3. Eleventh grader's timed essay, based on the prompt "Write a paper in which you examine how making a choice helped you or someone else discover something" (Michigan Educational Assessment Program, 1997)

syncratic, their use is quite complex and again not explainable by the average native speaker (or most English teachers, including us). No wonder English language learners may continue to have some difficulties with these systems, even long after they have, perhaps, become published writers.

Most of the research relative to acquiring English as a nonnative language has, in fact, involved children under the age of ten, so the patterns exhibited by older youth and adults are not so well documented. In any case, Gass and Selinker (2001) conclude that acquring a second language is not exactly like acquiring one's native language, but neither is it fundamentally different (p. 182).

The important question is whether English language learners' acquisition of mainstream grammatical features of English can be accelerated by our teaching. Gass and Selinker (2001, pp. 317–320) discuss the natural development of a nonnative language in the classroom, including research demonstrating that traditional direct instruction, based on behavioral principles, is less effective than conversational interaction. Krashen (2003) comes to the same conclusion. Mackey found that conversation focused on structural (grammatical) features could increase the pace of acquisition to some degree, but could not push learners beyond their level of developmental readiness: "There are constraints on learning such that even pedagogical intervention is likely to be unsuccessful in altering the order of acquisition" (quoted in Gass & Selinker, 2001, p. 319).

Overall, there are some important points to be made about interlanguage and teaching ELL students the syntax of English:

1. To some extent there is a natural order of acquisition (Corder, 1967; see also the research summary in Krashen, 1985), an order that we may see among speakers of diverse language backgrounds, such as Chinese and Spanish. (Dulay and Burt, 1974a, a study of 55 Chinese and 60 Spanish children's developing English, shows that the order of acquisition of several grammatical morphemes, like noun plural and past tense, was very similar, though the Spanish children had somewhat greater mastery.)

2. An individual's interlanguage may reflect such processes as language transfer, overgeneralization (such as *goed* for *went*), simplification, and creative innovation.

3. Despite the similarity in the order in which some language features—some basic grammatical endings and forms, and words like the basic conjunctions *and* and *but*—are acquired, each individual's interlanguage is idiosyncratic—that is, unique in its totality (e.g., Gass & Selinker, 2001, p. 49).

4. The ELL students in any given classroom will therefore have not only unique interlanguage patterns but also unique needs; however, where there are common language features (such as absence of a noun plural or past tense ending, misuse of common prepositions, or issues with subordinate clause structures), we can group together such students for instruction.

5. No matter in what order certain grammatical elements might be taught, they will not necessarily be acquired in that order (Terrell, 1991).

6. Overall, what is taught—even under the best of circumstances—may not necessarily be learned to the point of application, because the learner may not be developmentally ready, or the cognitive demands of communication may override attention to mainstream grammatical features of English that have not yet become automatic.

7. Furthermore, certain language features seem almost impervious to any kind of instruction. Mastery of the prepositional system of English is difficult for nonnative English speakers, and mastery of the system for using articles before a noun—*a, an, the*, or nothing—is so complex that many ELLs never really master it, even if they

command most other features of English grammar. It's virtually impossible to acquire the English article system through instruction—and there are differences, too, between American English and British and Canadian English!

These observations give rise to a constructivist view of language acquisition and support a constructivist approach to teaching features of mainstream English to English language learners, as exemplified in Chapter 15 of this book.

Promoting a low "affective filter"

Crucial to developing constructivist approaches to helping students acquire English is what Krashen refers to as a "low affective filter." Basically, an "affective filter" is the emotional factor controlling the extent to which learners of a nonnative language will be able to acquire its grammatical and other structural features from comprehensible input. It also affects language learners' willingness to risk using the target language. In our classrooms, English language learners have to be confident they will not be made to look dumb as they risk expanding their use of English in class discussions. Taking these risks requires a *low* affective filter, with little concern about being "wrong."

Correction may be appropriate in specific role-playing situations for which students have had the opportunity to write scripts and get editing help, but in most situations, students need to be able to use their emerging English freely, without fear of embarrassment: in speaking, journal entries, and other first-draft writing. Otherwise, our English language learners may have a *high* affective filter and limit their English use in order to avoid embarrassment—thus retarding their progress. We need first to emphasize fluency and clarity in expressing meaning, reserving a focus on "correctness" for nonthreatening contexts. This is why we suggest focusing on teaching students to convert interlanguage features to mainstream English features as part of helping students edit their written work, especially writing that is to "go public."

English language learners have to be confident they will not be made to look dumb as they risk expanding their use of English in class discussions.

Principles to guide the teaching of standard English features

This chapter has offered several principles we believe should guide us in explicitly teaching ELL students to switch certain interlanguage features to their counterparts in standard English. We summarize them here:

1. Avoid an error-correction approach that involves marking students' papers with corrections. This doesn't work even with speakers of a mainstream variety of English, much less with those who are just

learning English and are especially unlikely to understand the point of the corrections.

2. Avoid the behavioral approach that involves teaching, practicing, and testing grammatical features of mainstream English in isolation; this has little effect on language use.

3. Adopt the linguistic perspective that the grammatical features and patterns of ELL speakers' interlanguage are merely characteristics, neither positive nor negative—not "errors."

4. Treat ELLs' language—their native language and their emerging English—with respect, just as you treat the learners themselves with respect.

5. Create a language-rich environment in which students can express themselves without fear of correction or disapproval, and a literacy-rich environment in which students are generously exposed to appropriate written texts. This alone won't teach students all the grammatical features of mainstream English, but it promotes fluency and clarity and mastery of some of the more global grammatical constructions. (See Krashen, 2004.)

6. Teach the kinds of features we're discussing in conjunction with helping intermediate ELL learners edit their writing. (Extensive reading may be the best solution for those at all levels of English mastery—see Krashen 2003 and 2004).

7. Analyze the patterns in your students' writing that contrast with corresponding features of mainstream English. Choose the most frequent and/or the most stigmatizing interlanguage features and prioritize what to teach first, next, and so forth. Group students as needed for such teaching.

8. Be careful not to overemphasize the learning of grammatical forms to the point of limiting students' willingness to take risks in their speaking and writing.

9. Keep your expectations realistic. When students are struggling to communicate meaning, they may not use the grammatical features you have previously taught and they seemingly mastered as you guided them in editing their writing. Since nonnative language acquisition is a gradual process, with or without any kind of instruction, reasonable expectations, patience, and repeated guidance are crucial.

10. Remember that respect and patient persistence are two of a teacher's greatest assets.

Rescuing Expository Writing from the Humdrum

From Rhetoric to Grammar

At a recent professional development session at a local high school, Jonathan led teachers in a series of grammatical activities illustrating our concept of grammatical instruction that enriches student writing. Afterward, a teacher came up to him and said, "All this was really interesting, but I don't teach creative writing. Do you have anything for me?" This was a flabbergasting question, since we consider the aspects of grammar taught in the preceding chapters to be appropriate for many forms of writing—see, for instance, the examples at the end of Chapter 6. Yet the incident also reminds us that many teachers draw more distinctions between major genres of writing—expository, creative, and journalistic—than we do. It reminds us even more that we need to be able to show teachers directly how grammar can be a tool for their students in all of these genres.

Throughout this book, we have looked at grammatical elements and strategies at a microlevel, showing how specific grammatical structures and teaching practices can be considered and applied throughout the genres. This chapter, however, focuses on a detailed discussion of expository writing, a genre that's generally considered—wrongly, in our opinion—to be the most unvaried and formulaic and thus, at least on the surface, the least amenable to our previous recommendations for teaching grammatical structures.

The idea of expository writing first appears in Alexander Bain's 1866 *English Composition and Rhetoric*. Bain posited that writing consisted of five modes: poetry, narration, description, exposition, and persuasion. Although four of these modes can still be found in many modern composition texts (poetry, sadly, couldn't cut the mustard), we've come to understand that they are not as unrelated as Bain once believed. Rhetorical scholars, most notably James Kinneavy, have been advancing and modifying these modes ever since. Kinneavy, in *A Theory of Discourse* (1980), revises the modes into a set of four: narration, description, evaluation, and classification. The expository mode as it is most traditionally discussed in classrooms includes elements of all these under the broader aegis of information dissemination.

Recently Jonathan asked several first-year writing instructors to poll their students for a definition of expository writing. One teacher had her students, in small groups, derive a consensus based on individual responses such as "writing that conveys information," "writing that argues," and "English class writing." After a series of arguments and negotiations, the most common consensus was "writing we do in school." A lot of discussion focused on formulas and whether exposition was synonymous with the ubiquitous five-paragraph essay. There was a general perception among many students that they knew what expository writing was but could not adequately verbalize it as a genre. The one thing that all students agreed on, without much debate, was that creativity and flexibility were limited and that all expository text was subject to much more restrictive standards than other writings, both informal and formal.

Perhaps the best way to define expository writing is to discuss what it is generally considered not to be—informal, passionate, exploratory, literary, or expressive. In academic settings, the writing generally termed "expository" includes three primary forms, all of which come under the category of what James Britton and colleagues (1975) called *transactional writing*—that is, writing to achieve a practical goal:

- *Informational writing:* designed to convey information to an audience, with a need for close attention to clarity, organization, and content. This can include presenting factual information about a topic, describing a process or event, clarifying the nature of—or misunderstandings about—something, and so forth.
- *Research writing:* designed to present the results of formal or informal investigation of a particular question, concept, or topic. In school, research writing often focuses on other people's original research, not the writer's own.
- *Persuasive writing:* designed to persuade an audience of a particular view, or to provide a well-reasoned presentation of facts and arguments with close attention to tone, organization, and support. Argumentative writing is a subgenre, with a point-counterpoint structure that itself is often formulaic (see, for example, Baker & Yarber, *The Practical Stylist*, 1997).

These three forms of writing may have more in common than not. For example, informative pieces and research papers are often written to persuade. Furthermore, some of the most effective published writing uses elements of creative writing with expository, transactional intent, as we shall see later in this chapter.

Unfortunately, narrow conceptions of expository writing can lead to overly general advice about style and grammar. Generally speaking, when teachers speak of expository writing from the traditional perspective, a series of rules, expectations, or requirements like these is offered:

- *Focus:* Should have an identifiable thesis statement, preferably in the introductory paragraph.
- *Structure and organization:* Should have an identifiable introduction, a body, and a conclusion that restates or summarizes.
- *Content:* Content should follow explicitly from the thesis sentence.
- *Tone:* Should use third person exclusively; straightforward text designed for straightforward understanding.
- *Conventions:* Should never deviate from rules of standard edited English.

These stipulations are a summary of common guidelines. There are many teacher's guides, individual project materials, and other resources that will gladly break them down into minutiae for teachers, students, and anyone else willing to listen. See, for example:

http://www.geocities.com/SoHo/Atrium/1437/expo.html
http://www.arcanum-butler.k12.oh.us/Expository_Page.html
http://www.sbac.edu/~idylwild/writingtips.html
http://www.studygs.net/wrtstr3.htm

To illustrate some of these rules and their limiting nature, let's look at an example of expository writing.

Following a formula for persuasive writing

Here's an expository text—meant to be persuasive—that follows all these basic exhortations for expository writing. The result is straightforward, easily understood, and focused. It is also a pretty bad example of the genre—perhaps so bad as to be unrealistic—but it helps us make a point about school writing.

Game Day Soccer Coaching: A Guide

Soccer is a game in which coaches need to trust their players. During a soccer game, coaches need to sit back and let the players play. They should do their coaching during practices.

A recent informal survey of local soccer fields showed a lot of coaches running up and down the sidelines of the soccer fields yelling instructions to players. The players were not listening. Many players are so focused on the game that they don't even hear their parents yelling. They are so busy playing the game that they don't have time to listen to people telling them what to do.

Coaching behavior like this is also distracting to fans. One coach was yelling so much that he was keeping people from watching the game. He was running in front of parents and making them look around him as he yelled at his players.

If players do not know what to do once a game starts, it is already too late. A game is not the time to try to tell players what to do. Coaches should coach in practice and let the players play during the game.

In short, coaches are teachers. A game is like a test in school. Teachers don't try to teach during a test. Coaches shouldn't try to yell instructions during a game.

This essay follows the time-honored rules, the formula, for a five-paragraph theme. From that point of view, it succeeds.

But what's missing is voice, style, convincing evidence, and passion, among other things. The support could be strengthened with specific details and images—perhaps including statistics or more details from the informal survey referred to, sensory details about the "one coach" mentioned, imagined examples, an analogy between teaching some specific school subject and coaching soccer and so forth—all of which would help make the essay interesting. As written, however, the essay has no voice—or perhaps we might say it has a "student" voice. It sounds—and is—contrived to follow "the rules."

Of course, many English teachers encourage their students to break some of the traditional rules, especially the one about using third person. Here's just one example of how a five-paragraph theme might begin with a different voice that addresses the reader directly and begins to set a different tone:

It's Saturday afternoon; you're eight years old; you've been looking forward to playing soccer all week. But when the whistle blows and the game starts, all you can hear is "Kick it!" "Cover that side!" "Don't forget to pass!" It's your coach. She won't shut up. You like soccer, but she makes it not fun anymore. Annoyed, you do the best you can to ignore her and enjoy yourself. I know I'm not the first person who has ever experienced this frustration of the overly zealous coach. Too many coaches, parents, and passers-by have lost the original point of recreational sports:

recreation! Goals of fun and exercise are bypassed by a need for the kids to succeed; to win; and to play well. The American Youth Soccer Associations (AYSO) says, one of their goals is "to create a positive environment based on mutual respect." It does not say anything about playing to win. We all need to find ways to restore the fun to kids' sports.

Revisions of this nature break some of the time-honored rules and make the essay much more interesting, but the use of the five-paragraph structure—with explicit thesis statement and its explicit repetition in the conclusion—still places it in the genre of school writing. The structure may be useful as a step in helping students learn to write a cogent argument, but why not push beyond these bounds? Why not help students write more like published writers? (See Chapter 12, where we suggest this as a stage beyond the five-paragraph theme.)

Abandoning the formula to make writing more persuasive

The following piece takes a different tack. By being addressed to someone in particular—coaches—the essay immediately signals both an audience and a voice, the writer who is giving advice to coaches. The strict rules for the structure of a five-paragraph theme aren't followed: There's no easily identifiable opening thesis followed by data lined up in logical support. In fact, the effective structure isn't easily apparent, because the essay flows instead of the structure calling attention to itself. It also doesn't follow certain oft-repeated "rules" about conventions.

Coaches: "Sit Down, Relax, and Enjoy the Game"

A few years ago I was coaching one of my first basketball games. We were losing badly and I was out of timeouts. Nervous about my team and my own ability as a coach, I found myself yelling ridiculous directions at my team as they brought the ball down the court: "Spread out!" "Set the screen!" and even "Don't forget to shoot!" Suddenly, the young boy who was our point guard, without stopping his dribble, turned to me with a big smile and said something spectacularly profound: "Coach, don't worry. We've got it."

I was stunned for a second, and then I realized the wisdom of what he had said. Properly chastised, I chuckled and quietly sat down on the bench to watch the game. He was right. I needed to shut up and enjoy watching the kids put into action what we had practiced. No, we didn't win, but we came close. I learned a valuable lesson about coaching. The games are for the kids. Coaches need to teach in practice and trust in the players' ability to play when game time comes. Got it.

But later the same year, coaching soccer, I found myself violating this important rule again—running on the sideline, yelling to players, shouting instructions, and, quite simply, coaching as if the game depended on me more than the players. After the game, a wise referee took me aside.

He told me two important things to remember: first, that kids very rarely hear their coaches during games, and, second, even if they do hear, they often have no idea what the coach is talking about. (He was right; at the next practice, I asked my players what instructions they remembered: the response, a resounding "I dunno."). He then gave me a great piece of advice: to bring a lawn chair to the games—and sit in it. "Relax and enjoy the game," he told me, "You deserve it."

Why mention this? This past weekend, I witnessed a lot of overaggressive coaching at a recreational youth soccer league. I spent some time watching the disturbing histrionics of one coach in particular; he wasn't abusive in any way, but, without a doubt, he was drastically overcoaching his players—going back and forth down the field, continually yelling, directing, cajoling, and instructing throughout the game. It adds an ironic twist that from the opening whistle, his team, while not playing perfectly, was clearly going to win the game.

He was so focused on controlling the actions of his players that he was even walking back and forth in front of parents and families. Sometimes his advice to his players, given continually during the action, like mine years ago, was inane: "Kick the ball!" "Pass it!" "Run and get it!" Other times, what he was yelling was clearly too technical: "Watch out for the offsides!" I saw a few players looking back quizzically as he yelled, trying to figure out what he meant. Most, thank goodness, like mine years ago, simply played the game heedless of his instructions.

As I strolled around the fields to watch other games, I heard and saw similar coaching taking place all around me. Coaches were running up and down fields, continually yelling instructions at players, and generally making a nuisance of themselves as the kids tried to play.

I've done a lot of coaching since those early days, and now, if I'm tempted to get up out of my lawn chair and start yelling advice again during a game, a voice sometimes comes into my head to remind me: "Coach, don't worry. They've got it." They usually do. But if they don't, we always have something to talk about at halftime or work on during the next practice.

And then I sit back, relax, and enjoy the game.

Stylistic options that enrich the writing

Before we get to "rules," did you notice the many present participial phrases in this piece—the *-ing* phrases that show coaches yelling, players running, and so forth? The out-of-order adjectival phrases? An occasional appositive? Other stylistic devices like the commentary "thank goodness"? Here are some examples:

Present participial phrases set off by punctuation

Later the same year, <u>coaching soccer</u>, I found myself violating this important rule again—<u>running on the sideline</u>, <u>yelling to players</u>, <u>shouting instructions</u>, and, quite simply, <u>coaching as if the game depended on me more than the players</u>. [This use of a series of the same kind of construction, called *parallelism*, is often found in effective prose, whether creative or expository.]

I saw a few players looking back quizzically as he yelled, <u>trying to figure out what he meant</u>.

Miscellaneous out-of-order adjectival phrases

<u>Nervous about my team and my own ability as a coach</u>, I found myself yelling ridiculous directions. . . .

<u>Properly chastised</u>, I chuckled and quietly sat down on the bench to watch the game.

Sometimes his advice to his players, <u>given continually during the action</u>, <u>like mine years ago</u>, was inane: "Kick the ball!" "Pass it!" "Run and get it!" [Here there are two adjectival phrases, both occurring after *advice* and describing it—technically, "modifying" it.

Appositive

Sometimes an appositive occurs right after a colon:

(He was right; at the next practice, I asked my players what instructions they remembered: the response, <u>a resounding "I dunno."</u>) [This appositive is unusual, because the comma before it seems replaceable by the word *was*: *the response was a resounding "I dunno."* Using the appositive, a noun phrase clarifying the previous noun, calls attention to "I dunno," making it more likely that it will make an impact on the reader.]

He then gave me a great piece of advice: <u>to bring a lawn chair to the games—and sit in it.</u>

The kinds of adjectival phrases emphasized in the previous chapters abound in this piece because the writer has used narration in service of her persuasive argument.

Contrasting these two approaches to persuasion

Now let's compare the two essays in relation to the "rules" of expository writing we stated previously:

	Rule	Essay #1 *Game Day Coaching*	Essay #2: *Coaches: "Sit Down, Relax, and Enjoy the Game"*
Focus:	Should have an identifiable thesis statement, preferably in the introductory paragraph.	First paragraph: *"During a soccer game, coaches need to sit back and let the players play. They should do their coaching during practices."*	No discernable thesis statement. Point is never explicitly stated. Closest possibility, middle of essay: *"Why mention this? This past weekend, I witnessed a lot of over aggressive coaching at a recreational youth soccer league."*
Structure and organization:	Should have an identifiable introduction, body, and conclusion that restates or summarizes.	Five-paragraph structure is clearly followed. Conclusion restates thesis after three support paragraphs.	Structured as a narrative, with stories followed by personal comments. Concluding paragraph is a single sentence, referring to anecdote.
Content:	Content should follow explicitly from the thesis sentence.	Writing rarely deviates from stated point. All content serves to support thesis. Facts developed and cited: *"a recent informal survey."*	Content focuses on personal observations. Otherwise, factual evidence is missing.

	Rule	Essay #1 *Game Day Coaching*	Essay #2: *Coaches: "Sit Down, Relax, and Enjoy the Game"*
Tone:	Should use third person exclusively; straight-forward text designed for straightforward understanding.	Uses third person. Tone is distant and clinical. Personal details are related as impersonal facts.	Uses first person. Tone is engaging and personal. Uses grammatical constructions that convey details and a sense of "being there."
Conventions:	Should never deviate from rules of standard edited English.	Conventions are followed.	Paragraph lengths vary. Fragments are used. Sentences begin with *and* and *but*.

The first essay follows the rules, the still-recommended formula, for logical argument, including the five-paragraph structure with thesis statement, three paragraphs of support, and a conclusion restating the thesis. The second complete essay deviates from this structure as well as the other traditional rules. The first sounds like a student essay and would still exemplify that genre if it included specific details and a first-person voice. The second, with its unique structure, sounds more like published writing—and indeed, a shortened version was published as an opinion piece in the *Kalamazoo Gazette*!

Use of ethos and pathos in service of logos: A rhetorical decision

Teachers have often been taught, or exhorted, to view students' persuasive writing through "the rules" for the five-paragraph expository theme: Does the paper follow the rules or not? We can, however, look at the second complete soccer coach piece through many different lenses—psychological, feminist, cultural, and so forth. We'll choose the classic rhetoric lens, which values argumentation and exposition developed around the concepts of ethos, pathos, and logos. *Ethos* is generally defined as "credibility," the trait that gives the writer authority; *pathos* as the development of concepts via emotions; and *logos* as the use of logic and logical arguments. These approaches are not mutually exclusive, though: For example, ethos and pathos can be used in the service of logos, or logical argument, as in "Coaches: 'Sit Down.'"

Instead of beginning with a thesis, the writer first moves to establish her authoritative voice by relating an anecdote from previous coaching—ethos. She thereby weaves a "been-there, done-that" tone that evokes a casual, "I know all about it" approach to coaching—in ironic contrast to the hyperactive coaching she demonstrates in the first paragraph. Primarily, though, the essay weaves its argument by the use of *pathos*, an emotional appeal. This appeal relies on common feeling and emotional engagement. The author paints a picture of a coach ruining the playing experiences of young children, bringing up an archetypical image of the overzealous and abusive coach.

Interestingly, the essay's least obvious appeal is the one most emphasized in traditional notions about expository writing. This is, of course, logos, the rhetorical appeal of logic. Some readers might argue that logos is entirely absent, that the author builds the argument solely on pathos and ethos. But the author does add an implicit logical argument for the ineffectiveness of this kind of coaching when she relates the anecdote about the inappropriateness of overactive coaching and her players' negative responses to her question, "What did I tell you during the game?" The writer's authoritative tone, though, derives mainly from her rhetorical decision to use pathos and ethos in service of logos, her implicit logical argument.

We suppose that, like us, most readers find the second essay, which doesn't follow the touted "rules" for expository writing, to be vastly superior to the first. The greater appeal of the second essay derives partly from its nonformulaic structure; it doesn't creak. Like other effective writers, the author of "Coaches: 'Sit Down'" has focused on higher-order concerns of audience, purpose, and content, then let these concepts guide the lower-order concerns of organization, grammar, and style. This is what published writers do.

In addition to the use of personal experience and anecdotes, what other factors do we think elevate "Coaches: 'Sit Down'" above the humdrum? Here's our entire list:

- Use of ethos to establish credibility and pathos to appeal to emotions.
- Use of narration, with various adjectival phrases that occur after the noun modified or as sentence openers. (Adverbial phrases, too, but we haven't discussed these.)
- Overall structure that is primarily associational, encompassing an implied compare/contrast structure (what I did "before," what I did "after" I learned how not to coach).
- Clear flow from associational elements into logical appeal—logos, with cohesive devices that link new information with old.

- Use of effective stylistic/rhetorical devices, such as an occasional fragment or a sentence that begins with *but* or *and*.

These features work together, creating a whole that establishes an "I'm one of you" tone that makes the argument more credible. The writer made rhetorical decisions about how best to persuade her audience, which in turn influenced her grammatical choices.

Writers make rhetorical decisions about how best to tie things together within a piece of writing. Will we, for instance, use heavyweight connectors like *however* and *therefore*, or lightweight connectors like *but* and *and*? Will we repeat key phrases verbatim, or perhaps modify the wording slightly for variety or emphasis? Each decision is guided, though often without conscious thought, by the writer's decision about what is most suitable not only for the topic but for the audience.

Cohesion in "Coaches: 'Sit Down' "

We made a quick trip through this piece, identifying the cohesive devices that had been used (see the shaded words and phrases in Figure 10–1). Of course, these choices are arbitrary to some degree, and sometimes you won't recognize something as a cohesive device until you see its echo later. What we noticed right away were some rather traditional devices:

> time connectors: *after, now, and then*
> sequencers: *first . . . second*
> contrasting pairs: *sometimes . . . other times*; *a few . . . most*
> coordinating conjunctions at the beginning of paragraphs: *but* and
>   *and*
> fragments: *got it* standing alone at the end of a paragraph; *why mention this?* at the beginning of another

as well as several phrases that are unique to the piece:

> *enjoy watching . . . enjoy the game . . . and then I sit back, relax, and enjoy the game.*

Why mention this? is the most important cohesive (and transitional) device, because it links the past with the present, the first personal experience with the recent one, thus completing the implicit argument that during games, coaches should not teach but rather trust their players, sit back, relax, and enjoy the game.

What is rhetoric?

In Chapter 3, we paraphrased Aristotle's original definition that rhetoric is the effective use of the available means of persuasion within a given context or situation. We also quoted Francis Christensen's point that grammar maps out the possible, while rhetoric narrows the possible down to what is most effective—especially for the audience and purpose. We might also say that rhetoric is the art of selecting and using language to engage the reader's mind, heart, imagination, and/or spirit. Rhetorical decisions lead to a particular style and to a particular authorial voice.

Coaches: "Sit Down, Relax, and Enjoy the Game"

A few years ago I was coaching one of my first basketball games. We were losing badly and I was out of timeouts. Nervous about my team and my own ability as a coach, I found myself yelling ridiculous directions at my team as they brought the ball down the court: "Spread out!" "Set the screen!" and even "Don't forget to shoot!" Suddenly, the young boy who was our point guard, without stopping his dribble, turned to me with a big smile and said something spectacularly profound: "Coach, don't worry. We've got it."

I was stunned for a second, and then I realized the wisdom of what he had said. Properly chastised, I chuckled and quietly sat down on the bench to watch the game. He was right. I needed to shut up and enjoy watching the kids put into action what we had practiced. No, we didn't win, but we came close. I learned a valuable lesson about coaching. The games are for the kids. Coaches need to teach in practice and trust in the players' ability to play when game time comes. Got it.

But later the same year, coaching soccer, I found myself violating this important rule again—running on the sideline, yelling to players, shouting instructions, and, quite simply, coaching as if the game depended on me more than the players. After the game, a wise referee took me aside.

He told me two important things to remember: first, that kids very rarely hear their coaches during games, and, second, even if they do hear, they often have no idea what the coach is talking about. (He was right; at the next practice, I asked my players what instructions they remembered: the response, a resounding "I dunno."). He then gave me a great piece of advice: to bring a lawn chair to the games—and sit in it. "Relax and enjoy the game," he told me, "You deserve it."

Why mention this? This past weekend, I witnessed a lot of overaggressive coaching at a recreational youth soccer league. I spent some time watching the disturbing histrionics of one coach in particular; he wasn't abusive in any way, but, without a doubt, he was drastically over-coaching his players—going back and forth down the field, continually yelling, directing, cajoling, and instructing throughout the game. It adds an ironic twist that from the opening whistle, his team, while not playing perfectly, was clearly going to win the game.

He was so focused on controlling the actions of his players that he was even walking back and forth in front of parents and families. Sometimes his advice to his players, given continually during the action, like mine years ago, was inane: "Kick the ball!" "Pass it!" "Run and get it!" Other times, what he was yelling was clearly too technical: "Watch out for the offsides!" I saw a few players looking back quizzically as he yelled, trying to figure out what he meant. Most, thank goodness, like mine years ago, simply played the game heedless of his instructions.

As I strolled around the fields to watch other games, I heard and saw similar coaching taking place all around me. Coaches were running up and down fields, continually yelling instructions at players, and generally making a nuisance of themselves as the kids tried to play.

I've done a lot of coaching since those early days, and now, if I'm tempted to get up out of my lawn chair and start yelling advice again during a game, a voice sometimes comes into my head to remind me: "Coach, don't worry. They've got it." They usually do. But if they don't, we always have something to talk about at halftime or work on during the next practice.

And then I sit back, relax, and enjoy the game.

FIGURE 10–1. Cohesive devices in "Coaches: 'Sit Down'"

Cohesive devices and traditional connectors

To our surprise, only one of the subordinate clauses in Figure 10–1 initially leaped out as a connective (subordinating) device because it begins a new paragraph: *as I strolled around the fields to watch other games.* We noticed this one because it reminded readers that the narrator, who had stepped out of time to critique the other coach, was still on the field, so to speak. But we didn't notice the other adverbial clauses that began with *as, when,* and *if.* Nor did we notice most instances of *and* or *but.*

Why mention this? Because it's important for us as teachers to help students learn to create flow and cohesion within a piece of writing by using a variety of devices, some of which—like repetition of a key word or phrase—are likely to be idiosyncratic. In other words, when we teach ways of conjoining and subordinating sentences and connecting sentences and paragraphs, our guidance in using cohesive devices must go beyond traditional grammatical categories like conjunctions and conjunctive adverbs. Chapter 11 presents a generous list of commonly used transitions that include those categories and more, organized by meaning or purpose rather than by grammar. Still, no prepackaged list covers all the territory.

Rules that don't rule

In Chapter 2, we briefly discussed some "rules that don't rule," a phrase borrowed from Ed Schuster (2003). One of these dealt with the prohibition against sentence fragments, and the other with the prohibition against starting a sentence with *and* or *but.* The "Coaches: 'Sit Down'" piece breaks both these rules, to good effect.

The "frumious fragament"—or fragments reconsidered

One rule that effective professional writers increasingly ignore is the prohibition against the use of sentence fragments. As Stephen King (2000) writes, "*Must* you write complete sentences each time, every time? Perish the thought" (p. 120).

Sentence fragments often occur in fiction, but also, though to a lesser extent, in nonfiction. Fragments can be especially useful as transitional devices at the end or the beginning of a paragraph. But they can occur anywhere within a paragraph, too. For example, here is the third paragraph from the authors' introduction to their book *What the Bleep Do We Know!?* (Arntz, Chasse, & Vicente, 2005):

> Or rather, we went on a trip. We trooped around the country interviewing all these brilliant people so we could get on film what they had to say. <u>Turns out we wanted to get on film what we thought they had to say and soon learned that what they really did have to say was different.</u> <u>Different from some of our notions, different from each other, different from what we were taught in school, different from what was preached in church and what we see on the nightly news.</u> And in the end we were the ones to decide. <u>To decide for ourselves where the truth lies and what to try out in our lives.</u> (p. ix)

Thanks substantially to the fragments, the tone is deliberately breezy, designed to draw in potential readers—whom the authors address as *you* in their very first sentence. The subject, however, is quite serious, focusing first on discoveries from quantum physics. Obviously the authors made a rhetorical decision to try to offset the "heavy" content with a light tone, one that would say to the reader, "You can understand this."

In "Name Dropping: Want to Be a Star?" Philip Plait (in *Skeptical Inquirer,* 2006) starts two new sections—not just paragraphs—with a fragment. Here is one:

> <u>And what of "my" star, Philip Cary Plait?</u> (p. 54)

This informative article, too, has a rather light tone, with fragments; sentences beginning with *but* and *and*; word choices like *hogging*; phrases like *they really, honestly*; *I* used as the narrative voice, along with *you* and *your* to address the reader. The article has definitely engaged *us* as readers!

What particularly alerted us to fragments as transitions were instances we noted in David Bodanis' *The Secret House: The Extraordinary Science of an Ordinary Day* (1986). We've included the preceding sentence, or sentences, in each case. Here's the first example:

> Aside from the oils and detergents in the ink there is also a high concentration of antimicrobial poisons worked in. It's good for keeping ink stores fresh when they're waiting at the painters, but here, splattering loose on the table, it's what causes the frantic riot of fleeing pseudomonads we started with.
>   <u>So far so good.</u> (p. 18)

Wouldn't you agree that Bodanis may have used this fragment as a break from the scientific details of his explanation of the science in ordinary lives? It appears he's tried to lighten his scientifically weighty subject with fragments like these. In the next example, the "shock" of the grammatical fragment is used artfully to emphasize the shock of the information:

In time they [minute marine organisms] ended up in the geological layers our present water supplies pass through. Regular amounts leach out and are carried to the house, where, just as regularly, the water is used and sent out again without these ancient chemical tombs being disturbed.

Except, that is, in the heating kettle, chugging away merrily in preparation for the needed drink. (p. 27)

Recovering from our own shock, we now show you a stretch of text that includes two paragraphs, each beginning with a fragment (in the paragraph just before, Bodanis concludes by mentioning the sulfuric acid that seeps into a house and even into women's nylons):

Back to the male. The shirt is finally on, and now only the problem of getting the trousers pulled up remains to be faced. The ancestor of trousers was the skirt, and that noble garment has always been easier to manoeuver. But a skirt that has been sewn into two narrow tubes, and is held together by an unwieldy saddle-shaped wedge of cloth at the top, is certain to demand yanking and tugging to get it in place. There is even, though the dresser doesn't know it yet, tearing.

Not great crackling rips, not the sort to make one spin around at parties and hastily seek the nearest sofa refuge to hide the damage. These universal early morning tears are smaller. (p. 42)

We've occasionally used the "back to" ploy ourselves to start a new paragraph. As for the other fragment, we've noticed over time that it's not uncommon to begin a paragraph with a fragment expressing a kind of negative, in contrast to the preceding paragraph.

Of course, not all examples of fragments in nonfiction prose are designed to create a light tone, even sporadically, to lighten technical content. Here are two examples, both occurring at the *beginning* of a paragraph:

Then why the recent spike in performance? (Barbara Kiviat, "Investing by the Numbers," *Time*, 2006, p. 83)

Got psi? Richard Shoup of the Boundary Institute spoke on "Physics Without Causality: Theory and Evidence." (Robert Sheaffer, "Time Flies Like an Arrow, but Fruit Flies Like Bilked Bananas," *Skeptical Inquirer*, 2006, p. 32)

The use of a question to start a new paragraph is fairly common, and such questions may well be fragments, grammatically speaking.

Here's a different kind of example. After a sentence on President Bush's veto of expanded funding for stem cell research as he stood surrounded by a bevy of children who had once been "a frozen embryo in a lab," writer Bruno Maddox (in *Discover* magazine, 2006) ends his paragraph with the following fragment:

> As if anyone had argued that frozen embryos couldn't be grown into people given the right care and feeding and a few hundred grand's worth of special treatment by the very people whose funding he was now freezing. (p. 29)

Perhaps the author's sarcasm—another effective rhetorical device—is also responsible for his starting three of his twelve paragraphs with fragments that begin with *which*. One of these fragments is a paragraph by itself, prefaced below by the last sentence in the preceding paragraph:

> More likely, the young doctors of 1858, like everyone else drawing breath in the English-speaking world at that time, simply liked to unwind after a hard day by gawping at the deformed.
> Which they did, famously, for a reason: they were worried.
> (p. 28)

Are we suggesting, then, that students be encouraged to pepper their paragraphs with sentence fragments? Of course not.

Even though there's a complete sentence after the colon, we include this as an example of a fragment not only because the part before the colon is grammatically incomplete but also because it *works* like a rhetorical fragment does, sharpening a particular point, shocking the reader, or—in this case—signaling a drastic shift in tone or content. Is it acceptable, or should we chastise this author? True, when we were in school, we were especially cautioned against fragments beginning with *which*—yet we see this occasionally in today's highly respected publications, not only the relatively informal but the more formal. In this particular instance, the rule-breaking iconoclasm fits well with the title and description of the article, "Blinded by Science," in which "we visit a museum of medical oddities and ask if future freaks will be bioengineered" (p. 2).

Are we suggesting, then, that students be encouraged to pepper their paragraphs with sentence fragments? Of course not. Neither do most published writers overuse fragments, at least not writers of nonfiction; indeed, many use few fragments or none at all. Still, we have a real problem with teachers' insisting that students must learn to avoid fragments before they can be allowed to use them in their own writing. We strongly disagree. Teachers can give their students pieces of published writing, including nonfiction—or excerpts from such writing—that make effective use of fragments. Students themselves—together with their teachers!—can discover some of the patterns that we have noted. Such discovery fits natu-

A word about standardized tests

Standardized tests of revision and editing skills, like the multiple-choice part of the SAT's writing test and the ACT's English test, require writers to identify fragments as "wrong." Interestingly, many of these "fragments" seem to be garbled sentences in which the writer has lost track of the grammar. It is easy to identify these as incorrect. Other examples on such tests, we have found, are so obviously ineffective that most students would reject them. In fact, the fragments from such tests may make a good contrast in the classroom to the effective examples we have cited. In any case, we urge teachers not to prohibit their writers from using an occasional sentence fragment as professionals use them, or an occasional sentence beginning with *and* or *but*. Students capable of doing well on standardized tests are also capable of understanding that rules don't completely govern expository writing, even though how they answer questions on these tests is based on the fiction that the rules always apply.

rally with the exploration of tone in writing: what rhetorical decisions the writer has made about the audience and how to address that audience on that particular topic. A writer's topic and audience may call for fragments, whether the writing is informative or persuasive. And isn't informative writing almost always persuasive, anyway—just as persuasive writing will inform, in one way or another?

What style we use, what stylistic devices we use, and even what genre we use depend crucially on our rhetorical decisions about audience, purpose, and topic. Just as young children quickly learn to differentiate between their mother's expectations and their father's, so our middle and secondary students can learn to differentiate between effective fragments and those that don't work. More and more teachers are now convinced that the kind of instruction given to "gifted" students will often also work best for students who are seen as below average, perhaps even as "special needs" students. Similarly, the more challenging task of differentiating between effective and ineffective fragments may motivate many students more than the task of avoiding fragments altogether.

Rhetorical/stylistic use of but or and to start a sentence

The use of *and* and *but* to begin a paragraph or other sentence can be an effective rhetorical technique that creates emphasis and cohesion while making a smooth transition from one sentence or paragraph to the next. Following are examples from newspapers as well as creative and expository writing.

An important caveat: In most cases, these stylistic options are rhetorically effective if, and only if, they are used sparingly. Otherwise, they themselves can become humdrum and lose their rhetorical power.

In journalism

We first began to notice the use of sentence-opening *but*s and *and*s in journalism—not just in feature articles and editorials, but in news articles as well. We discovered, in fact, something we hadn't consciously noticed before: Writers use these rhetorical/stylistic devices at least as often at the beginning of new paragraphs as elsewhere.

Using *but* and *and* in this way connects a concept with one previously discussed; these words function as transitions. Following are examples of *but* starting new paragraphs in some randomly selected front-page articles from Kalamazoo, Michigan's *Kalamazoo Gazette*, beginning with examples from "Impact of Affirmative-Action Ban Unfolding," by Judy Putnam (2006):

> "To unscramble the egg in the middle would be unfair to everyone, especially when nobody knows what the amendment requires," Washington said.
>
> But Attorney General Mike Cox last week said the universities' request was more than a temporary delay. (p. A1)

Here *but* moves the reader from point to counterpoint. But *but* can also be used to introduce a point that leads simply to clarification. For example:

> But what exactly does compliance mean? Washington argues that the universities are considering race in admissions but aren't giving preferences. (p. A1)

In both cases, the sentence beginning with *but* serves a legitimate purpose—to create coherence and ease the transition from one topic to another.

Here is another example, from "Smooth Handoff Essential" by Julie Mack (2006):

> Although the board plans a national search, they say they haven't ruled out internal or local candidates or nontraditional applicants with a background outside K–12 education.
>
> But on one issue they are clear, Brown's successor must be someone who can continue the momentum jump-started by the Kalamazoo Promise and school reforms implemented in recent years. (p. A1)

In this instance, *but* is used to emphasize a particular point. *And* can serve a similar role at the beginning of a paragraph or other sentence.

Instead of creating a counterpoint, though, *and* may create an extended argument or continued support. Consider this use of *and* from another article in the *Kalamazoo Gazette* ("Magnificent Animals," 2006):

> "When they weigh 1,200 pounds, they can do quite a bit of damage," he said. "They are animals of reaction, rather than action, and they respond immediately to a stimulus with fight or flight. Defense is teeth and hooves, flight is run—so you'd better duck out of the way."
>
> <u>And</u> yet, Connell said, "I don't think God put any prettier creature on earth than a horse." (p. A4)

And, we might add, both *and* and *but* can be found in concert. Consider a front-page article from another newspaper, the *Detroit News* ("Brandon Banks Is 6 Years Old. He's Trying to Save His Sister's Life," by Amber Hunt, 2006):

> Brandon Banks couldn't muster a smile Monday as strangers filled his Detroit home and lavished him with praise.
>> "You're such a brave boy."
>> "You're special, you know that?"
>> "God has a place for angels like you."
>
> <u>But</u> while 6-year old Brandon, dressed in a striped shirt and tie, politely shook the hands of those who flattered him, he kept his eyes low. Clearly, he was scared.
>
> <u>And</u> with good reason: Today, he'll lie in a hospital 250 miles from home in Cincinnati, get stuck with a needle and have some of his bone marrow sucked from his body and injected into his little sister's in an effort to save her life. (p. 1A)

Such rhetorical use of *and* and *but* is common not only in journalism, but in other genres too: fiction and nonfiction, creative and expository writing.

In creative and expository writing

Teachers often think nonfiction expository writing has to be straightforward, rule-conforming, and lacking in style. Not so. The expository examples of fragments that follow come from several nonfiction sources.

First, we turn to nonfiction literature for young people to illustrate the use of *and* or *but* to start a sentence. Let's begin with a favorite informational picture book, *Starry Messenger: Galileo Galilei,* by Peter Sís

(1996). Galileo, you remember, discovered that the earth revolved around the sun instead of the sun revolving around the earth. The Roman Catholic Church put him on trial and punished him for his scientifically demonstrable claims that challenged its own beliefs. Here is a paragraph in which both *but* and *and* are used to begin sentences:

> Galileo was condemned to spend the rest of his life locked in his house under guard. But he still had stars on his mind, and no one could keep him from thinking about the wonders of the skies and the mysteries of the universe. And even when he went blind, no one could keep him from passing his ideas along to others until the day he died. But still the ideas lived on. (np)

Our additional examples demonstrate the use of these cohesive devices at the beginning of paragraphs. These first instances come from *The Librarian Who Measured the Earth*, by Kathryn Lasky (1994), a picture book about the childhood interests and adult accomplishments of a Greek named Eratosthenes, who lived more than two thousand years ago.

> And in the evening, when he looked out the window of his bedroom, he wondered why the stars stayed in the sky. (p. 6) [This sentence was a paragraph in itself.]

> And two thousand years ago, books were handwritten on scrolls of animal skins or papyrus, paper made from a tall grass that grows along the Nile. (p. 24)

> But knowing that was still not enough. (p. 40)

> But it wasn't. (p. 40)

The following examples are from *Dinosaur Ghosts: The Mystery of Coelophysis*, by J. Lynett Gillette (1997):

> But in the summer of 1947 Colbert's team began finding dozens and dozens of *Coelophysis* skeletons, buried in 225 million-year-old rocks from near the end of the Triassic period. (p. 7)

> But why were all these dinosaurs buried in one place? (p. 22)

> And there's another idea to consider. (p. 22)

In this picture book, there are two more paragraphs beginning with *but*, yet no others beginning with *and*. We suspect that using *but* to start a sentence is generally more common, because the only good alternative is the heavyweight conjunctive adverb *however*. There are some less ponderous alternatives to *and*, depending on the meaning intended: For instance, *also* or *in addition* will work in some contexts.

Instances of *but* and *and* to start paragraphs occur in some of the articles in the magazines from which we drew examples of fragments as transitions and cohesive devices, as well as in both nonfiction adult books featured in Chapter 6: *Nickel and Dimed* (Ehrenreich, 2001) and *The Secret House* (Bodanis, 1986). Here are some examples of paragraph openers from *Nickel and Dimed*:

> But there can be too much freedom and certainly far too much motion. (p. 104)
>
> But Holly's ancestors win out over mine. (p. 111)
>
> But misdirected rage is not an easy thing to hold on to; the last sparks of it get snuffed out, as they deserve to be, in the icy waters of humiliation and defeat. (p. 114)
>
> But on Tuesday, when the post–Memorial Day week begins, my life seems real enough again in a gray and baleful way. (p. 134)
>
> But no job is as easy as it looks to the uninitiated. (p. 155)
>
> But now I know something else. (p. 175)

(Looking at these sentences out of context, it occurs to us that students might enjoy writing a paragraph that could have come before these transitions! We're not fond of decontextualized writing activities, but in this instance we're tempted.)

In examining nonfiction, we've noticed that sentences—and paragraphs—may start with a coordinator and *also* consist of a fragment:

> *But* so what?
> *And* more.
> *Or* not.
> *So* who, then?

Here is a published example (from *A Grand Canyon Journey*, by Peter Anderson, 1997), with preceding context that includes another fragment:

> As the earth's plates move, continents change shape. So do our oceans and seas.
> And so do rock layers like the ones we are walking through in the Grand Canyon. (p. 16)

A main verb, *change*, is understood from context, but these underlined "sentences" are grammatically incomplete—yet highly effective.

Overall, the use of the coordinating conjunctions—*and*, *but*, and sometimes *or* or *so*—to begin sentences and paragraphs has become commonplace among many published writers today. Should we, then, insist that our students follow the old rule about not starting a sentence with *and* or *but*? Not if we want our students to avoid the humdrum in their expository writing.

True, young children may overuse this stylistic device—starting new afterthought phrases and sentences with *and*, in particular, as they add to their previous thoughts by means of a sentence or fragment. Young writers may grow out of this tendency naturally, or they may need some instructional guidance in not starting so many sentences with *and*—or *but*. Nevertheless, just because young writers often go through such a phase doesn't mean that we have to ban all use of *and* or *but* to begin a sentence. Once again, we can help students—especially those beyond the intermediate grades—investigate published writers' effective use of this device.

What does all this mean for teachers of writing?

We admit that teaching the rule-bound five-paragraph essay may have its value—but mainly as a steppingstone to writing that is more interesting, more likely to catch and hold the attention of uncoerced audiences. Informational and persuasive writing can be enlivened in many ways, especially these:

- Narration (and description) to inform or persuade by pathos, not "just the facts, ma'am"
- A wide range of adjectival phrases that occur after the noun or as sentence openers and a variety of adverbial phrases before the main subject and verb (the latter are discussed in Chapter 11)
- Comparison/contrast within a piece if and as needed, not as the overall organizing structure of the piece
- Rhetorical/stylistic devices that break the traditional rules of grammar
- Grammatical parallelism and certain grammatical constructions especially useful in explanation or persuasion: "cleft" and other inverted sentences, in particular (see Chapter 12)

Informative writing is much more interesting, and persuasive writing much more persuasive, when writers are not held to the traditional forms of the five-paragraph essay or the structures often taught for a "logical" approach to the argumentative essay.

In her teaching, Connie first saw this particular light when conferring with a freshman who was writing her research paper on lupus and wanted to combine her personal experience with factual information she had researched, including articles she had read as a teenager. Cindy had developed this life-threatening condition at the age of twelve but had never told anyone—until she shared this confidence with Connie, her writing teacher. Not knowing anything then about lupus, Connie asked and was told that those who develop lupus in their youth rarely live beyond the age of thirty. Suddenly inspired, Connie suggested that Cindy write as if she were now thirty years old, rediscovering in the attic some old magazine articles about lupus and reading some new, updated material that she could now understand. At the end of the semester, Cindy was so proud of her paper that she shared it—and her medical condition—with the entire class.

From then on Connie began urging her students to use narration and even poetry in their informational and persuasive writing. In her course on the reading process and its implications for practice, as well as in her grammar-in-writing course, she received many original position papers, such as an unmailed letter to a school principal with whom the writer had just had a job interview, explaining why the writer could not accept a job teaching reading at his school. Some were parodies of other works. Each fall term, someone in the reading course inevitably rewrote Dickens' *A Christmas Carol* to feature the Ghosts of Reading Past, Present, and Future. (In the grammar-in-writing class, they became the Ghosts of Grammar Past, Present, and Future.) Each winter/spring term, someone in each course invariably produced a parody of either *The Sound of Music* or *The Wizard of Oz*. Other papers were unique: a variety of stories and plays; an extensive rap poem from the reading class; and from the grammar-in-writing course, a paper titled "Out of the Janitor's Closet," in which the writer imagined himself initially banished to the janitor's closet for teaching grammar in isolation from writing.

We and our students later discovered the highly effective multigenre paper as taught and promoted by Tom Romano—see especially his *Blending Genre, Altering Style* (2000) and the more recent Putz (2006). Toward the end of Connie's teaching career, she was suggesting four different rhetorical structures as possibilities for her students' persuasive position papers on the teaching of grammar:

- A traditional argumentative paper.
- An "I-search" paper, more or less as characterized by Ken Macrorie (1988): a paper for which the reader genuinely wants to search out information—not reproduce or re-search other people's work (Macrorie called this style of research writing fishy prose, or Engfish). Often, the writer uses varied, nontraditional sources: not only print material, but first-hand investigations, including interviews, questionnaires, personal observation, TV shows and ads, and so forth. Written in the first person, such papers chronicle the writer's process of discovery as well as reflect on what was learned.
- A creative paper in which narration or poetry is used to persuade—as in "Coaches: 'Sit Down, Relax, and Enjoy the Game'" or the kinds of papers just mentioned. Often, these papers involve two or more voices. For example, the primary organizational structure might be a series of imagined or real journal entries about teaching, alternating with classroom scenes and/or later reflections; panel discussions; teacher conversations in the staffroom; letters to and from a friend in English education at another university—you name it, and Connie or the students probably thought of it.
- A multigenre paper, a la Tom Romano. Such a paper might be a potpourri of genres, including the kinds of items typically found in a magazine or newspaper: news article, feature article, editorial, letters to the editor, classified ads, a sports article. Consciously using grammatical options while describing writing as a sport? You bet!

Some students chose the traditional argumentative paper, but most experimented with another option. It is amazing how hard students will work on a paper that is structurally and stylistically unique, instead of the formula-driven humdrum. As Donald Graves once said, children—everyone, really—will work much harder on a piece of writing when they are truly engaged with it and truly eager to share it with a wider audience: They will, in fact, work harder than we'd ever dare ask them to. Instead of sparse, boring prose, they produce pieces that entertain, that delight, that eloquently persuade, that drip with "juicy details." In our English education classes, we ask students to write position papers that are so specific and so well crafted that they might genuinely persuade other educators of their position—on teaching reading or teaching grammar to enrich and enhance writing. By writing with passion—the title of one of Tom Romano's earlier books (1995)—they engage the reader passionately, too. What more could we ask of good writing?

A final word

We'll let one of our students from the grammar-in-writing course have the last word. Here are two excerpts from a multigenre position paper by Gretchen Rumohr-Voskuil, a high school teacher currently finishing her doctoral work in Western Michigan University's English Education program:

Obituaries/Memorials

Sophie Schoolmarm-Penn
200 B.C.-2003

Dearest Sophie,

We stil remember the way you sat, red pen in you're hand, correcting our essays in the curagiuos attempt to learn us all real good. We red the grammar books you left us evry day and no that writing is a real serious subject. We wuld like to right more but we're afraid that our righting just don't measure up. You will be part of our lifes for a real long time.

Sincerely,

Your former students
A. F. Raid, Knots Smart, I. Cant and Bro.
"Ken" Spirit

It's a bird....

It's a plane.....

It's...........

Grammarwoman!

By harnessing the power of verbs, drawing on the forces of motivation, and channeling the strength of experience, this superteacher is . . .

. . . able to fight the ineffective antics of traditional grammarians such as Grammardittowoman;

. . . able to inspire students to use brush strokes while writing imaginative, original creative sentences;

. . . able to teach grammatical concepts with only minimal grammar terminology;

. . . able to discern when to correct students' grammar and when to leave it alone;

Do not fear . . . Grammarwoman is here! With her academic X-ray vision, she can spot the grammar needs of any desperate student. Call on her for help and your students' writing skills will go

Up,

Up,

And STAY!!!

Grammar
Rocks and Mortar

11

Grammatical elements can be likened to the rocks and mortar from which we build stone houses, walls, and waterfalls. Why rocks, rather than bricks? Building with bricks, we tend to use mostly bricks of the same design—a formulaic approach, if you will. Rocks are unique. In Michigan, particularly farther north, we have rocks, even boulders, affectionately known as "puddingstone" or "puddin' stones" (because the rock was originally glacial silt of puddinglike consistency before it hardened). Technically, these rocks are grayish-brown "conglomerates," essentially glommed-together silt in-fused with colored pebbles of brick red (jasper), brown, black, and white. We might think of the brown and black pebbles as the noun and verb construc-tions that are basic to a sentence, and the red and white pebbles as the ad-jectivals and adverbials that adorn the basic structure, enhancing it with color—in fact, the jasper puddingstone (said to look like suet with cherries in it) is primarily used for decoration. The mortar, then, is what's used to cement the colored rocks together to keep the exterior of a stone house sturdy, a stone wall from collapsing, and a waterfall's boulders and slabs from slipping and sliding. Except for the obvious fact that conglomerate

Sample of Hertfordshire puddingstone
Photo courtesy of D. M. GAC Fossils

185

rocks are formed haphazardly and good writing is carefully crafted, the analogy works.

This chapter offers new examples of adjectivals (previously discussed in Chapters 5 and 6) and adverbials (introduced in Chapter 8), then focuses on the use of grammatical elements that conjoin and subordinate sentences, as well as those that connect them by clarifying the meaningful relationships between them (the transitional and cohesive devices). This information needn't be taught to students as it is presented here, but teachers need these basics in order to understand the rhetorical patterns, transitions, and other cohesive devices that will enable them to use the chart of developmental trends in the next chapter. Also, standardized tests like the ACT and the SAT require students to *recognize* (in the multiple-choice section) and *use* (in their written essay) transitions that are appropriate to their meaning and punctuated conventionally. Although these tests don't ask students to define such transitions or analyze sentences and label the transition words, we believe teachers should know more than their students do. Our explanations here sometimes go even further, just to remind us how elegantly complex are even the basic phrases and sentences that we and our students understand and use every day as we listen and speak the language.

Adjectivals

Adjectivals include single-word adjectives before a noun or after a "linking" verb like *am, is, are, was, were,* in addition to adjectival clauses and the postnoun adjectival phrases discussed earlier. When we teach a particular construction in a writing class, we use its name, but only to help students get a sense of that adjectival option. We *don't* teach the detailed analysis of sentences. In the long run, what's important for students is learning to *use* a variety of adjectival constructions to enhance their writing. And having students imitate literary models may be the best way to teach these constructions anyway.

In the following examples, from Lois Lowry's *Messenger* (2004), a sequel to both *The Giver* (1993) and *Gathering Blue* (2000), we have underlined only the larger adjectivals, not the adjectivals embedded within other adjectivals.

The <u>blind</u> man, <u>Seer</u>, made his way through the lanes <u>of Village</u>, <u>checking on the populace</u>, <u>assessing the well-being of each individual</u>. (p. 17)

<u>Squatting</u>, it moved its <u>protruding</u> eyes around, <u>trying to sense more insects to devour</u>. (p. 19)

People tended him now, and he helped with <u>farm</u> chores, but his energy was gone, <u>taken away by the mysterious energy that lived in lightning</u>. (p. 39)

<u>Thick around a tall trellis</u>, a vine that had been <u>simply green</u> when he arrived the day before was now <u>profuse</u> with <u>opened</u> <u>blue</u> and <u>white</u> morning glories. (p. 129)

Now and then a <u>lone</u> citizen, <u>untouched by trade</u>, would go to the platform and try to speak. (p. 85)

Matty slipped into a group <u>that had gathered and was standing nearest to the platform</u>, <u>a simple wooden structure like a stage for many occasions when the people came together</u>. (p. 57)

She was describing a <u>small</u> tapestry <u>she had embroidered as a wedding gift for her friend Thomas, the woodcarver, who had recently been married</u>. (p. 119)

There was a knock on the door, and it was Jean, <u>her hair curlier than usual from the dampness that remained after the rain</u>. (p. 99)

The sounds <u>he heard</u> were the <u>raspy</u> croak <u>of a toad</u>, the <u>stealthy</u> movement <u>of a rodent in the bushes</u>, and <u>foamy</u> bubbles <u>belching from some <u>slithery</u> <u>malevolent</u> creature in the dark waters of the pond</u>. (p. 150) [Within this long participial phrase modifying *bubbles*, we have adjectivals within adjectivals, each modifying a following or previous noun.]

Not wanting to neglect expository prose, we include just a few of the adjectivals in Carl Sagan's informative essay "The Gaze of God and the Dripping Faucet," from his *Billions and Billions: Thoughts on Life and Death at the Brink of the Millennium* (1997). Sagan's popularizations of science are known for their accessible style, as you can see. Again, only the larger, "top-level" adjectivals are underlined:

On the other hand, most materials are <u>poor</u> absorbers <u>of visible light</u>. Air, for example, is generally <u>transparent to visible light</u>. (p. 40)

The human family—<u>originating in one small locale in East Africa a few million years ago</u>—wandered, separated, diversified, and became strangers to one another. (p. 35)

New waves are arriving at your end of the tub, <u>each generated by another drip of the faucet</u>. (p. 32) [Absolute]

The reversal of this trend—the movement toward the reacquaintance and reunification of the lost tribes of the human family, the binding up of the species—has occurred only fairly recently and only because of advances in technology. (p. 35)

It takes 20 minutes to receive a message from a spacecraft favorably situated in Martian orbit. In August 1989, we received pictures, taken by the *Voyager 2* spacecraft, of Neptune and its moons and ring arcs—data sent to us from the planetary frontiers of the Solar System, taking five hours to reach us at the speed of light. (p. 36)

Sentences like the last one invite the kind of visual sentence chunking suggested at the beginning of Chapter 6, as readers unravel *what* describes *what* within the sentence.

The benefits of chunking

Chunking helps us understand the opening sentence of E. L. Doctorow's beautifully written, spellbinding historical novel *The March* (2005), which describes General Sherman's devastating march across Georgia with his sixty thousand troops toward the end of the Civil War. The elaborated introductory phrase, which ends with a colon, makes the sentence especially challenging. Notice the wealth of adjectivals, particularly absolutes:

> At five in the morning someone banging on the door and shouting, her husband, John, leaping out of bed, grabbing his rifle, and Roscoe at the same time roused from the backhouse, his bare feet pounding: Mattie hurriedly pulled on her robe, her mind prepared for the alarm of war, but the heart stricken that it would finally have come, and down the stairs she flew to see through the open door in the lamplight, at the steps of the portico, the two horses, steam rising from their flanks, their heads lifting, their eyes wild, the driver a young darkie with rounded shoulders, showing stolid patience even in this, and the woman standing in her carriage no one but her aunt Letitia Pettibone of McDonough, her elderly face drawn in anguish, her hair a straggled mess, this woman of such fine grooming, this dowager who practically ruled the season in Atlanta standing up in the equipage like some hag of doom, which indeed she would prove to be. (p. 4)

Why might Doctorow have made the rhetorical decision to open the novel with so lengthy and complex a sentence? Perhaps he wanted the first sentence to recapitulate, grammatically, the upheaval and chaos being described. Prose stylists would call this a *labyrinthine sentence*: "not a lawless, poorly punctuated run-on sentence, but a finely crafted aggregation of words that weaves in and out, accruing information, riding rhythms, and tacking on ideas" (Juriaan, 2007).

Adverbials

The other kinds of pebbles in our grammatical conglomerate are adverbials. An *adverbial* is any word or group or words that works like an adverb to describe/modify a verb or, more often, an entire subject-verb unit. (Anything that modifies an adjective—as happens in some of the preceding example sentences—is also said to be an adverbial.) Sometimes, an adverbial is a single word (often but not always ending in -*ly*). The single-word adverbs in the examples below modify the verb:

> Move <u>slowly</u> and <u>carefully</u>.

> Let's go <u>home</u>. [*home* tells where we'll go]

Often, however, the single-word adverb can be seen as modifying the entire main clause, in which case it can occur at the beginning of a sentence:

> <u>Cautiously</u>, we edged our way past the sheer drop.

> <u>Oddly</u> but <u>fortunately</u>, the drop didn't frighten the driver as much as the rest of us.

> <u>Tomorrow</u>, we'd better return to the safety of the main highway.

Typically the single-word adverbs tell *how* (in what manner); *how often*; *how long* or *how far* (to what extent); or *when, where,* or *why* (for what reason or purpose) with respect to the action. That is, they describe or modify the verb or the subject-verb unit that expresses the action. Other meanings of adverbials are indicated by certain kinds of connectors; these functions are included in the list of cohesive devices or "transitions" from Lunsford (2003), reproduced later in this chapter. Here we illustrate, without comment, a variety of meaning functions with examples from the previously cited essay by Carl Sagan (1997). Only the larger adverbials are marked, not those within other adverbials.

> <u>Once every second</u>, say, a drop falls <u>into the tub</u>. (p. 31)

> <u>On the other hand</u>, most materials are poor absorbers of visible light. (p. 41)

> <u>Rather than traveling like a bullet in a straight line</u>, the waves spread from the two slits <u>at various angles</u>. (p. 37)

> <u>Remarkably</u>, a typical anthocyanin is red when placed in acid, blue in alkali, and violet in water. (p. 43)

> And yet <u>for most purposes</u>, light is similar to sound. Light waves are three-dimensional, have a frequency, a wavelength, and a

speed (the speed of light). But, <u>astonishingly</u>, they do not require a medium, like water or air, to propagate in. Light reaches us from the Sun and the distant stars, <u>even though the intervening space is a nearly perfect vacuum</u>. (p. 37) [The final adverbial qualifies the main subject-verb, "Light reaches us . . ."]

<u>When we were hunter-gatherers</u>, language became essential for planning the day's activity, teaching the children, cementing friendships, alerting the others <u>to danger</u>, and sitting <u>around the fire</u> <u>after dinner</u> watching the stars come out and telling stories. (p. 34)

If you don't recognize all of these constructions as adverbials modifying a verb or subject-verb unit or can't decide exactly what meaning they convey, don't worry: Our purpose is simply to demonstrate that a wide variety of constructions can function adverbially. And our *major* purpose is to illustrate that in effective writing, adverbials that modify the whole subject-verb unit often occur at the beginning of the sentence or clause, setting the scene for what follows. Instructionally, one major way we can help students revise or avoid awkward sentences is to guide them in moving such modifiers to or toward the front, where they don't interrupt or limp along after the main statement.

An aside on prepositional phrases

Prepositional phrases consist of a *preposition* plus a nominal, whether it be a noun or pronoun, a single word or a phrase or a clause. Here is a list of words that commonly—though not always—function as prepositions.

**Words Commonly Used as Prepositions
(several function in other ways, too)**

about	beside	for	opposite	till
above	besides	from	out	to
across	between	in	outside	toward
after	beyond	inside	over	under
against	but	into	past	underneath
along	by	like	plus	unlike
among	concerning	near	regarding	until
around	considering	next to	respecting	unto
as	despite	of	since	up
at	down	off	than	upon
before	during	on	through	with
behind	except	onto	throughout	without
below				

Prepositional phrases function as either adjectives or adverbs. Fortunately, writers do not need to distinguish between them: They only need to *use* both kinds to add details to their writing.

To illustrate, here again are the last two Sagan quotes, with the prepositional phrases underlined (some of the adverbials modify a preceding adjective, a function we haven't emphasized):

And yet <u>for most purposes</u> [adverbial, modifying subject-verb unit], light is similar <u>to sound</u> [adverbial, modifying adjective *similar*]. Light waves are three-dimensional, have a frequency, a wavelength, and a speed (the speed <u>of light</u> [adjectival, modifying the noun *speed*]). But, astonishingly, they do not require a medium, <u>like water or air</u> [adjectival, modifying the noun *medium*] to propagate in. Light reaches us <u>from the Sun and the distant stars</u> [adverbial, modifying *reaches* or the entire subject-verb unit], even though the intervening space is a nearly perfect vacuum. (p. 37)

You may have noticed what looked like another prepositional phrase, the phrase *to propagate in.* This is an infinitive phrase (*to* plus the base form of the verb) modifying *medium.*

The mortar: Meanings of cohesive and transitional devices

We especially like the table of cohesive devices that Andrea Lunsford labels "transitions" in *The St. Martin's Handbook* (2003, pp. 126–127). This list, reproduced here, labels common connecting words and phrases according to their meaning—their rhetorical use as connectors—rather than according to grammar. Many of them enable us to make effective rhetorical moves as we try to inform or persuade an audience.

Transitions to signal sequence: again, also, and, and then, besides, finally, first . . . second . . . third, furthermore, last, moreover, next, still, too

Transitions to signal time: after a few days, after a while, afterward, as long as, as soon as, at last, at that time, before, earlier, immediately, in the meantime, in the past, lately, later, meanwhile, now, presently, simultaneously, since, so far, soon, then, thereafter, until, when

Transitions to signal comparison: again, also, in the same way, likewise, once more, similarly

Transitions to signal contrast: although, but, despite, even though, however, in contrast, in spite of, instead, nevertheless, nonetheless, on the contrary, on the one hand . . . on the other hand, regardless, still, though, yet

Transitions to signal examples: after all, even, for example, for instance, indeed, in fact, of course, specifically, such as, the following example, to illustrate

Transitions to signal cause and effect: accordingly, as a result, because, consequently, for this purpose, hence, so, then, therefore, thus, to this end

Transitions to signal place: above, adjacent to, below, beyond, closer to, elsewhere, far, farther on, here, near, nearby, opposite to, there, to the left, to the right

Transitions to signal concession: although it is true that, granted that, I admit that, it may appear that, naturally, of course

Transitions to signal summary, repetition, or conclusion: as a result, as has been noted, as I have said, as mentioned earlier, as we have seen, in any event, in conclusion, in other words, in short, on the whole, therefore, to summarize

Such a list cannot be complete, of course, nor does it seem productive to try to categorize all these words and phrases as to their grammatical function—especially since some can function more than one way. However, the major grammatical categories are discussed in the next section, in which we emphasize the importance of understanding the correlations between different types of connectors and punctuation.

The mortar: Grammatical categories

Prepositions are one kind of mortar. Others are coordinating and correlative conjunctions, conjunctive adverbs, subordinating conjunctions, and the pronouns used in introducing adjective and noun clauses. We discuss these kinds of mortar in conjunction with punctuation, focusing on the practical rather than on mere classification.

Many "mortar" words relate one clause to another. A *clause* can be defined simply as a subject plus a complete verb unit. Thus *Abi is running* would be a clause, but in mainstream English, *Abi running* would not. An *independent clause* is one that can stand alone grammatically as a complete sentence: Not only is it grammatically complete, but it is not subordinated to another clause or to something within another clause. Here are some instances wherein *Abi is running* functions as a subordinate, not an independent, clause:

> Because Abi is running, we're confident our team will win the relay. [Adverb clause telling why we're confident]

The 100-yard dash that Abi is running will be more challenging. [Adjective clause describing *dash*; the word *that* is optional here]

That Abi is running is a miracle. [Noun clause, subject of sentence]

Once again, we see that the same construction can sometimes have more than one grammatical function in a sentence.

Let's begin with the kinds of grammatical mortar used in connection with independent clauses. (We'll come back later to subordinate clauses and the grammatical mortar associated with them.)

Coordinating conjunctions, correlative conjunctions, and conjunctive adverbs

We've already noted that an *independent clause* is simply a subject-predicate unit that can stand by itself as a grammatically complete sentence. Thus the terms *independent clause* and *simple sentence* are synonymous. Particularly when there is more than one clause in a sentence, an independent clause is often referred to as a *main clause*.

A *punctuated sentence*—what occurs between the initial capital and the final period—may include more than one independent clause. These independent clauses may be joined by a comma plus a *coordinating conjunction*:

The currents swirled, and the raft capsized.

Rollie leaped, but Connie fell.

(When the independent clauses are short and very closely related, as in the above examples, the comma is often omitted.) The other common coordinating conjunctions are *or, so, yet,* and sometimes *for* or *nor*. Most of these coordinators may also be used to conjoin other grammatical elements of the same kind—that is, grammatically parallel elements.

Words That Often Function as Coordinating Conjunctions (but not always)

and	yet
but	for
or	nor
so	

Pairs of coordinators that work together are called correlative conjunctions. They join equal elements:

You will receive <u>either</u> a car <u>or</u> cash if you're the lucky winner.

<u>Just as</u> we recommend teaching only those aspects of grammar that are genuinely useful for students, <u>so</u> we recommend sentence production rather than analysis.

Correlative conjunctions

both . . . and	just . . . so	not only . . . but also
either . . . or	neither . . . nor	whether . . . or

Joining and separating independent clauses

Independent clauses may be joined and/or separated:

1. With a period, which obliterates any relationship, if indeed there is one:

   Daryl scored the winning touchdown. Afterwards the team went out to celebrate together.

2. With a comma plus a coordinating conjunction (*and, but, or, so, yet,* and sometimes *for* or *nor*):

   Daryl scored the winning touchdown, <u>and</u> his teammates carried him off the field on their shoulders.

   Daryl scored the winning touchdown, <u>but</u> he didn't take credit for winning the game.

3. With a colon, when the first simple sentence serves as a "trumpet" introducing the second one:

   It was amazing: Even some members of the losing team cheered the winners.

4. With a semicolon, which both separates and relates (think of the top part as a period, to separate, and the bottom part as a comma, to relate):

   The cheerleaders jumped and shouted<u>;</u> the crowd roared.

5. With a semicolon plus a conjunctive adverb:

   Daryl tried to avoid the media<u>; however,</u> three reporters immediately stuck their microphones in his face.

Daryl tried to avoid the media; three reporters, <u>however</u>, immediately stuck their microphones in his face.

6. With a period, which separates, followed in the second simple sentence by a conjunctive adverb, which joins:

Daryl tried to avoid the media. <u>However</u>, three reporters immediately stuck their microphones in his face.

Daryl tried to avoid the media. Three reporters, <u>however</u>, immediately stuck their microphones in his face.

Conjunctive adverbs join like coordinating conjunctions do, but they and the clauses they introduce typically have an adverbial sense. Sometimes conjunctive adverbs occur *within* rather than at the beginning of the second simple sentence, as in the second example in items 5 and 6. Some conjunctive adverbs need to be set off by a comma or commas; others don't. By reading a sentence aloud, you can usually tell whether the conjunctive adverb needs to be set off.

Conjunctive adverbs got their name because they join together—that is, <u>conjoin</u>—two simple sentences, but they also have an adverbial meaning, and indeed they all can work as adverbials within a one-clause sentence.

Words and Phrases That Commonly Serve as Conjunctive Adverbs (or as regular adverbials)

also	accordingly	as a result
besides	consequently	for example
hence	furthermore	for instance
indeed	however	in fact
instead	meanwhile	of course
then	moreover	on the other hand
thus	nevertheless	
	therefore	

When the word *then* joins two simple sentences, it is considered a conjunctive adverb, and therefore the conservative rule calls for it to be preceded by a semicolon, not a comma:

The climbers ascended most of the way with precarious handholds and toeholds; <u>then</u> they resorted to pitons and ropes to reach the peak.

The same is true of *thus*, as well as all the other connecting words and phrases in the preceding list.

Creating adverbial clauses

There are three kinds of subordinate clauses, functioning as three different parts of speech: adverb, adjective, or noun. An adverbial clause is introduced by a subordinating conjunction. To express it differently, we can make an independent clause into a subordinate one by putting a subordinating conjunction in front of it:

He bought lottery tickets every week. He never won anything.

Although he bought lottery tickets every week

Possible resulting sentences:

He never won anything, *although* he bought lottery tickets every week.

Although he bought lottery tickets every week, he never won anything.

A comma is required after an introductory adverbial clause but is usually—not always—omitted before a final adverbial clause. A comma was included before the final adverbial clause in the first of the above example sentences to signal a significant pause—thus giving the reader time to think about the main clause before going on to the subordinate *although* clause.

Words That Commonly Function as Subordinating Conjunctions (some have other functions as well)

Time	Cause	Condition	Contrast
after	as	as if	although
as	because	assuming that	even though
as soon as	in order that	if	rather than
before	since	in case	though
since	so that	unless	whereas
till		when	while
until		whether	
when			
while			

Creating adjectival clauses

To make a sentence into an adjectival clause, we cannot simply put the introducing word—known as a *relative pronoun*—in front of the sentence. Instead, we have to replace some word in the sentence with another appropriate word.

> The toys can be put away now. She's tired of ~~the toys~~.

> The toys <u>that she's tired of</u> can be put away now.

When an adjectival clause is not essential for identifying the entity being talked about, it is introduced by *which* for something that is inanimate—a thing or idea, for example.

> Those baby toys can be put away for now. She's tired of ~~those baby toys~~.

> Those baby toys, *which* <u>she's tired of</u>, can be put away for now.

The relative pronouns *who* and *whom* can be used to introduce either an essential (no comma before it) or a nonessential (comma before it) adjectival clause. Again, the relative pronoun can be thought of as replacing some element in an underlying sentence.

> Don't throw the ball to any player. ~~The player~~ is not paying attention.

> Don't throw the ball to any player *who* <u>is not paying attention</u>.

> Don't throw the ball to Hank. ~~He~~ isn't paying attention.

> Don't throw the ball to Hank, *who* <u>isn't paying attention</u>.

> That's the belly dancer. Hector hired ~~the belly dancer~~ for the party.

> That's the belly dancer *whom* <u>Hector hired for the party</u>. OR

> That's the belly dancer, *whom* <u>Hector hired for the party</u>.

In the next-to-last sentence, *whom* sounds overly formal; it could simply be eliminated.

Creating noun clauses

Some noun clauses are introduced by *who* or *whom*. The conventional choice depends on how the noun originally functioned in the underlying sentence.

I'd like to know SOMETHING. ~~SOMEONE~~ wants to go.

I'd like to know *who wants to go.*

Who is the subject of *wants*. However, in the following sentence, the replaced word is not a subject, so the object form *whom* is called for:

I'd like to know SOMETHING. You've chosen ~~SOMEONE~~.

I'd like to know *whom you've chosen.*

In noun clauses, the pronoun forms *whoever* and *whomever* work like *who* and *whom*:

Give those records to *whoever wants them.* (*Whoever* is the subject of *wants*.)

I'll give them to *whomever you have chosen.* (*Whomever* is the object of *chosen*.)

In casual speech and informal writing, we more commonly see the "incorrect" *who* in sentences such as *I'd like to know who you've chosen* and *I'll give it to whoever you have chosen.* On the other hand, standardized tests call for the use of *whom*.

Choosing your rocks and mortar

When people write, they choose grammatical connectors based on what they want to say and their assessment of the rhetorical situation: They make choices. To illustrate: Jonathan, with the help of his wife Erin, a secondary English teacher, wrote the following piece in the manner of an eleventh-grade paper. Effortlessly and for the most part unconsciously, they used all of the specific rhetorical devices mentioned in this chapter.

Choices

Life is full of choices. Should I watch TV or do homework? Clean my room or go outside? Study or try to cheat? Sometimes you make the right choice. Sometimes you make the wrong choice. Sometimes you make a choice that seems like the right one at the time but turns out to be the wrong one. When you make a choice like this, it is important to look back at it and learn so that you don't do it again. I made a bad choice recently—cheating. Luckily, however, I didn't get in trouble. More important, I learned from my mistake.

My wrong choice happened in geology class. We had a test, a very difficult one, coming up, and I knew I was going to struggle. It was all about minerals and rocks; we had spent lab time touching, feeling, even smelling different minerals in order to be able to identify them. We also were expected to be able to tell certain facts about how they were created, what they can be used for, and where they are often found. I have never been good at memorizing things, so I was pretty worried.

I'm more of a creative thinker; therefore, I had been struggling in this class. We had been memorizing things all year, and I had been doing poorly all year. I'm not a bad student, but I found myself becoming more and more lost in the class. My grades in geology have been the only thing keeping me off the honor roll. I knew that this was going to be just one more test where I flunked—or worse. I felt I had only one choice—it seemed like the right one at the time—to cheat. During the test, our teacher would pass different minerals and rocks to each table. We were sitting in our chairs, shielded by the table, so I would make a "cheat sheet." Using a code, I would write down shorthand versions of traits to help me identify some minerals I was worried about identifying, along with some important facts. When the minerals were passed to my table, I would just have to glance down at the sheet I put on my chair, in between my legs, and I would be able to answer any question that was asked.

I spent the next few days developing my cheat sheet. I didn't tell any of my friends. I was too embarrassed. I wrote and rewrote key facts, putting them in different formats, different fonts, and different colors, continually experimenting until I created the perfect cheat sheet—one that I could quickly read at a moment's glance. Finally, test day came. I was ready.

So what happened? It was a bad choice. (And, no, I didn't get caught!) When it came right down to it, I just couldn't do it. I had the cheat sheet in my hand, but I couldn't make myself put it down on the chair. Instead, I just crumpled it up and shoved it in my pocket. I realized that I'm not that kind of person. I'm not a cheater. I believe that honor is important. I don't like to lie. I don't like to cheat. I don't like to get away with things.

More important, I learned that I didn't need it. I aced the test. Aced it! Not quite 100%, but close. How? I had to rewrite the cheat sheet multiple times to make it fit the tight spot on my seat. I had to change things to make them fit in certain spaces on the papers. I had to recopy facts in different colors to make them easier to read. And you know what happened? While making the cheat sheet, I actually learned—about feldspar, about sandstone, about granite. I remembered all the key facts I was trying to write down and I knew almost everything on the test. Now I know how to study for geology.

Sometimes what appears to be a good choice is actually the wrong one. I made a bad choice. I was lucky enough to learn from it and not pay the consequences.

The worst choice we can make is to make the same mistake over again. I won't cheat again. I learned my lesson.

If you didn't notice many of the connectors, the grammatical mortar discussed in this chapter—well, that's the idea. Without calling attention to itself, the mortar highlights, by contrast, the pebbles within—thus bringing to the fore the ideas and voice of the writer.

Making Decisions That Make a Difference

Grammar and the "6 Traits" of Writing

12 ✧

Throughout this book we've echoed Rei Noguchi's assertion that when teaching grammar, less is more. The sheer number of grammar skills, concepts, and notions makes it impossible to teach them all in a single classroom—or ever. We question the efficacy of attempting to do so and view such a pedagogical decision—the "coverage" model—as one of the banes of grammar instruction.

The "coverage" approach rears its head whenever we talk to teachers about grammar skills—grammar to enrich and enhance writing. No matter what we've talked about, we often hear the response: "We've covered that." Sentence variation? "Covered it in September." Fragments and run-ons? "We cover that during the third quarter." Yet teachers also admit that their coverage hasn't had much effect on most students' writing, at least in heterogeneous classes (see Chapters 2 and 3). Instead of coverage, we need an in-depth approach:

- When teaching grammar, teachers must be selective—perhaps very selective—about what they teach.
- Once these choices are made, the teaching of grammar must be, as we say in Chapter 4, "a mile deep"—meaning that concepts and skills aren't taught just once but are practiced, reviewed, reconsidered in published writing, redeveloped, and made rich through repeated application: the antithesis of "covered."

So how do we decide what to teach? As teachers, our decisions must be based on our own understanding of grammar (not the answer key provided with a grammar book), our goals for enhancing and enriching writing by teaching selected aspects of grammar, and the skills our students already possess or haven't yet mastered. We advocate teaching grammar strategies and skills for rhetorical purposes, in depth and in conjunction with and in the context of writing, because this pedagogical strategy is most effective and efficient.

More specifically, why do we want to teach grammar in conjunction with and in the context of writing? To enhance students' *sentence sense*, *sentence variety*, and *syntactic fluency*? To promote the use of appropriate *conventions* for writing? Yes, of course. But, as we've said before, there are other reasons, too:

- To generate details—that is, rich *content*—by using key grammatical constructions to elaborate on general or abstract *ideas*.
- To use transitions and other connectors that relate ideas appropriately: in other words, that make the *organization* of a piece clear and coherent.
- To use *voice* and *style* appropriate to purpose, content, and audience.

Together, these factors constitute five of the popularly acclaimed "6 traits" of writing (Spandel, 2005; Culham, 2003). The sixth is word choice. By whatever names others may call them, these are the characteristics of writing that are most valued.

Grammar on standardized tests

As we use various procedures for teaching less grammar but teaching it more intensively, we can incorporate much of what is expected on state or other large-scale assessments of writing. An examination of scoring rubrics often shows we need not be nearly as picky as we think. We can also incorporate into the teaching of writing, almost painlessly, what is actually emphasized on the tests of English that may be administered. It pays to examine such tests carefully, because many teachers have assumed certain things are tested, or tested extensively, when in fact they aren't. The ACT and SAT, for example, don't test students' ability to analyze sentences and label parts of speech. And even on the multiple-choice English questions, they pay much more attention to grammar as it relates to organization, rhetoric, and style than to editing to eliminate errors. See, for example, Connie's informal analysis of some ACT tests in her *Grammar Plan Book* (2007, pp. 65–69). The SAT multiple-choice questions include more than twice as many items on sentence and paragraph revision (taken together) as on correcting errors in grammar and usage.

What should we teach when?

By helping us determine students' level of competence, the schematic in Figure 12–1 helps us decide where to go next in our teaching. It may look, walk, and talk like a rubric, but it isn't meant to be used that way. Although most of the grammatical features in a given paper may reflect the same level of competency, there are always exceptions. We felt it necessary to give some specific examples, yet the chart becomes less reliable the more specific we get: Our examples must be taken only as suggestions. Furthermore, we have strong concerns about rubrics in general, believing that they can be used in such a lockstep, formulaic way as to stifle individuality and encourage teachers to turn a blind eye to good and even outstanding writing if it doesn't include every characteristic listed at whatever level seems to predominate. We've found that teachers sometimes use rubrics this way even when they are aiming for a holistic score.

What's this guide good for, then, if not to evaluate writing with a score? *To help teachers decide what to teach next*, in terms of grammatical elements that will promote the expression of ideas, organization, voice and style, word choice (effective nouns, verbs, adjectives, adverbs), conventions, and, of course, sentence dexterity. This may seem like a fine distinction, since you obviously need to look at students' writing to determine what kind of guidance they might benefit from most. Nevertheless, the distinction is important one. You could use the guide to:

- Help you notice patterns of grammatical development
- Confirm your existing sense of writers' grammatical development
- Help you determine where to go next in helping students use grammar to enrich and enhance their writing

The guide can give you sufficient additional background to read students' writing quickly and determine impressionistically which aspects of grammar to teach next—in order to help students make their writing more detailed and therefore more compelling, not just to deal with faulty this or faulty that. We've used this guide (and others) to help us sort students' writings into three, four, or five piles before deciding what to teach next to each clearly identifiable group. In other words, we don't use the guide to grade or label individual students' writing, but rather to plan for instruction. We often have *more than three groupings* to capture the gaps between the three levels indicated.

Once you have a sense of what's involved in each column and cell of the guide, you can use just the overall statements characterizing the three levels for holistic sorting, while keeping in mind the specifics they represent

Try it yourself

Examine two or three student papers that reflect different levels of quality overall. Does the use of grammar differ noticeably among the writers? Our guide typically reflects what teachers already perceive intuitively but may not have verbalized consciously about increasing sophistication in the use of grammar. Bringing our intuitive sense to conscious awareness helps us make instructional decisions about what to teach next.

What Should I Teach Next?

ENRICHING writing through grammar

		High—*highly effective*	Middle—*competent*	Low—*basic*
Sentence Sense • Variety • Fluency	**Ideas • Details**	Sentence structures and lengths are varied; sentences flow effectively throughout the paragraph. Rhetorical devices add flavor to the writing.	Sentences are sometimes varied in length and structure, with some variation in connective and cohesive devices. Occasional use of a rhetorical device.	Simple, short sentences occur regularly, with minimal sentence variation and basic kinds of transitions/connectors, if any.
		• If or when sentences in sequence start the same or nearly the same way, they have a clear rhetorical effect, for emphasis.	• Some sentences are compound: they have two or more independent clauses. Some are complex: they include one or more subordinate clauses.	• Many sentences follow the basic subject + verb + object pattern, often with the same subject, such as *I, he,* or *she.*
		• Generous use of various grammatical and stylistic tools for flow or other effect, such as—but not confined to—participial phrases, appositives, absolutes, etc.	• Noticeable and varied use of introductory phrases and subordinate clauses; substantial and varied use of prepositional phrases to describe and elaborate upon nouns as well as set the scene.	• Minimal use of adjectives and adverbs; prepositional phrases more often used to set the scene for what's going on than to describe someone or something.
Voice • Style • Tone	**Organization • Structure**	• Transitions/connectors are diverse—and, *if* appropriate to both the genre and the tone, may include some conjunctive adverbs like *meanwhile, thereafter, simultaneously, moreover, nevertheless, regardless,* and *granted that,* and correlative conjunctions like *both . . . and, either . . . or, neither . . . nor, not only . . . but also.*	• Transitions/connectors include use of subordinating conjunctions like *when, because, if, until, while,* and—depending partly on the genre—some others like *afterwards, thereafter, even though,* and *although.* May include conjunctive adverbs like *however, for example, for instance, of course, on the other hand, then, thus,* and the word *so* to indicate consequence.	• Transitions/connectors, if present, mostly deal with time or sequence—*then, next; first, second*—or joining of elements with *and* or *but, also, in addition,* and such.

		• Other cohesive devices to start a sentence or paragraph include rhetorical devices like
		   • a fragment
		   • *but* or *and*
			• Other cohesive devices across sentence and paragraph boundaries include more than just the basics, such as
			   • conventional words and phrases like *as soon as, in the meantime, in contrast, in spite of*
			   • phrases unique to the piece
				• Other cohesive devices across sentence and paragraph boundaries, if present, are mostly limited to pronouns like *he, her, my, they,* etc.; the words *this, these, that, those;* and some repetition of words and phrases previously used.

		• Other rhetorical devices may include
		   • multiple instances of parallelism
		   • varied sentence lengths
		   • inverted, "cleft" sentences
		   • other sentences that put the most important information last
			• Other rhetorical devices may include
			   • minimal use of parallelism
			   • occasional variation in sentence length
			   • a few sentences that put the important information last	

Note: While "connector" is not a traditional grammatical term, we find it useful to cover not only the traditional transitions but also any cohesive device that seems to connect one part of a text with another, either within or across sentence and paragraph boundaries.

FIGURE 12–1. What should I teach next? A guide for examining the grammar of student writing

ENRICHING *writing through word choice*

High—*highly effective*	Middle—*competent*	Low—*basic*
Infrequent use of common, bland, general words; frequent use of precise, "just right" words.	Some use of precise words, though many words are common, bland, or general.	Frequent use of common, bland, general words throughout.
• Verbs such as *loped* instead of *ran*, nouns like *curator* instead of *director*. Phrases like *feisty cocker spaniel* instead of *dog* or *in a flash* instead of *suddenly*.	• Some effective use of specific nouns, active verbs, and uniquely descriptive adjectives and adverbs.	• Vague nouns; imprecise, dull verbs; minimal use of adjectives and adverbs that describe.
• Inverted and "cleft" sentences that add *is, are, was,* or *were* are effective and not overused.	• Infrequent use of *is, are, was, were,* instead of a more powerful verb. Possible overuse of inverted and "cleft" sentences that include one of these verbs.	• Common use of *is, are, was, were* instead of a more powerful verb.

Ideas • Details

Voice • Style • Tone

ENHANCING *writing through punctuation and usage*

High—*highly effective*	Middle—*competent*	Low—*basic*
Hardly any errors in punctuation, though the writing may have occasional errors in using more sophisticated punctuation, such as semicolons and colons.	Some errors in punctuation, perhaps reflecting a clear and specific pattern, but these errors do not usually interfere with comprehension.	Errors in punctuation are frequent and/or make it difficult to read the piece.
• Semicolons, when used, are almost always used appropriately.	• Within compound sentences, a comma usually occurs before a connecting *and* or *but*. A semicolon, if used, may or may not be used appropriately.	• Sentences may not all have end punctuation. Run-on sentences may occur.
• Colons may be used as introducers, when a sentence shifts from general to more specific.		
• Comma use is mostly conventional, though a comma may be added to separate parallel parts of a long phrase, even when no "comma rule" supports such use.	• The writing may not necessarily include the commas conventionally associated with longer introductory elements and/or other nonessential descriptive phrases.	• Commas are seldom used, or used randomly.
• The writing shows clear and bold experimentation with stylistic devices, such as emphatic fragments, run-ons to capture stream of consciousness, dashes to separate and emphasize, juxtaposition of two voices, use of punctuation or type font for special effects.	• One or more sentences may simply be malformed; the writer may have lost track of the sentence structure while writing.	• Fragments, if they occur, consist of garbles or occur before what they refer to, not after.
• There are few errors in punctuation, none of which interfere with the construction of meaning.	• Errors may amount to frequent occurrences of one, two, maybe three patterns, such as comma splice sentences, faulty subject-verb or pronoun-referent agreement, or excessive use of unneeded commas.	• Writing may have features associated with informal English, such as *ain't*; multiple negatives; and lack of basic subject-verb agreement, as in *he don't* or *we was*. Such features may or may not be associated with particular dialects or the add-on learning of English.
• Dialect features, if used, serve a clear rhetorical purpose.		

Conventions and Voice • Style • Tone

as well as the possibility that there may be more levels in *your* students' writing. As you work with the guide, feel free to email us and share your own observations.

Interpreting the guide

The very lowest level of writing would consist mostly of false starts and garbles—or virtually nothing! Our low level starts a bit higher, with patterns we have seen in student writing at all levels, from kindergarten into college. The gap between the low and middle range is large, to emphasize that development from one level to the next will be gradual. The middle range is also especially broad, running the gamut between beginning use of some constructions and proficient use. The column labeled high includes features that tend to make us, as teachers, say "Wow!" about a student's use of language.

We drew not only on our own experience as teachers and teaching consultants, including a wealth of student papers, but also on research into the development of children's written language (see Chapter 3). As you read the guide from right to left, from low to high, you'll find that some features listed for the middle level are not included at the low level, and some features listed at the high level are not included in the lower levels. In effect, the chart suggests a hypothesis: that features new to the high level are not likely to appear often in a writer's work until his or her writing has demonstrated automatic use of features new to the middle level, and so forth. Still, we caution you not to take too seriously the examples of specific transitions/connectors (we'll explain our rationale shortly). Here's how we broadly characterize the levels in our chart:

High *Highly effective*	**Middle** *Competent*	**Low** *Basic*
Demonstrating appropriate voice/style	Ranging from above low to proficient	Possibly very weak in some areas

For the high level we chose the descriptor *highly effective* rather than *outstanding* or *superb*, because we wanted to emphasize that high-level writing has a clear voice designed to reach a clearly defined audience. You may find it helpful to divide the middle level into low-middle, mid-middle, and high-middle, or to make some other distinctions within or between the categories. We find these distinctions easy to spot when looking at individual papers but too idiosyncratic to specify in a chart.

There are five categories labeled vertically at the side of the chart:

1. Ideas/details
   - Grammatical options
   - Word choice
2. Organization/structure
3. Voice/style/tone
4. Sentence sense/variety/fluency
5. Conventions

This list includes all six major traits of writing, with sentence sense, variety, and fluency also relating to each of the other five. Under "Ideas/details," note that not only "just right" words but also grammatical options like phrases and dependent clauses add to the specificity of the text. The only aspect of conventions we've emphasized in our chart is punctuation as it relates to grammar; most other grammatical aspects of usage don't lend themselves to specification by level.

You can skip the following explanatory discussion if you already have a good sense of what the categories entail, but our comments will help you understand why this chart—and any rubric—should be used thoughtfully rather than mechanically, as if cast in stone.

Enriching writing through grammar

The first section of the guide deals with ideas/details, organization/structure, and voice/style/tone as affected by sentence sense/variety/fluency.

Grammatical options

Below the boldface overview statements, the first and second descriptors in each column deal with grammatical structures and options within a sentence. Here are the second statements at the low and middle levels:

Low: Minimal use of adjectives and adverbs; prepositional phrases more often used to set the scene for what's going on than to describe someone or something.

Middle: Noticeable and varied use of introductory phrases and subordinate clauses; substantial and varied use of prepositional phrases to describe and elaborate upon nouns as well as set the scene.

These statements reflect the fact that very young, emergent writers tend to use prepositional phrases adverbially, especially to indicate time or location, but they may not make as much use of prepositional phrases to describe nouns. The corresponding high-level statement includes the kinds of adjectival modifiers emphasized in Chapters 5 and 6. We are not sure to what extent older but still very basic writers follow this pattern.

Organization/structure

This category includes a set of statements dealing with transitions and other connectors—not only those that operate within a sentence, but also those that clarify meaning relationships and add cohesion across sentence boundaries.

We haven't been able to disentangle genuine writing development from the sequence in which modes and genres are typically taught in schools. We've assumed that the most basic writing will be expressive, with a descriptive or narrative flavor that favors connectors indicating time or sequence rather than, say, subordination of ideas or sophisticated logic. But this limitation depends partly on what teachers are having kids write. If we compare students' narrative pieces with their persuasive pieces—as Connie did in an earlier investigation (1982)—we will find subordinating conjunctions used: not only those like *when* and *until*, indicating time, but ones like *because* and *if*, which are commonly used in persuasive writing. In fact, *because* and *if* are common in the persuasive writing of even first graders.

So where should connectors like *when, because, if, until,* and *while* be listed? In the middle level, where we've put them? In the low level? Perhaps ideally in the gap between the two levels? You may need to modify this transitions aspect of the chart to reflect the writing that students in your own classrooms are producing, since we've tried to cover the gamut from kindergarten to college in only three levels.

Our rationale for listing certain conjunctive adverbs at the high level rather than the middle is this: While some are relatively sophisticated words for time relationships, most are more likely to be used in argumentative writing, the specific kind of persuasive writing that often emphasizes logos, or logic, and that's usually not taught until at least junior high. This is a prime example of grammatical "development" reflecting not just age, but mode and genre as well as instruction.

Parallelism

Parallelism, as we've said, refers to using a series of the same kind of grammatical construction. "The same" can mean repeated exactly or be construed more loosely. Rhetorically, grammatical parallelism calls attention not only to the structure but also to the content of the items in the series, which often are meant to surprise or shock, inflame or inspire. Sometimes just two items will have that effect, though usually a series is thought of as having three and sometimes more items. Following are some examples from *Night* (1960), by Elie Wiesel, an autobiographical novel based on the author's horrific experiences as a Jewish teenager during the Holocaust.

Clearly parallelism is a rhetorical device that Wiesel uses with craft and care:

They said he was a charming man—calm, likable, polite, and sympathetic. (p. 7)

Several days passed. Several weeks. Several months. Life had returned to normal. A wind of calmness and reassurance blew through our houses. The traders were doing good business, the students lived buried in their books, and the children played in the streets. (p. 4)

I had asked my father to sell out, liquidate his business, and leave. (p. 6) [The *to* is understood before *liquidate* and *leave*.]

I looked at our house, where I had spent so many years in my search for God; in fasting in order to hasten the coming of the Messiah; in imagining what my life would be like. (p. 16)

Perhaps they thought that God could have devised no torment in hell worse than that of sitting there among the bundles, in the middle of the road, beneath a blazing sun; that anything would be preferable to that. (p. 14)

One by one they passed in front of me, teachers, friends, others, all those I had been afraid of, all those I once could have laughed at, all those I had lived with over the years. They went by, fallen, dragging their packs, dragging their lives, deserting their homes, the years of their childhood, cringing like beaten dogs. (pp. 14–15)

"Each person will be allowed to take only his own personal belongings. A bag on our backs, some food, a few clothes. Nothing else." (p. 11)

At the ineffective extreme—clearly the overuse of parallelism—are the seven sentences beginning with "his" this or "his" that, in the student's second version of "The Big Guy" (see page 125). The sentences have the same basic structure, yet their overuse characterizes the writer as emerging rather than highly competent.

What of the series of sentences that start the same in "Choices," the essay Jonathan wrote for Chapter 11 in an attempt to illustrate effective writing typical of an eleventh grader? You be the judge!

A note about infinitives and gerunds

We have not specifically illustrated infinitives or gerunds up to this point because we believe they contribute little to style except when they occur in parallel phrases. An *infinitive* consists of *to* + the base from of a verb, as in *to go, to think, to flee*. However, infinitives don't function as main verbs; they generally work like nouns, adjectives, or adverbs. Here are some examples from *Night* of infinitives in a series:

> We began to look for familiar faces, to seek information, to question the veteran prisoners . . . . (p. 45)

> We were no longer allowed to go into restaurants or cafes, to travel on the railway, to attend the synagogue, to go out into the street after six o'clock. (p. 9)

> The idea of dying, of no longer being, began to fascinate me. Not to exist any longer. Not to feel the horrible pains in my foot. Not to feel anything, neither weariness, nor cold, nor anything. (p. 82)

In the last example, the infinitives are preceded by *not*. They occur as fragments.

We saw in Chapter 5 that verb forms ending in *-ing* often modify a noun, in which case they are called participles. When an *-ing* verb form works like a noun, it is called a *gerund*. We skimmed *Night* several times, looking for series of gerunds or gerund phrases. All we found however, were sentences with two:

> The idea of dying, of no longer being, began to fascinate me. (p. 82) [Actually, it's the prepositional phrases that are parallel, but they both have a gerund within them.]

To further illustrate some gerunds in a series, we have generated two sentences that relate to *Night*:

> The Jews of Sighet had a history of ignoring warnings, going about their daily business as usual, and pretending they were safe. But simply waiting, praying, and pulling the wool over their own eyes were fatal mistakes.

If you feel you must teach infinitives and gerunds—perhaps because they're listed in your state standards—we suggest you teach them in parallel series as a part of effective style.

"Cleft" and other inverted sentences

By putting the "new" and/or most important information at the end of our sentences, we can make the information more prominent and therefore more memorable. There are many ways to do this—for example, it helps simply to put adverbial modifiers at the beginning of sentences whenever possible.

Here is a different kind of example. Which of the following three sentences do you find most memorable?

> To note that the ISR was never directly indicated anywhere on Martino's page is interesting.

> That the ISR was never directly indicated anywhere on Martino's page is interesting to note.

> It's interesting to note that the ISR was never directly indicated anywhere on Martino's page.

We consider the third, published (Plait, *Skeptical Inquirer,* 2006, p. 54) version superior, because it doesn't limp off into the sunset with the "interesting" commentary but rather ends with the interesting statement itself. This and the following examples are all from popular magazines.

More common are sentences beginning with *it is true* or *it is true that, the idea is, the solution is,* and others. Here's an example:

> <u>The truth is that</u> this prophecy, like one that supposedly predicted the September 11, 2001, attacks, was a recent creation. (Gámez, *Skeptical Inquirer,* 2006, p. 12)

Such a sentence would be very awkward if reworded so as not to begin *The truth is.*

Here's an inverted sentence structured a little differently:

> And <u>it is here</u>, with Narayan finishing high school, <u>that</u> the diverting particulars of childhood—the monkeys and peacocks, the colonial cruelties, the academic misadventures—run dry. (Mason, *The New Yorker,* 2006, p. 89)

The word *that* has been added as the sentence is inverted, putting *here* near the beginning rather than at the end. Such a sentence is called a "cleft" sentence because it is divided, or "cleft," by an added word (in this case, *that*). Here are slightly different examples with the added introductory *what* underlined, along with the added *is* or *was*:

> <u>What</u> this means <u>is</u> that for the foreseeable future we will be unable to ascertain what goes on in places like Guantánamo without taking some extraordinary measures. (Griswold, *Harper's,* 2006, p. 41)

<u>What</u> he knew then, what we all know now, <u>is</u> that 1,600 miles away in Colorado he had a considerable ace up his sleeve. (Lacayo, *Time,* 2006, p. 77)

<u>What</u> passed for investigation in earlier times <u>is</u> illustrated by a "true" ghost story related by Pliny the Younger (ca. 100 AD). (Nickell, *Skeptical Inquirer,* 2006, p. 23)

The structure of such sentences catches a reader's attention, thus emphasizing the important content at the end. Such sentences often connect not only the old with the new but also one paragraph with another. In their original sources, each of these *what* cleft sentences occurred at the beginning of a new paragraph. All the other example sentences did, too!

Shouldn't we offer students models of such sentences and encourage their judicious use? Cleft and other inverted sentences occur in published writing—both fiction and nonfiction. They make some sentences less awkward and, in general, help a writer emphasize what's most important in the sentence.

Enriching writing through word choice

Why include word choice in a guide featuring grammatical elements? Because when we talk about using concrete, interesting, and precise words, we're talking about words that work as nouns, verbs, adjectives, and adverbs—in other words, particular parts of speech. With pressure from various citizen groups, some states have put back into their content standards the expectation that students will use, and perhaps also "know," these functions. Not all states test the ability to recognize them, nor do the SAT and ACT assessments. But the rubrics for large-scale writing assessment do include some attention to word choice—which makes sense, since good writers choose their words carefully. Instead of focusing on analyzing sentences to label the parts of speech, why not focus on making effective word choices in writing: on *using* these grammatical elements to good effect and learning their names while doing so? Again, we suggest *production* rather than analysis.

"Just right" words

At the heart of word choice is the "just right" word, a word of such specific detail and tone that nothing else will do as well. (The "just right" concept can be extended from the single word to the simple phrase.) Specifically, we want to get our students away from vague nouns; imprecise, dull verbs; and minimal use of descriptive adjectives and adverbs (low-level characteristics) and toward frequent use of precise words and phrases.

Teachers can show students the power of specific imagery in words and phrases. Take, for instance, the following example from *The New York Times Magazine*:

> Moments before a recent show in Peoria, Ill., the world's No. 1 preschool band appeared on two projection screens flanking a stage already set with a drum kit, an electric guitar, a Spanish Galleon, and a smiley face house. Calling into the camera with their standard welcome—"Hi everyone, we're the Wiggles. I'm Greg . . . I'm Murray . . . I'm Jeff . . . I'm Anthony"—the Australian quartet seemed to come straight toward the audience in a cartoony red car, smiling, waving, and giving everyone a big thumbs up. (Scott, 2006, p. 36)

So which words and phrases are "just right"? Let's rewrite without them and see what's missing:

> The band of colorful and energetic men appeared on two screens and introduced themselves to the crowd and gave hand signals.

All the style, voice, description, and detail are gone. Find the words that add those elements and you've found the "just right" words and phrases. The "just right" elements enhance the overall image presented, adding both depth and strength to a scene that sets the tone for the article. Even if they are not parents of toddlers, readers can feel the setting that makes the children's band the Wiggles so popular among its target audience.

Here's another example, taken from *The Atlantic Monthly*:

> At the age of twenty-two, Hamid Hayat appeared to be adrift on two continents. He slacked, by turns, in his hometown of Lodi, California, and in his family's home country, Pakistan. Having lived for roughly equal amounts of time in each, he seemed without direction in either. But on June 5, 2005, the young American offered up alarming evidence of personal initiative: after hours of questioning at the FBI's Sacramento office he confessed that he had attended a terrorist training camp in Pakistan and returned to the United States to wage jihad. In quick succession came his arrest, a packed press conference, and his indictment—and suddenly, it was all over but the trial. (Waldman, 2006, p. 82)

Again, we see the use of precise, "just right" words and phrases. Readers can make their own decisions about which ones are most powerful in adding to the tone of the writing. While the previous example used such elements mainly to add to a scene, this piece uses them to convey both credibility and tone. We are particularly taken with the specific dates and places—*Lodi, California; Pakistan; FBI's Sacramento office; June 5, 2005*—in addition to the descriptive elements like *adrift on two continents* and *slacked*.

So, what are "just right" words? Let's summarize with what they aren't. They aren't vague, dull, or generic. They are words carefully chosen by the author to convey specific points, information, tones, or feelings. They are words chosen with care and thought. They aren't "just good enough"; they are "just right."

Forms of the verb to be

The chart also mentions the use of forms of the verb *to be*, specifically ones for present or past tense: *is* and *are, was* and *were*. Writers are often admonished to eliminate these verb forms whenever possible. But sometimes this advice is better ignored than followed. For example, what about the title of Nora Zeale Hurston's book *Their Eyes Were Watching God* (1937/1991)? Phrased this way, the action is described as continuous over time. In the simple past tense, "Their eyes watched God," the main verb alone, without *is*, suggests a single point in time—apparently not what Hurston meant.

We're also often told to avoid the passive voice, in which the subject of the sentence is not the doer. But what about *Garbage is collected on Mondays*? Isn't that better than the *is*-less but wordy phrase *Garbage collectors collect the garbage on Mondays*?

And some cleft and other inverted sentences also require *is* or *are, was* or *were*. We suggest in our chart that these, if not overused, are a high-level characteristic.

Enhancing writing through punctuation and usage

There are three particular points to be made about this last section of the chart:

1. When writers are learning a new grammatical construction or way of conjoining or subordinating sentences, they often don't use the punctuation associated with it, even though we may have taught the punctuation too. Missing or misused commas and semicolons (the first two bulleted items in the middle level) are examples of new kinds of errors that may initially accompany progress (discussed more generally in Chapter 3).

2. While a paper may contain many errors, there may be far fewer error *patterns*: multiple instances of comma splices, for instance, or

A cautionary tale

A few years ago, one of Connie's students who was doing his intern teaching was asked by his supervising teacher to correct the capitalization and punctuation in her high school students' papers. Unsure of the rules himself, he asked Connie if she would teach him the rules needed. Dutifully, they went through one paper together, error by error, rule by rule. Of course the intern teacher needed to learn the rules, but was this the right approach to the writer's paper? Embarrassed at having fallen so easily into the trap of correction, Connie suddenly exclaimed, "What on earth are we doing? We could correct every single error in this paper and it would still be a level 1 paper [on the state writing assessment], because it has no real content!!" We need to tame the Error Beast and our own tendency to try to slay it through corrections and prohibitions. We need to develop a much richer concept of the role that grammar can play in making writing effective: in helping to generate ideas, use "just right" words and phrases, organize, create voice and style—all in the process of making sentences and paragraphs and whole pieces flow more smoothly, with sentence variety and finesse.

excessive use of unneeded commas (see the last bulleted item under the middle level). A related point is that even highly effective writing is not necessarily error free.

3. While dialect features likely reflect a writer's inability to eliminate them—at least from one-draft-only writing—or the writer's deliberate choice to resist emulating mainstream conventions, there are also positive uses for dialect features. Think, for example, of *Huckleberry Finn* or the novels of Nora Zeale Hurston and Toni Morrison—or Will in the TV sitcom *The Fresh Prince of Bel-Air* (see Chapter 3).

Using the "nonrubric" with caution

The "What Should I Teach Next?" guide can help teachers evaluate students' writing to determine their current skills and decide where to go next instructionally—always keeping in mind, though, that any one paper is just that: a single snapshot that may or may not be representative of the student's work. Another important thing to remember is that the guide is not grade-level specific. It is not just for high school or for middle school or elementary school. It includes not only developmental levels but multiple age ranges and grade levels.

The guide spans three broad categories:

- *enriching* writing through grammar
- *enriching* writing through word choice
- *enhancing* writing through punctuation and usage

Basically, the guide helps us verbalize quick insights about the use of grammar in a student's paper, but we have to be careful not to let our overall impression of the piece—led perhaps by its content, organization, and support for ideas or lack thereof—mislead us into thinking that the writer's use of grammar is stronger or weaker than it really is. Indeed, one purpose of the guide is to help us be more objective and more consistent with other teachers' determinations about writers' use of grammar, even while some decisions will surely be debatable and debated.

Our observations can all too easily become judgments about what the writer "ought" to have done, when we ourselves couldn't do it differently.

Though we aren't really interested in *labeling* whole papers as high, middle, or low with respect to the use of grammar, our guide nudges teachers in that direction. We also need to realize that our observations can all too easily become judgments about what the writer "ought" to have done, when we ourselves couldn't do it differently. We might notice, for example, that the writer has often used the verbs *is* and *are* or *was* and *were*. But in how many of these instances can we ourselves see a good way to replace the allegedly "weak" form of *to be* with a stronger action verb? Thus it may help to append explanations to some of our observations. We need to remember, too, that we are observing the writing, not trying to get inside the writer's head—though especially with the high-level papers, we couldn't resist at least drawing inferences about the writer's excellent or even exceptional writing abilities.

One more reminder: We recognize, of course, that teachers do not often have the time to do such thorough on-paper analyses. However, some experience working with other teachers to do more detailed descriptions and discuss where to go next instructionally can at least give us the means to more quickly group student writers for instruction and assistance.

Applying the guide

We'll now model how to use the guide by applying it to three eleventh-grade persuasive writing papers. We'll describe—objectively in some instances, but with inevitably personal judgments, too—what we particularly notice about the writers' use of grammar in these papers, followed in each case by some possible areas for what to teach next. With all but the high-level paper, we've included specific instructional suggestions for each of the three categories—enriching writing through grammar, enriching writing through word choice, and enhancing writing through punctuation and usage—thus making it obvious that there are options for grouping this writer with others for future guidance.

Paper 1: The Silent Assassin

What's your favorite part about going to eat dinner at a neighbor-hood restaurant with your family and friends? Is it the cheerful chattering with friends? The juicy double bacon cheeseburger, which you cherished every bite of? The mountain of chocolate, which you shared with your date for dessert? Or was it maybe the lungful of nicotine you got from the kind, considerate people sitting a few tables away with a mound of cigarette butts in their ashtray? What's the point of a smoking section that is only five feet away from the "non smoking" section in some areas? Oh but some restaurants are kind enough to put up a little 4-foot "walls" to separate the two areas. WOW! Thank you so much for putting up a tiny fence for the deadly gas to easily travel over and go straight to work on blackening my lungs! And yes I did say deadly gas. Not only does smoking ruin your meal and experiences in public places but secondhand smoke from cigarettes is also very unhealthy and dangerous. Thousands of non-smokers die each year as a result of secondhand smoke. Smoking should not be allowed in public places, especially restaurants.

The first and most important reason why I believe smoking shouldn't be allowed in public places is the health problems caused by secondhand smoke. I don't think smokers realize that when they are smoking a cigarette they aren't just destroying their own lungs, but everyone's around them. The surprising fact is that side-stream smoke—secondhand smoke—has higher concentrations of noxious compounds than the mainstream smoke inhaled by the smoker (T. Raupach, p. 382). This shows that people who smoke in public places are putting others' health at risk even more than their own. Secondhand smoke is involuntarily inhaled by nonsmokers, lingers in the air for hours after cigarettes have been extinguished and can cause a wide range of adverse health effects, including cancer, respiratory infections, and asthma. And it doesn't just affect your lungs as most people think; it can also cause serious damage to your heart. Secondhand smoke causes approximately 3,000 lung cancer deaths and 35,000-62,000 heart disease deaths in adult nonsmokers in the United States each year (ALA,

p. 1). What's worse than dying from another person's pleasure and addiction? Secondhand smoke is like a silent assassin sent for you from all those people smoking around you. And it isn't just adults that fall victim to this killer. Is is especially harmful to young children. Secondhand smoke is responsible for between 150,000 and 300,000 lower respiratory tract infections in infants and children under 18 months of age, resulting in between 7,500 and 15,000 hospitalizations each year, and causes 1,900 to 2,700 sudden infant death syndrome (SIDS) deaths in the united states annually (APA, p. 1). Secondhand smoke is not something that should be taken lightly any longer.

Nevertheless, smokers will say it's a free country and it's their right to smoke if they want to. It's just a "small pleasure" they need in life. And that's just fine with me if smokers want to sit at home and slowly destroy their own internal organs, but when they go to public places with tons of people around that's a totally different story. Smoking in public ruins everyone else's experience and is very unhealthy and dangerous. Who really wants smoke surrounding their table at lunch on Sunday after church? Or when they're pushing their daughter on a swing at the park? This "small pleasure", smoking, takes thousands of lives each year, and that's not including the actual smokers. Are a few puffs of chemicals and gases really worth this many lives?

I really hope I have opened your eyes to the dangers of secondhand smoking. With so many problems resulting from smoking and secondhand smoke, why is it still allowed in public places? When people's lives are at stake, there needs to be a change. There needs to be laws regarding smoking in public places and soon. How many more must fall victim to secondhand smoke before something is done? So the next time you go to a restaurant to eat with your friends or family, just think about what the guy puffing away at his fifth or sixth cigarette is doing to your health and, more importantly, your children's.

Applying the guide to paper 1

ENRICHING *Writing Through Grammar*

Definitely rates high. The writing includes varied sentence structures. A satirical tone in the first paragraph pulls us in as readers. The rhetorical use of question marks, the beginning of sentences with *and*, and the use of fragments reveal a writer who is comfortable with experimentation. Transitions and connectors are sometimes highly effective: *not only . . . but . . . .*

ENRICHING Writing Through Word Choice

Again, high. We are impressed with the writer's choice of "just right" words, particularly nouns and noun phrases: *the mountain of chocolate; deadly gas; the juicy double bacon cheeseburger*. The use of statistics rather than just generalities adds to the overall description.

ENHANCING Writing Through Punctuation and Usage

High, with effective use of parallelism as well as dashes and semicolons. Lapses from conventional punctuation are scarcely noticeable.

This is a very strong paper. We would group it among the highest within this set of writings. Instructionally, we would help the writer experiment with adjectival phrases as discussed in Chapters 5 and 6. We would also offer examples of other organizational schemes that break out of the traditional introduction/body/conclusion mold.

Paper 2: Smelling Like a Dirty Ashtray

Have you ever walked into a restaurant and been so anxious to sit down and get dinner but there is a line? Then the waiter asks if you prefer smoking or non - and at this point you just want to eat as fast as you can - so you say first available. Then you try to enjoy your meal but there's one problem; your food now smells like a dirty ashtray, and there's no joy in spending thirty dollars on dinner that smells like tobacco.

Nowadays smokers have some restrictions on where they can light up at, for example: In Overland Park, Kansas they have now put a smoke free establishment rule into effect, where really only pubs, some restaurants and clubs are they only places where smoking is allowed inside. And to be quite honest, I feel that it is a good thing in our society to stamp out the use of tobacco once and for all. Here is why I think smoking in public should be banned.

First off, cigarette smoking is the leading cause of cancer, obviously in the lungs, and one of the leading causes of death in our country. I don't understand how someone can do something to their body, so often, when they know there will be long term consequences!! And another thing that makes me furious is the use of nicotine, that's how the head honchos make more of their money; people who start have a hard time putting them down. Personally, I think that smoking cigarettes should be banned totally. I can't stand the smell, and it has been proven to be a cause of global warming.

No one expects perfection

Even our high-rated examples have grammar errors and aspects of the writing that could benefit from some enriching. We remind teachers that high doesn't equal perfection, especially in timed situations. Rather, a high rating says that the writer is very effectively using grammar to enrich and enhance his or her work, using many of the available grammatical tools to craft sentences, paragraphs, and text for the desired audiences and purposes.

Global warming will probably not affect us in our life-time, but it will way on down the road, in the next 100,000 years or so, no one knows for sure. People who smoke cigarettes are actually being very selfish, because their actions will end our world that much sooner. Yes, a smoker would argue that driving cars or other use of petroleum products is just as bad, but gasoline doesn't kill people because they smoke it, cigarettes do. I have seen the long term effects, and it isn't good, this is a personal experience:

You're nearing 78 years of age, and living in a retirement home in Florida. It might not sound like the bad life right now, but it gets so much worse. You have to be hooked up to an oxygen machine twenty-two hours a day and you've been trying to rid yourself from smoking cigarettes for nearly two decades and you just cannot stop your addiction, its almost like there is no cure. You can't even lie off of the cancer stick for the four hours that your two nephews come from Missouri to visit, because you can't travel by yourself to the family reunions over the summer. You have to take your oxygen tank with you in public, and you constantly sound like you have a horrific sinus infection when you breathe.

That is what it was like visiting my Aunt Margaret, that's the main reason that I'm not in favor of smoking in public places. I feel that the Government should have regulations against it in all fifty states. I feel that first of all it would raise the life expectancy by a tremendous amount. Also, I think our environment would benefit greatly from the stoppage of the tobacco smog stinking up our planet. Besides, who really wants earth to turn into one big, giant ashtray anyways?

Applying the guide to paper 2

ENRICHING *Writing Through Grammar*

We see this piece of writing in the middle category. It includes some sentence variety, though few descriptive phrases. The writer has tried some rhetorical moves with his sentences—especially the use of questions. His use of transitions is competent, but not outstanding—*and to be quite honest, first of, also*. His use of *and* to begin a sentence isn't especially effective. The *you* in the fifth paragraph is confusing, at least until we realize that the writer is trying to get us to imagine ourselves in the situation of his aunt.

ENRICHING *Writing Through Word Choice*

Again, in the middle. The writing includes only a few strong words and phrases, notably *horrific sinus infection*, *head honchos*, and the metaphorical concept of people as ashtrays. Though the writing includes a lot of *is* and *was* sentences, not many could be readily changed to action verbs. There are a lot of general, nondescriptive nouns and verbs.

ENHANCING Writing Through Punctuation and Usage

In the middle—maybe high-middle because of the rhetorical use of question marks and the use of semicolons, dashes (mistyped, though), and two colons (one not quite conventionally used). Includes no basic errors, but has a pattern of ineffective comma splices.

This is a classic "average" essay—the ones we tend to see that neither wow anyone nor drive readers to despair—essays that nevertheless leave the author with plenty of room for improvement, grammatically and otherwise. The guide helped us verbalize some things we want the author to work on:

Sentences: We'd help him use a greater variety of introductory phrases and clauses—attention to sentence openers can enhance the flow of his sentences. (The use of a range of adjectival modifiers can come later.)

Transitions/connectors: We'd teach more fluid and complex means of connecting ideas. The writer makes abrupt, unannounced transitions, such as the switch from global warming to the retirement home in Florida. We would focus specifically on giving clues to readers about upcoming points and expressing these through clear transitions.

Words: We'd focus on more "just right" nouns and active, descriptive verbs.

Punctuation: We'd teach using colons appropriately, while reinforcing the judicious use of semicolons.

Paper 3: Polygamy Good or Bad

A man with multiple wives maybe ranging from 14 to middle 20's. Men with 26 or more children mostly all from the different women they marry. The men that are marrying these very young girls are ages ranging from, 30 to 40's. Is this the right thing to do? Would you allow your young teenager to marry someone more than half there age? Well in some Mormon practices people find this to be ok. As it is known the Mormons banned this practice if multiple wives in 1890. It was a banned practice or so we think.

But in July or 2005 general officials say about 20,000 to 40,000 or more people still practice polygamy in the U.S. The only reason the LDS church banned the practice of polygamy was because they were under pressure from the government. But still some LDS churches teach polygamy and say they can't wait for the day when this practice is legalized.

The women of this religion sometimes say that they feel safe and that they have security with their one husband and big families. But most of the women find it degrading and wish to escape the life were you are not the only women in your husbands life. There is a polygamist cult in Colorado City. There many women say their husbands rape them all the time. They must have sex with there husbands whenever the husband says or they will be severally punished. They cannot read any books or they will be punished for that as well. They are also taught at an early age to fear outsiders. They also get taught that the only right women have is to be obedient to there husbands. The police in the city don't stop any of these things from happening. They are allowing under aged marriage and rape and other abuse to just happen. The sad thing is that they know about it and they say that they don't want to get involved with these people and interfere with there lives so instead they just let these horrible things happen to women.

So is this any way to live. I do not think that is way of life is right it puts men in complete control of all there wives and all the many children they may have. I think these women need to have choices and salvation. They need to be respected not degraded. I think the police should step up and help these poor women that have to go through these emotional horrors everyday. They will continue to go through this until someone steps up so why not do it now and help the women of polygamy?

Applying the guide to paper 3

Keep in mind that we are looking only at the writer's use of grammar and related punctuation, not at the accuracy of his information.

ENRICHING *Writing Through Grammar*

Middle/low. This paper doesn't exhibit throughout the classic low trait of relying primarily on the subject-verb-object sentence pattern, but there is one particular paragraph in which the author has strung together several sentences beginning with *they*. In his favor, there are also a few attempts to break from the basic sentence pattern. The use of *but* at the beginning of paragraph 2 doesn't convey the meaning needed, though the sentence-opening *but* within that paragraph does work. Transitions between paragraphs are seldom supplied or effective, with the exception of the final paragraph's *So is this any way to live.*

ENRICHING *Writing Through Word Choice*

Low. A lot of bland, dull words. *Is, are,* and *was* could sometimes be changed to more specific verbs. *They* is overused.

ENHANCING *Writing Through Punctuation and Usage*

Low/middle. Use of *there* for *their* is frequent. There's some inconsistency in verb tense, too. Some patterns of using compound sentences without appropriate punctuation—none, or just a comma (run-on and comma splice sentences). There are some ineffective fragments.

Grammatically, this paper reflects low to middle characteristics in the use of grammar. How might we help the writer?

Sentences: As with the middle-level paper, this one suggests that the writer could benefit from assistance in learning to vary his sentence openers. We might guide the writer to use descriptive adjectives before some of his nouns, saving until later our instruction on using free modifying adjectival phrases.

Transitions/connectors: Focusing on using connectors that signal an appropriate meaning relationship may be helpful—at least if connectors are inappropriately chosen in other pieces of this student's writing.

Words: Definitely could benefit from help in choosing and revising for "just right" words, especially verbs conveying action. Might benefit from some help in revising sentences with *is, are,* or *was* as the verb when a stronger verb could be used instead.

Punctuation and usage: The writer needs to learn that *there* is not the right spelling to show that *they* own something. We'd help the writer avoid or correct run-on and comma splice sentences, showing that a coordinating conjunction needs to be used along with a comma to connect two independent clauses in a compound sentence.

Of course we would not work with the student on all these issues at once.

Further notes on using the guide

So far, we've used the guide to discuss three papers demonstrating a wide range of skills. However, the set was very limited in scope: They were all eleventh-grade persuasive/argumentative essays. Can the guide be used for other genres and at other grade levels? Yes! We have used the guide with the writing of mid-elementary students and upper-level undergraduates. We have also used it with various genres, from fiction and creative nonfiction to technical documents to academic essays. In each case, the flexibility of the guide has made it applicable for understanding the skills and instructional needs of the writers.

The following personal narrative is taken from the Michigan Educational Assessment Program's sample anchor papers (1997):

Paper 4: The First Time I Got Bit by a Cat and Went to the Hospital

All of this happened when we were in Georgia to witness my cousin's marriage. That was over now and my family and I had a couple of days to have some fun!

That morning, my aunt and uncle had already been at work for about 1 hour. It was my family's job to let my aunt's cat out of the basement. This cat was very mean. It's name is Alley.

"Now girls," my mom said to my sister and I. "When Alley comes up, you stay away from her." There was fright in my mom's voice.

My mom slowly opened the creaky, wooden door. I suddenly saw two bright green eyes peering out from the door. Alley walked out, looked around, and started rubbing my mom's leg, purring.

Before anyone could say anything, I scampered to where the cat was, and sat on the floor next to her, with my legs spread.

Alley daintly walked over and curled up in my lap. I carefully pet her, checking to see if she was being good. When I thought that she was, I started petting her more quickely.

All of a sudden, SNAP! A twinge of pain sliced through my whole arm, like a knife. I cried out in pain, not knowing that it was me making the high pitched noise.

"AHH!" I screamed. I calmed down a while, then looking at my bloody hand, I started screaming again, with wet tears streaming down my face, tasting like salt. It was then, I realized, that Alley had bit me.

My dad came to me with a plate of ice. I put my hand on it, after my sister had taken me to the bathroom to wash it off. She had been crying too. My mom was too shocked to say anything.

At the same moment, Alley flung herself at my dad and started gnawing on his leg. My dad threw the cat on the wall. Alley slid down the wall, shook her head, and came charging back.

Who knows how we got out of that house, but we did.

My family and I tried to go an amusement park, but my hand
hurt to hold it down.

Finally, I went to the doctor's office. They told me to go
straight to the hospital.

Once there, my hand was the size of a small plate. I got a lot
of presents, shots, too.

I found out that Alley had bitten into one of my veins.

I was in the hospital for two days and one night.

When I finally got out of the hospital, it was time to go back
home.

So much for a vacation!

The End

Applying the guide to paper 4

We found lots of evidence of the writer's extraordinary skill in using
grammar effectively to enrich writing.

ENRICHING *Writing Through Grammar*

This narrative clearly falls in the high category. The writing demonstrates highly effective sentence variety, with varied and appropriate
transitions. We notice the writer's ability to change the pace of the
writing by moving from long sentences to short and back to longer
sentences. She's related ideas and concepts with different connecting devices at the beginning of new paragraphs—*all of a sudden,
that morning, before,* and *who knows how we got out of that house,
but we did,* among others. She's also used two effective fragments:
All of a sudden SNAP! and, at the very end, *So much for a vacation!*
Most notably, she has used set-off adjectivals, such as *purring* and
three present participial phrases. She also has included two effective
absolutes, if we accept Francis Christensen's notion that when *with*
is put in front of an absolute construction, it's still an absolute: *with
my legs spread* and *with wet tears streaming down my face, tasting
like salt.*

ENRICHING *Writing Through Word Choice*

Word choices are also exceptionally strong—clearly deserves a high
rating. The writer demonstrates skill in using "just right" words in
place of less specific or dull ones. Some excellent word choices:

- Nouns and noun phrases—*the creaky, wooden door; two bright
green eyes; high pitched voice; a twinge of pain.*

- Verbs and adverbials: *scampered, daintily walked, sliced, flung, streaming,* and *gnawing.*

ENHANCING *Writing Through Punctuation and Usage*

High. Makes effective use of parallelism; two fragments and two exclamation points contribute to a clear voice. Few errors in punctuation or usage, none of which interfere with meaning.

This writer's grammar skills clearly fall into the high categories. She generously used varied sentence structures, including cohesive devices—transitions and connectors. Perhaps most notable is the use of present participial phrases and the absolutes introduced by *with* to add details and create flow. The writer uses many kinds of rhetorical devices to enrich and flavor the writing—especially some fragments for effect.

Of course this is not a perfect paper. Written in a timed testing situation, it dwindles off with few details toward the end and probably has not been proofread. But as we've noted, grammatical perfection is not expected even for the highest score, and certainly not on these standardized tests. Such perfection is seldom expected of anyone, in fact, except copy editors and maybe secretaries—and they too occasionally make or don't notice lapses from the conventions of Edited American English.

Does it surprise you to learn that the student who wrote this narrative—in limited time, on a state writing assessment—was a fifth grader?

We suspect that such writing resulted not only from good teaching, but also from wide reading. In *On Writing: A Memoir of the Craft* (2000), Stephen King devotes a couple of pages to grammar tips, but prefaces his advice this way: "One either absorbs the grammatical principles of one's native language in conversation and in reading or one does not" (p. 118). King exaggerates a little, we think—else he would not have given grammar tips, and we would not have written this book. In a softer tone, however, we echo his implication that well-written books are our greatest ally in teaching students to use grammar effectively to enrich and enhance writing. Those who read widely often pick up grammatical patterns unconsciously, as Connie's son revealed in his "War Death" poem, and as the fifth grader demonstrated in her essay. Thus promoting reading to strengthen writing is a positive, productive, and practical way to expand students' grammatical repertoire, along with providing guidance in using grammar throughout the writing process.

Well-written books are our greatest ally in teaching students to use grammar effectively to enrich and enhance writing.

Rethinking How to Respond to Students' Errors

SHARON MOERMAN
WATERVLIET MIDDLE SCHOOL, WATERVLIET, MICHIGAN

Recently in Connie Weaver's graduate grammar-for-teachers class, I read aloud the following essay written by one of my eighth graders in response to this Life Map Assignment:

My Grandfather's Death

by Chasity

I still remember my mom in the living room with her brothers as my grandfather took his last breath. I was only seven and I was the only kid there. I knew my grandfather was sick for awhile and that he may die soon, but I never thought that it would change my life that much.

My mom was the saddest. She was a daddy's girl, and as she rested her head on his arm, I couldn't even imagine what might be going through her head. As she walked in the kitchen, you could see the sadness and misery on her face.

The next day was very hard for her and the family. When we went to the funeral home everyone was hugging and kissing each other. I wanted to go up there and see him, but that being the first time I had ever seen a dead body, I was a little scared to, so I made my cousin Ashley go with me. He didn't look dead to me, he just looked like he always did except he was wearing a light blue dress shirt and he had a very peculiar smile. It was weird.

Note: This piece was originally published in 2001 as part of a *Voices from the Middle* article by Weaver, McNally, and Moerman.

Life map assignment

Make a list of at least 15 events that have occurred in your life. Then make a life map depicting those events on a 16-by-20-inch sheet of tag board. You can be as creative as you want, but you must start with your birth date and chronologically show at least 15 events, including the date, a word or two describing the event, and a symbol representing the event. Once everyone's life map is finished and displayed in the room, you will write the story of one of the events from the life map.

When "Amazing Grace" played, my mom burst out in tears with about seven other people that I saw. So I put my hand on hers thinking it would help, but she cried more. I couldn't even look at her.

When we went to the cemetery, my mom was staring at him going down, crying, but her eyes were glowing. I could tell she was thinking about what his last breath was: "I'll tell Mom you said hi." I knew she was happy he went where he wanted to be—with his wife.

My grandfather and I were very close. I sometimes think of me on his lap with hot cocoa watching Scooby-do. Sometimes I think he's still here with me, holding my hand, walking me through life.

Considering and reconsidering Chasity's piece

When I finished reading this piece, I noticed lots of tear-filled eyes. I was not surprised—I had the same reaction when I read it. Then I asked my classmates, "Would you *fail* this piece?" They looked at me as though I had just arrived from outer space. Then I put Chasity's piece—exactly as she had written it when she turned it in—on the overhead (see Figure 13–1). "*Now* what do you say?" I asked. This time they were silent for a different reason.

If a rubric were derived from the holistic scorepoint descriptions for grade eight of the Michigan Educational Assessment Program, Chasity would have earned the lowest score—1—for conventions, because the surface errors in this piece severely interfered with understanding. But what about content and ideas? Organization? Style? Just as clearly, Chasity would score well in those areas. Would it be fair for Chasity to fail based on the number of convention errors?

I have to admit when I first looked at Chasity's piece I was perplexed, and it took several attempts before I could decipher what she was trying to say. But once I realized the depth of her feelings, and her ability to articulate them, I was completely taken aback. Chasity was one of those students we call "resistant" and "reluctant." She didn't hand in a lot of work, and what she did hand in wasn't always up to par. I couldn't help thinking it was no wonder; she must be a discouraged student—and a discouraged writer. But this! This piece had style and voice. It had depth and feeling. Clearly she had created pictures in my mind, and she had evoked an emotional response. For the first time, Chasity had handed in a completed piece of writing. I wanted to support her, assure her that this really was a good piece of writing and that we could work on editing the piece together. I was sure that if I handed Chasity's story back to her full of correction marks, she would likely shut down again. She had taken a risk, and I did not want to discourage her.

This was our first serious piece of writing this year. We had already spent some time revisiting the writing process and had practiced prewriting, drafting, revising, and editing. Before getting started on this writing assignment, I had presented some minilessons on introductions and conclusions, and we talked about what it means to stay focused and organized. We read some personal narratives and discussed what was good, what we liked, and what we didn't like. I instructed them to make me laugh, make me cry, but make me do *something* when I read their papers. "Put me there! Make pictures in my head as I read your papers!" I told

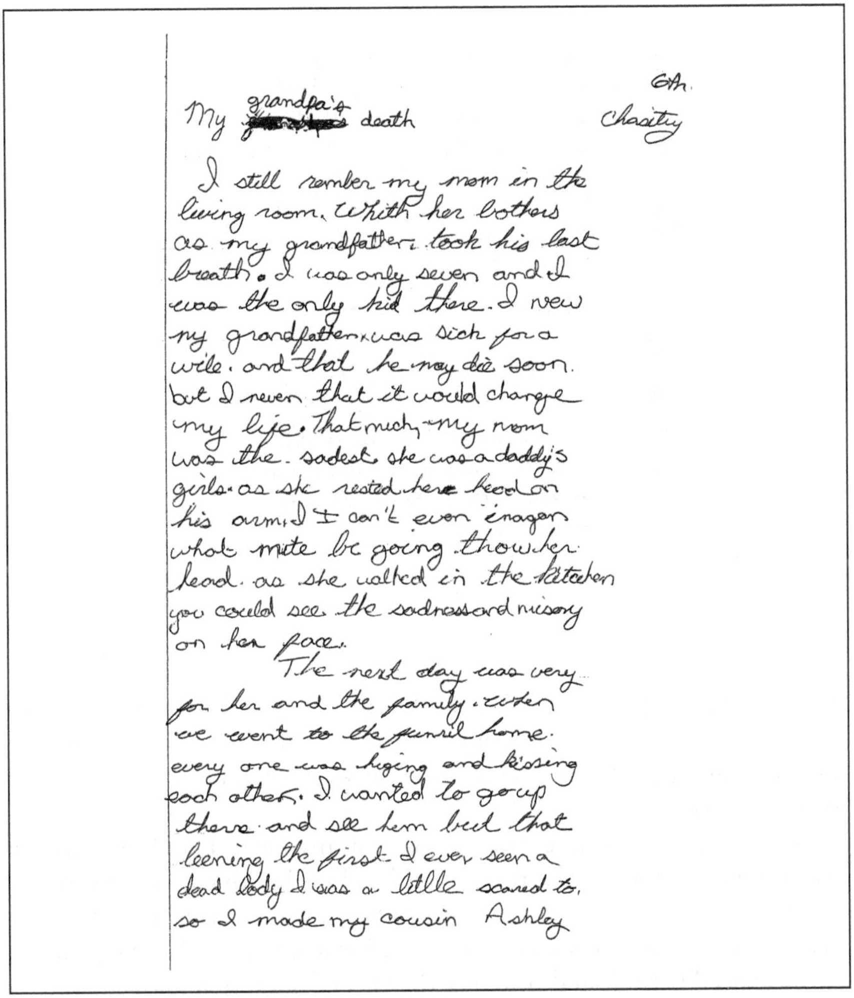

FIGURE 13–1.
Chasity's Piece

(continues)

FIGURE 13–1.
Continued

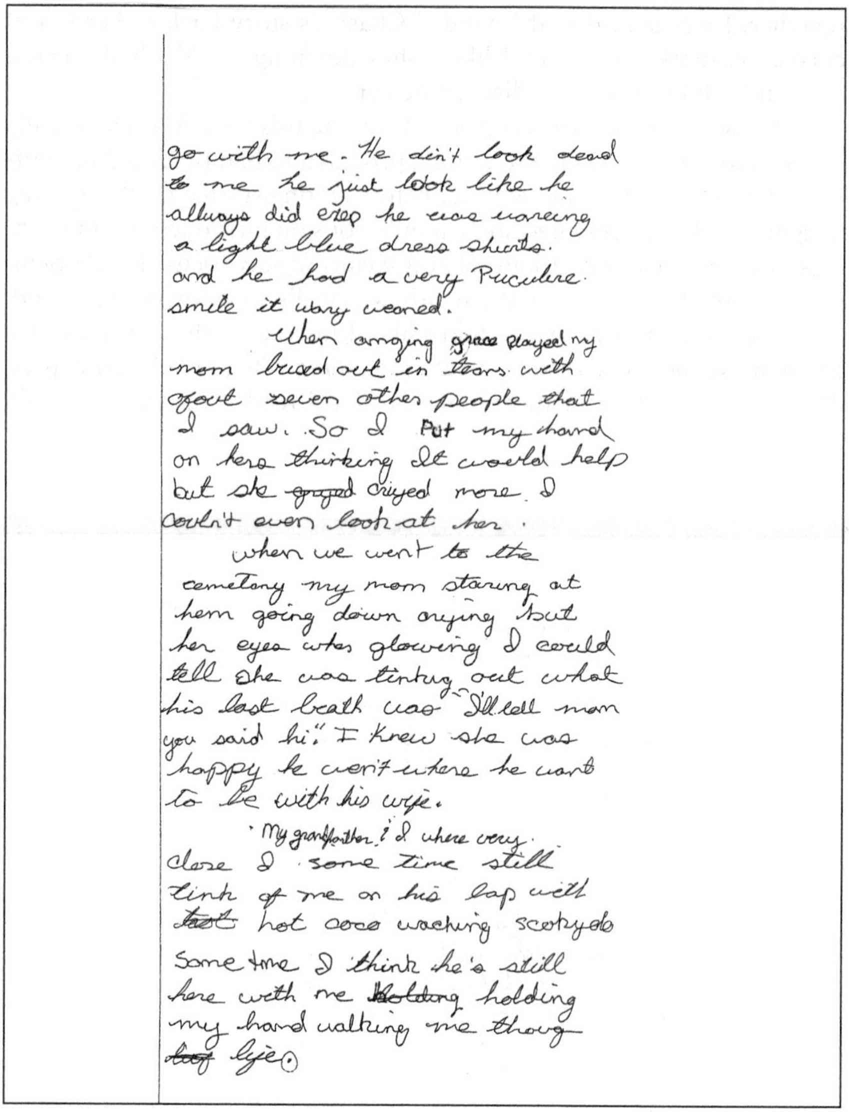

go with me. He din't look dead
to me he just look like he
always did even he was wearing
a light blue dress shirts.
and he had a very Ruculure
smile it was weared.
    When amazing grace played my
mom bused out in tears with
about seven other people that
I saw. So I Put my hand
on hers thinking It would help
but she cryed more. I
couln't even look at her.
        when we went to the
cemetary my mom staring at
hem going down crying but
her eyes was glowing I could
tell she was tinking out what
his last breath was "I'll tell mom
you said hi". I knew she was
happy he went where he want
to be with his wife.
    "My granfather & I where very.
close I some time still
tink of me on his lap with
hot coco waching scobydo
Some time I think he's still
here with me holding
my hand walking me thoug
life.

them dramatically. "Put a WOW at the end!" I gave them the "Life Map
Essay" rubric consistent with our state assessment for eighth grade (Figure 13–2) and asked them to score their own writing before turning it in
for me to score.

Chasity had, indeed, created pictures in my head. I could vividly see
her mother, a daddy's girl, resting her head on her dying father's arm. I
could feel Chasity's pain and confusion as she tried to console her incon-
solable mother, only to see her cry more. But what about the misspellings,
the misplaced periods and commas, the lack of quotation marks . . . ?

Life Map Essay Rubric

	Excellent, Outstanding, Brilliant (EOB)	Almost Excellent, Outstanding, Brilliant	Missed EOB, but is still very good	Missed EOB, but is adequate	Not adequate (You can do better)	Missing
Direct focus. (What the paper is about, without saying, "This paper is about . . .")						
Stays on target. (Doesn't go to the mall.)						
Well organized. (There is a sequence.)						
Richly developed supporting ideas. (It's as though the reader was there.)						
Vivid details and examples. (Use sensory images; make a picture in the reader's brain.)						
Writing holds reader's attention. (Reader didn't want to stop reading.)						
Wrting achieves a sense of wholeness. (No gaps in the story. No "huh?")						
Writer displays control over language. (Best choice of words.)						
Variety of sentence structures. (Not every sentence has the same number of words.)						
Few conventional errors. (PROOFREAD!!! Correct all the spelling, grammar, punctuation.)						

Writing Process

Prewrite

Draft

Revise

Proofread and edit

Published piece

Interesting essay

FIGURE 13–2. Life map essay rubric. From Weaver, McNally, and Moerman, 2001; used with permission. (Based on Michigan Educational Assessment Program Rubric.)

Chasity and research as my teachers

Like so many of my colleagues, I strive to be the best English teacher I can possibly be, so I persistently ask myself, "What is best for my students?" Research consistently shows teaching grammar in isolation does not work: Most students do not remember it, and they seldom transfer it to their writing. As Connie Weaver noted almost thirty years ago in *Grammar for Teachers* (1979):

> There seems to be little value in marking students' papers with "corrections," little value in teaching the conventions of mechanics apart from actual writing, and even less value in teaching grammar in order to instill these conventions. (p. 64)

Nevertheless, ten years later, in an article titled "Developing Correctness in Student Writing: Alternatives to the Error Hunt" (1987), Lois Matz Rosen observed:

> Although numerous research studies show that there is little or no transfer of learning from isolated drills to actual writing experiences and that the time-intensive practice of the teacher's "error hunt" does not produce more mechanically perfect papers, this 100-year-old tradition still persists. (p. 139)

Later in the same chapter, Rosen went on to say:

> Research has never been able to show that circling all the errors—the error hunt approach to marking—makes a significant difference in writing quality; instead it discourages the student whose paper is full of mistakes and focuses students on errors instead of ideas. Students are more likely to grow as writers when the teacher's primary purpose in reading student papers is to respond to content. (p. 149)

The grammar debate continues to rage, not only in English teacher journals, listservs, and classrooms, but also in my own head. Where does teaching grammar fit in? Should I teach grammar in isolation, skill and drill, and have students identify parts of speech on worksheet after worksheet? Based on current research, my experiences as a teacher, my participation in the Third Coast Writing Project, and improvement in my students' writing, I think not.

Research over the last two decades gives us no reason to challenge these conclusions. So I ask myself, "Why should I waste valuable classroom time fighting what has already been proven a losing battle?" The answer to this question was even more apparent when I read Chasity's piece about her grandfather. If Chasity had focused on conventions instead of content, I am not even sure she would have tried writing the piece. I recalled Connie's advice in *Teaching Grammar in Context* (Weaver, 1996):

> To avoid stunting students' growth as writers, we need to guide our students in the writing process, including the phases of revising and editing their sentences and words. It would also be helpful to avoid correcting the kinds of constructions that published writers use with impunity and indeed with good effect. And we need to respond positively to the new kinds of errors that reflect syntactic risk and growth. Time enough to help students correct these errors when they have gotten their ideas down on paper, experimenting with language in the process. In short, the Error Beast is to be welcomed and tamed, not slain. (p. 101)

Working with Chasity

I talked to Chasity before school the morning after I read her essay. I told her that she had done a terrific job of putting me there with her, making pictures in my mind, and evoking an emotional response. She seemed genuinely pleased. I explained that I was concerned about her editing, and asked her if she would confer with me individually so that we could edit it together. She agreed.

Chasity and I sat down together. I asked her to read the piece to me *exactly* as she wrote it. She read it, and as I suspected she would, she read it as she *intended* it to be read. We talked about conveying meaning and how important it is for the reader to understand the significance of her grandfather's death. Suddenly, conventions and correct spellings had *relevance*. She cared about correctly placing periods and commas. She agonized over her words and sentences. She corrected as she read, and as we conferred, she began to feel her way through her corrections. She was engaged in the editing process! She knew what she wanted to say, she just needed some help making the conventions correct. It was the first step in encouraging her to write more, read more, participate in class more. In other words, it was a step toward success. For me, it was confirmation that "taming the Error Beast" truly was better than trying to slay it.

I have come to realize that I simply must allow my eighth graders time to grow as writers, teach them to say what they mean first, encourage them to communicate their thoughts and ideas effectively. Writing is a process. It's ongoing and alive. Just like my kids.

Code-Switching

Teaching Standard English in African American Classrooms

REBECCA S. WHEELER
CHRISTOPHER NEWPORT UNIVERSITY, NEWPORT NEWS, VIRGINIA

While the examples I use in this chapter come from African American students, the basic insights and strategies offered are relevant to any group of students who speak a home dialect different from what's expected in formal, standard English. As I describe elsewhere (Wheeler & Swords, 2006), contrastive analysis and code-switching are relevant to students who speak diverse dialects of English (Southern, Pennsylvania Dutch, Appalachian, Bronx, African American, etc.) and students who speak diverse versions of international English (British, New Zealand, Asian, South African, etc.). Contrastive analysis and code-switching may also be relevant to students who speak English as a nonnative language. These techniques are even relevant to mainstream-English-speaking students who need to move on from the patterns of casual spoken standard English to the patterns of written standard English (fragments versus full sentences; slang or instant-message abbreviations versus formal diction).

In a downtown elementary school on the Virginia peninsula, third grader Tamal writes about the moon's cycles (see Figure 14–1). He's making good progress on the content of the piece. Soon his teacher, Janet, will address the conventions of standard English usage. How will she assess her student's grammar knowledge and performance?

Dollars to doughnuts, Janet will believe that Tamal has forgotten his word endings—endings on his verbs (subject-verb agreement: *waxing mean_*) and endings on his nouns (showing plurality: *24 hour_*; *moon cycle_*)—that he's confused about grammar, that he doesn't know "the right way" to show agreement, or plurality.

Nine blocks north of Tamal's elementary school is Downtown Middle—96.6 percent of the students African American, 87.8 percent of the

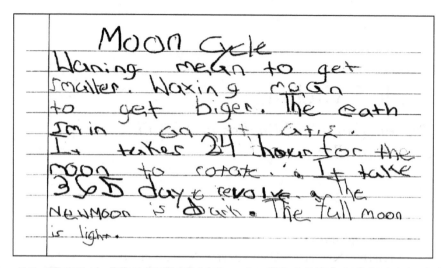

Moon cycle

Waning mean to get smaller. Waxing mean to get biger. The eath is in a[n] orbit. I takes 24 hour for the moon to rotate. It take 365 day to revolve. The newmoon is dark. The full moon is light.

FIGURE 14–1. Everyday English grammar: Subject-verb agreement and plural marked by context

students receiving a free or reduced-price lunch. Student writing at Downtown Middle shows very good growth in overall composition, development, elaboration, and sentence variety (see Figure 14–2). This isn't too surprising as teachers there are well supported in guiding students through the bulk of the writing process. However, what about standard English grammar?

If the essay in Figure 14–2 is representative (and I am assured that it is), middle school students continue to "leave off endings" and "struggle" with grammar: *I have plan_, it make_ sense, give us so[me] idea_,* and *the person_ poem.* The same grammar issues continue to pepper the writing of developmental students in community college. Examples drawn from my consulting work with community college students in New Orleans show the same grammar issues teachers corrected in elementary and middle school: *violence on TV make kids believe . . .* ; *Ms. Goodman theory of adding the consequences may help future generation but not today generation.*

K–16 teachers work hard to teach standard English. They reach for the red pen, circling what they see as student errors, inserting "forgotten" endings, adding "missing words," correcting "wrong words," in hopes of showing the student "correct" standard grammar. Figure 14–3 is fairly typical of how teachers respond to the vernacular grammar of middle school students.

We see the same style of corrections in high school. In Figure 14–4, a high school teacher corrects various mechanical issues. Among other comments, we see that she inserts two *-ed*s to show past time. Interestingly, although she was focusing on showing past time, two other, perhaps less

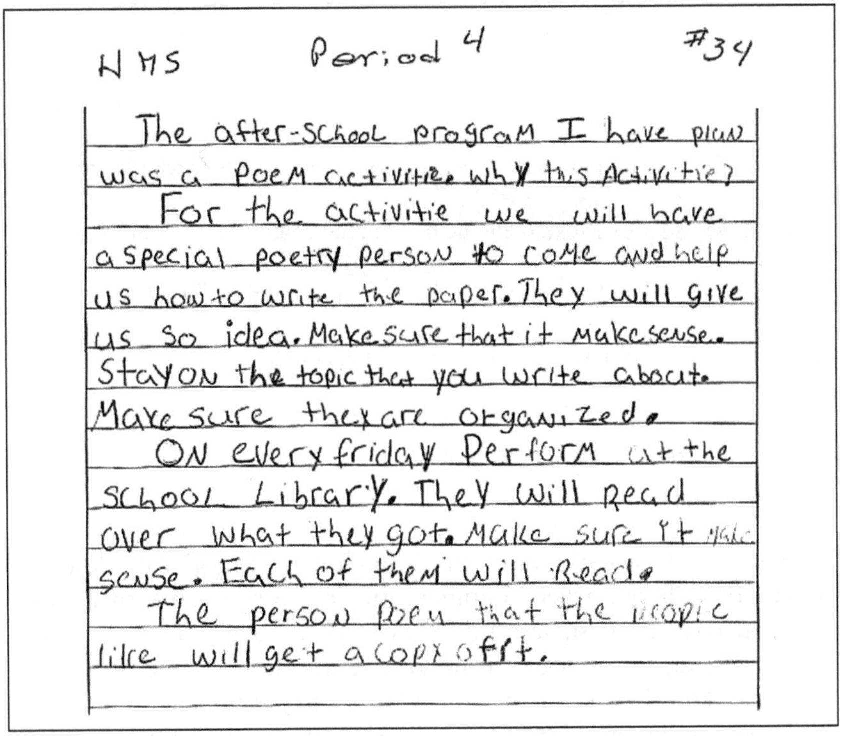

HMS Period 4 #34

The after-school program I have plan was a poem activitie. why this Activitie? For the activitie we will have a special poetry person to come and help us how to write the paper. They will give us so idea. Make sure that it make sense. Stay on the topic that you write about. Make sure they are organized. ON every friday Perform at the school Library. They will read over what they got. Make sure it make sense. Each of them will Read. The person poem that the people like will get a copy of it.

FIGURE 14–2. Eighth-grade essay illustrating student vernacular grammar

familiar, vernacular verb patterns slipped under the radar: *we had pick* and *I seen.*

Clearly the point of the teacher's insertions is to alert the student to the standard grammar rules. But haven't teachers been inserting these end-

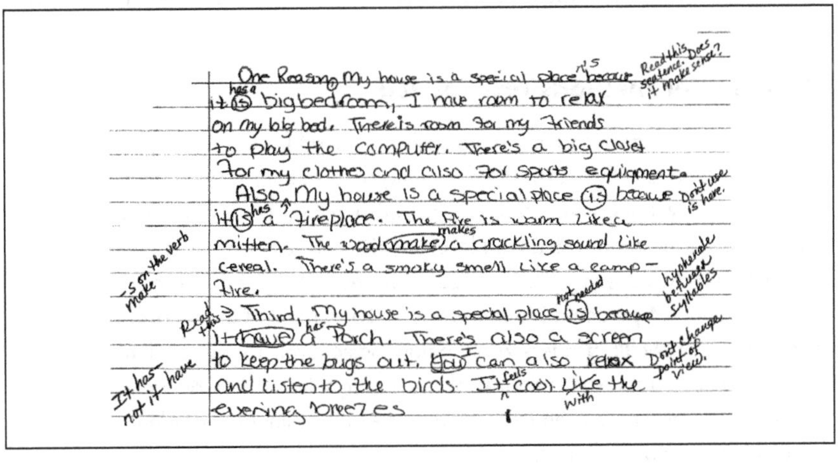

One Reason my house is a special place becaus it is big bedroom, I have room to relax on my big bed. There is room for my friends to play the computer. There's a big closet for my clothes and also for sports equipment. Also, my house is a special place is becaus it is a fireplace. The fire is warm like a mitten. The wood make a crackling sound like cereal. There's a smoky smell like a camp-fire. Third, my house is a special place is because it have a Porch. There's also a screen to keep the bugs out. You can also relax and listen to the birds. It cool like the evening breezes

FIGURE 14–3. Middle school teacher corrects student grammar

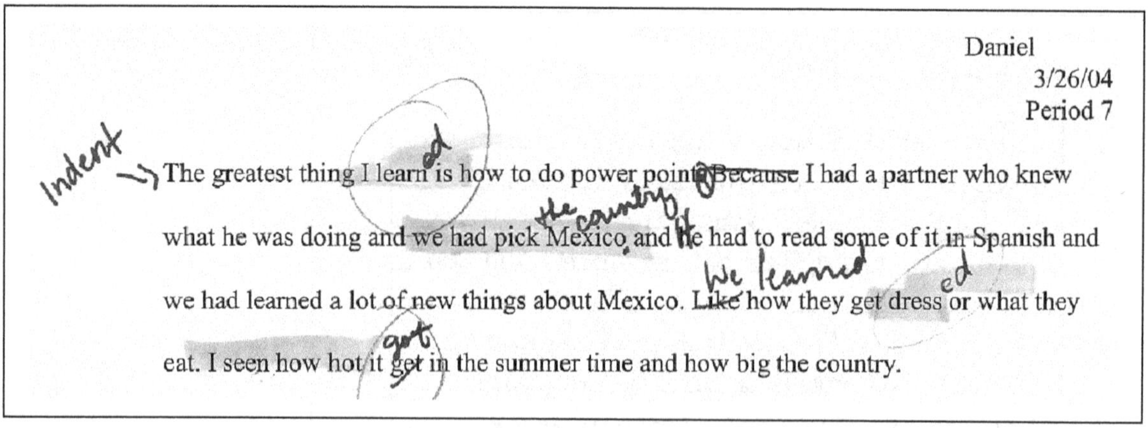
Daniel
3/26/04
Period 7

The greatest thing I learn is how to do power point. Because I had a partner who knew what he was doing and we had pick Mexico, and he had to read some of it in Spanish and we had learned a lot of new things about Mexico. Like how they get dress or what they eat. I seen how hot it get in the summer time and how big the country.

FIGURE 14–4. High school teacher corrects student grammar

ings, correcting and adding words, each and every year from elementary through middle school and on up through high school? And don't the community college teachers continue with their corrective marginalia too?

From coast to coast, across decades, teachers have corrected students' writing, trying to teach urban minority students the standard English they'll need for life and work in the wider society. Yet students just don't seem to learn. Despite persistent correction, students continue to "leave off the apostrophe *s*" and they continue to "forget their past tense *-ed.*" Teachers see their methods failing, assume that the reason for failure is the student's inability to learn, begin to expect less of their students, and witness negative self-fulfilling prophecies of student academic performance across the board (Delpit & Dowdy, 2002; Sweetland, 2006).

The fact that correction just doesn't work to teach standard English grammar comes as no surprise to anyone familiar with linguistic research: While "various strategies can be useful for learning Standard English

Why better methods are needed

Students are not gaining the writing skills they need for the worlds of work and enterprise. Indeed, the 2002 NAEP writing assessment revealed an overall decreasing level of command in writing: 28 percent of fourth graders performed at proficient or advanced levels, while only 24 percent of twelfth graders did. Basic level skills were cause for even greater concern. The NAEP revealed that 14 percent of fourth graders, 15 percent of eighth graders, and 26 percent of twelfth graders wrote below basic level. That is, students do not get better at writing across their twelve years in school. They actually lose ground. The picture is even more bleak for African American students who speak a stigmatized dialect.

equivalents . . . one that does not work is correcting vernacular features" (Wolfram et al., 1999, p. 122; Sweetland, 2006). Longstanding student performance and research show that the traditional correction methods fail to teach African American students skills of standard English usage. Observation and research show that the same is true for American students whose native language is other than English (see Chapter 15).

How can we stop this downward spiral? The answer lies, first, in correctly identifying what's really going on in student writing.

Key sociolinguistic concepts relevant to the writing classroom

Teachers assume that students who speak and write using stigmatized forms don't know grammar and that they struggle with possession, verb agreement, plurality, and so on. However, over forty years of linguistic research unequivocally shows that students who use vernacular language (*my goldfish name is Scaley*) *do know* possession, plurality, verb agreement, and so forth. How can that be?

A cluster of notions from applied linguistics lays the foundation for correctly assessing student writing needs: Key terms include *dialect, language variety, register,* and *style.* Three insights about language underlie all of these terms:

- Language is structured.
- Language varies by circumstance of use.
- Difference is *distinct from* deficiency.

A *dialect* is "variety of the language associated with a particular regional or social group" (Wolfram & Schilling-Estes, 2006, p. 350). Since everyone is associated with a particular regional or social group, everyone speaks a dialect. Also known as *language varieties*, dialects vary in structure (sound, vocabulary, grammar, and social conventions for structuring conversations) on the basis of the speaker's "age, socioeconomic status, gender, ethnic group membership, and geographic region" (Wolfram et al., 1999, p. 37; also see MacNeil & Cran, 2005). Notice that this means that so-called Standard English is a dialect of English. Contrary to popular understanding, "'dialect' does not mean a marginal, archaic, rustic, or degraded mode of speech" (Pullum, 1999, p. 44).

Even so, a dialect has variations within it—of both register and style. *Register* refers to the ways in which language varies by specific speech situations (e.g., newspaper headlines, rituals, recipes, technical writing, even baby talk). *Style* more often refers to the specific choices a writer makes to create voice.

Longstanding student performance and research show that the traditional correction methods fail to teach African American students skills of standard English usage.

While variation in language structure is always present, a different kind of variation lies in the public's *attitudes* toward language. "Standard" English is often called "good" English while "nonstandard" English is considered "bad." These judgments are based not on linguistic grounds but on sociopolitical considerations. Thus, what we call the *standard* is the language variety "associated with middle-class, educated, native speakers of the region" (Wolfram & Schilling-Estes, 2006, p. 315). People regard this variety as good because they regard its speakers as meritorious, but this judgment has nothing to do with an inherent structural superiority of "standard" English. (See also Lippi-Green [1997], who rejects the concept of "standard" English entirely, replacing it with "mainstream" English.)

Vernaculars (aka nonstandard varieties) are those "varieties of a language which are not classified as standard dialects" (Wolfram & Schilling-Estes, 2006, p. 13). They contain socially stigmatized features such as the so-called double negative in English (*I ain't got none*) or irregular verb forms (*I seen it*). Just as the public holds standard varieties in high regard because of high regard for their speakers, the public holds vernaculars in low regard and typically views its speakers with disdain. The judgment of "badness" is sociopolitical and has nothing to do with any structural inadequacy of vernacular dialects.

Finally, "standard" English is a misnomer, implying that only one standard exists. Yet we can readily identify a range of standards, from formal standard English (the written standard English of grammar books, reference works, and many established mainstream authors), informal standard English (a spoken variety defined by the absence of socially stigmatized structures), to regional standard English (the accepted dialect of English in a particular region) (Wolfram & Schilling-Estes, 2006).

Although the issues of language standardization and instruction are complex, our core points remain: Language is structured, and its structure varies by circumstance. But to perceive this, we must let go of blinding conventional assumptions. Only then can we build on the strengths of the language each child brings to school.

In sum, what teachers have traditionally called "mistakes" and grammar "errors" are often instances of grammatical patterns (rules) from a vernacular variety of English. Teachers' understanding of these key concepts from sociolinguistics can transform the dialectally diverse classroom.

Vernacular grammar patterns in student writing

Coming to a new understanding of the language context makes all the difference. Students who speak and write in a stigmatized dialect are not struggling with possession, plurality, and so forth. They are not making mistakes in standard English. Instead, they are following the grammar patterns of their everyday English, the language of nurture.

"Standard" English is a misnomer, implying that only one standard exists.

That is, African American students—particularly those from low-income and/or urban areas—may arrive at school speaking the structurally unique language variety that linguists term African American English (AAE). AAE is a system of sounds, words, and sentence structures; meaning and structural organization of vocabulary; and other information (Rickford, 1999; Green, 2002) and is spoken to some degree by some (but not all) African Americans:

> The fact is that most African Americans *do* talk differently from whites and Americans of other ethnic groups, or at least most of us can when we want to. And the fact is that most Americans, black and white, know this to be true. (Rickford & Rickford, 2000, p. 4)

Linguist John Baugh (2000) conducted an experiment regarding our abilities to ascertain a person's race by the way she or he talks. He found that people can identify a person's race in just seconds of speech. How do we do this, and why does it matter in school?

While a complete answer would fill volumes, the simple answer is this: We are aware of the distinctive sounds, intonation, word choice, grammar, and rhetorical patterns of a person's discourse—not just patterns that are unique to that individual, but the patterns of the dialect or language group(s) to which he or she belongs. Taken together, these patterns make up a distinct language variety known by many names over the years—for example, Negro dialect, nonstandard Negro English, Negro English, Black dialect, Black English, Black English Vernacular, African American Vernacular English, African American language, and African American English (Green, 2002, p. 6). Currently, linguists refer to the variety by one of the latter three terms.

African American English (or any of the other names) is almost a misnomer, given its limitations. In particular, John Rickford (1999) characterizes *who* speaks AAE *when*:

> Not every African American speaks AAVE, and no one uses all of the features . . . 100 percent of the time. Although it is often said that 80 percent of African Americans speak AAVE (Dillard, 1972, p. 229), this is a guesstimate. . . . In general, [characteristic] phonological and grammatical features [of AAVE] . . . are used most often by younger lower- and working-class speakers in urban areas and in informal styles, but the extent to which this is true, and how often the features are used varies from one feature to another. (p. 9)

We also know that students of other ethnic groups adopt some AAE features in their casual speech, if not their writing. But the crucial insight here is that students who write as in Figures 14–1 or 14–2 are following the grammar of a language variety linguists have analyzed extensively across the past forty years (Wolfram, 1969; Labov, 1972). In my work with the schools, I use the terms informal English and everyday English because these terms are readily understood and accepted by students, teachers, school administrators, and the lay public.

Teaching standard English in African American classrooms: Code-switching and contrastive analysis

Since the child who uses his or her everyday English in writing is not making "mistakes," then correction is not the right tool! Instead, a different response is appropriate. Specifically, we use insights from second language and second dialect acquisition: contrastive analysis (CA) and code-switching (CS). In *contrastive analysis*, the teacher draws on the linguistic insights that all language is patterned and that dialects systematically contrast with one another (Rickford et al., 2004; Wheeler, 2005; Wheeler & Swords, 2004, 2006). In *code-switching*, students learn to choose the language style to fit the context—to fit the time, place, audience, and communicative purpose. While the concepts of contrastive analysis and code-switching were originally associated with behavioral teaching methods, we use them with the recognition that students will not mimic and memorize but construct concepts collaboratively in the classroom.

In code-switching, students learn to choose the language style to fit the context—to fit the time, place, audience, and communicative purpose.

Let's observe a teacher operating from a sociolinguistic perspective toward teaching grammar. Tamara, a veteran middle school teacher in an urban school with predominantly African American students from low-income families, receives paper after paper from her students with sentences like these:

My goldfish name is Scaley.

I don't understand my little sister work.

Ellen Goodman essay tell all about violence on TV.

It is not the children fault.

She knows that her children are writing as they speak. As she reads the papers, she sees the same issue happening over and over (on a range of grammar fronts). In the preceding sentences showing possession, something feels the same to her about each example, some pattern that each student is following. She tries to figure out the pattern: *What is going on? I know these convey an idea of possession. But how? Where?* So she underlines the places where possession seems to live and looks again. *Gold-*

fish name, little sister work, Ellen Goodman essay, children fault. That's it! The pattern jumps out at her. The owner sits right before the thing owned. That's the grammar rule! In this language variety we signal possession by the pattern *owner + thing owned.*

Tamara has an epiphany: The students are not "leaving off" the standard English apostrophe *s*; they are successfully following a different grammar rule for possession—and *that* pattern does not call for an apostrophe or an *s*. To show possession inside this form of everyday English, you put the owner right before the thing owned.

Then, using *contrastive analysis,* Tamara prepares graphic organizers called *compare and contrast charts* (or *code-switching charts*) that help urban minority students become conscious of this and other common grammar patterns of everyday English that crop up in their speech and writing. Figure 14–5 shows an example of a compare and contrast chart for possessives.

After discovering the explicit contrasts in grammar between the language of the home and the language of wider communication, students learn to *code-switch,* to choose the language variety to fit the context—typically formal English for school, though not always. If a student is writing a narrative with dialogue, surely she will choose human-being speak, not academic language, to bring voice to a character. On the other hand, if a student group is preparing a research report on a community project for presentation to the mayor, they will likely choose the conventions of standard English, as that's what the business world expects. In the home community, with family and friends, students will likely choose to speak and write more casually, in informal English.

Showing Possession

Informal	Formal
I played on Derrick team	I played on Derrick's team
You were going to say that boy name	You were going to say that boy's name
You step on someone foot by accident	You step on someone's foot by accident
. . . in some old people neighborhood	. . . in some old people's neighborhood

The Pattern

owner + what is owned	*owner + 's + what is owned*

FIGURE 14–5. Showing possession in formal and informal English

Research proves this contrastive approach is far more successful in teaching standard English than the traditional correction model (for research results, see Fogel & Ehri, 2000; Taylor, 1991; Rickford, 1999; Sweetland, 2006; Wheeler & Swords, 2004, 2006). Indeed, according to Professor John Rickford, former Martin Luther King Jr. Centennial Professor at Stanford University, "Teaching methods which DO take vernacular dialects into account in teaching the standard *work better* than those which DO NOT" (Rickford, 1996). That's what our work does, as we use students' existing knowledge (everyday English) as a foundation on which to add standard English to their linguistic repertoires.

Contrastive analysis and code-switching: Powerful tools for standard literacy

Sometimes teachers are impatient with this approach, saying, "Oh, stop with all this time-consuming political correctness! English is right or it's wrong! And those students are making mistakes, plain and simple, so correct them! I don't have time for this." Yet as a collaborating teacher I work with, Rachel Swords, points out, with a code-switching approach it actually takes *less time* to teach grammar because her kids get it, and powerfully so.

With a code-switching approach it actually takes less *time* to teach *grammar because kids get it, and powerfully so.*

One day, half of Rachel's class was participating in a read-aloud in another third-grade room. In the other room, Ms. Jones kept interrupting one of her students as he read out loud. Where the book showed "The boy walks to school in the morning," the child said, "The boy walk to school." The teacher interrupted: "Read what's on the page!" The student took another try: "The boy walk . . . " "No!" Ms. Jones interrupted. "Pay attention to the end of the words! *WalkS*. There is an *s* on the end of the word, say it!" Of course, by this time, the child was demoralized, embarrassed, and well on the way to shutting down and disengaging from learning in school. Tamisha, one of Rachel's students, leaned over and whispered, "The book uses formal English. You're using informal, like you do at home. Ms. Jones wants you to use formal English when you're reading. So be sure to look at the ends of the words and say them out loud." That's pretty deep command of language for any age, let alone a third grader.

A few years ago, teachers at Rachel's grade level asked her, "How do you do it? Your kids *get* subject-verb agreement. I've been over it and over it, and *still* my kids are confused. What are you *doing* in your classroom?"

Realizing that the traditional correctionist techniques just don't work, three of the four other teachers at Rachel's grade level also began using a sociolinguistic approach to student writing. In classes where teachers adopted code-switching, students scored considerably above the passing rate: 88 percent, 85 percent, and 83 percent. Rachel's students scores were even higher, with 100 percent of her students passing reading and math, and 94 percent passing social studies and science. Indeed, 100 percent of her African American students passed 100 percent of the subjects tested under No Child Left Behind (NCLB); the one failing child was white. Her class was preponderantly minority students (eleven African American, one Asian, one American Indian, two Hispanic, and four white). In the class where the teacher did not adopt code-switching, students languished, scoring 64 points on year-end tests under NCLB.

Code-switching in the classroom

Now that we've had a preview, let's observe a sociolinguistically informed classroom in more detail. The classroom is again that of Rachel Swords, an urban second/third-grade teacher in a district where a majority of the students are African American. Each year Rachel helps her students discover that we *all* vary our self-presentation, situation by situation.

Setting the stage

"What do you think might be an informal kind of place?" Rachel asked.

Taquisha's hand went up. "Home or the mall."

Jamal added, "The neighborhood with your friends."

"Good!" Rachel affirmed. She organized her children's responses on a tree map. The children explored formal/informal places, formal/informal clothing, formal/informal behavior, and so on. After they finished, the set-up for formal/informal places looked like this:

Places

Informal	Formal
home, neighborhood	jobs
street with friends	school
church	church

To reinforce the idea that variation is natural, Rachel had her children draw pictures of themselves in formal and informal clothing (see Figure 14–6). Children also used cutouts from magazines to illustrate how we all vary our clothing to fit the setting. A wall chart made by a student who lived on the rural Eastern shore of Virginia is shown in Figure 14–7. (You might also invite students to draw illustrations or select cut-outs of formal versus informal dress and contexts, as in Figures 14–8 and 14–9.)

FIGURE 14-6.
Yasmine's picture of
herself wearing formal
and informal clothing

After students explored formal and informal clothing, places, posture, behavior, and so on, Rachel made the link to language, leading them to explore how their language might differ between formal and informal situations. The students explained that "yes, sir" and "excuse me" were formal and that "yo, wuz up?" and "he ain' nobody" were more informal. The class thought back to an exchange between two students. One student had exclaimed, in excitement, "Yo, Mz. Swords! Dat junk be *tight!*" A second student intervened to set the language right. "McKinzie! You ain' sposed ta talk t' Mrs. Swords dat way." "Oh, okay. Ms. Swords. Dat

FIGURE 14-7.
Formal and informal
clothing from
magazine cut-outs

FIGURE 14-8. Middle school illustration of formal and informal clothing and setting

FIGURE 14-9. Middle school illustration of formal and informal clothing and setting

stuff be cool!" Clearly, students had come to school already having a good grasp of language *style* (often the variation language shows in levels of formality) within their own variety, in this instance AAE. In this way, students used their own prior knowledge to define formal and informal language.

Code-switching minilessons illustrated

Rachel then applied that understanding of code-switching to the grammar of sentences. Using chart paper, she created two columns of sentences drawn from her students' own writing, the left one written in vernacular English (*I have two dog*), the style many students speak, and the right showing the same sentences written in Standard American English (*I have two dogs*) (see Figure 14–10). Rachel labeled the SAE examples "formal" and the vernacular examples "informal." She began with plural patterns, because she knew that her students would immediately see the difference between the formal and informal usage.

The class then compared and contrasted the grammar of the informal sentences with the grammar of the formal sentences. In doing so, they were applying the most successful instructional strategy—comparison and contrast—to grammar itself (Marzano et al., 2001). Immediately, one child said, "Oh, that's wrong. All the ones on that side [informal] are wrong and the ones on the other side [formal] are right."

FIGURE 14–10. Discovering the rules for plural patterns across language varieties

Plural Patterns

Informal	Formal
I have two dog.	I have two dogs.
Taylor likes cat.	Taylor likes cats.
All the boy are here today.	All the boys are. . . .

How to show "more than one"

Number words   *-s*

Other words
- *in the paragraph*
- *in the sentence*

Common knowledge

Rachel reminded students about their explorations of formal and informal styles of clothing and of how language varies by region of the country. She talked about how she switches her language to suit the setting. For example, at home she might say, "I'm fixin' to go the store—ya'll need anything?" but she wouldn't ask fellow Virginia teachers, "I'm fixin' to make copies—ya'll need any?" However, she might still keep the question casual by omitting the subject and part of the verb in the second clause: "I'm gonna make some copies; need any?" Rachel talked to the students about how she changes her language by setting and told them that when she makes these language choices, she is *code-switching*.

Moving back to the chart, Rachel asked students if they understood what each sentence meant and asked if the informal sentence *I have two dog* had the same meaning as the formal *I have two dogs*. The class agreed they did, so, using the scientific method of generating data, she asked, "If we can tell what the sentences mean, what differences do you see between the two columns?"

One child explained, "In this one [the formal form], the noun has an *s* on it." Rachel asked, "What does that mean? What is the *s* doing there?" Students replied, "It's making it more than one." They talked about how adding the *s* makes it more than one. Rachel then explained that this is the way we show "more than one" in formal language. To help guide children, she created a heading—*How to show more than one*—for the contrastive patterns they were discovering and wrote *-s* under the formal column.

Then the class explored the informal example's patterns. Reminding the children that the examples had the same meaning, she asked how the informal sentence shows us that the number is more than one. One student said, "You know it's more than one because it has the number *two* in it." Rachel wrote *number words* in the informal column and said, "Number words show there's more than one."

It's very important to check each example, to be sure students have discovered the full grammar rule at hand. So Rachel asked the children to look at the next sentence, "Taylor likes cat." She observed, "There's nothing in that sentence that tells you it's more than one cat." The children explained, "You have to look at the whole paragraph." So Rachel wrote *other words in the paragraph* as she said, "Other words in the paragraph can show there's more than one." Next the class looked at "All the boy are here today." Rachel asked, "What tells you there is more than one boy?" Someone replied, "The other words in the sentence—*all*." Rachel wrote *other words in the sentence* on the chart. Another boy patiently explained, "Mrs. Swords, you can't have part of a boy, so of course you have all of one boy. So, this hasta mean more than one boy!" Rachel added *common knowledge* to the plural chart (the final version is shown in Figure 14–10), which remained up on the classroom wall for easy reference.

Rachel has transformed her classroom. The tools of her trade? She understands and lives the conviction that:

- English comes in different varieties.
- Each variety is structured, rule-governed, and grammatical.
- We choose the language features to fit the time, place, audience, and communicative purpose.
- Language is not "correct or incorrect," "right or wrong," but instead works or doesn't work in a setting.

Rachel uses contrastive analysis charts and the scientific method to lead her children in active, inductive discovery of the grammar rules underlying students' everyday English and standard English.

Making code-switching work for you and your students

What works for Rachel can work for you. First you need to categorize the structural features in your students' writing that differ from standard English and recognize them as consistent features of the students' dialect.

Seeing student writing as data

Upon receiving your first set of papers, take a different approach to usage issues. That is, do *not* insert "missing" letters or endings. That's hard not to do—we're so accustomed to marking "corrections" in the margin. But when students write, "My goldfish name is Scaley," they are not forgetting the apostrophe *s*; instead they are following a different grammar pattern— the rule for possessive in their everyday English.

Instead of correcting student writing, circling words, or inserting endings, view the writing as data, data you will use to plan upcoming grammar minilessons for your writing workshop. Identify the most frequent vernacular patterns in student writing. To give you a head start, look at the top ten grammar patterns characteristic of the vernacular spoken by African American students (shown in Figure 14–11; Wheeler & Swords, 2006). Raimes (2007) shows how native speakers of Arabic, Bengali, Chinese, Farsi, French, German, Greek, Hebrew, Hindi, Japanese, Portuguese, Russian, Spanish, Swahili, Tagalog, Thai, Turkish, Urdu, and Vietnamese (among other languages) who are learning English often transfer the grammar patterns from their first language into spoken or written American English. Certain basic patterns are the same, whether English is being acquired as a first or second language (see Chapter 9).

Code-Switching Shopping List for Differentiated Instruction

Class: _____ Day: _____ Time: _____

As you read student essays, note which students need work on which everyday English patterns. Use this tool to form peer-editing groups of students who have similar gammar needs.

Informal v. Formal English Patterns	Students
Verb Patterns	
1. Subject-verb agreement she walk v. she walk<u>s</u>	
2. Showing past time (1) I finish v. I finish<u>ed</u>	
3. Showing past time (2) she <u>seen</u> v. she <u>saw/had seen</u>	
4. A form of the *BE* verb understood (such as *is, are, was, were*) he cool with me v. he'<u>s</u> cool with me	
5. Making negatives she <u>won't never</u> v. she won't <u>ever</u>	
Noun Patterns	
6. Plurality: "Showing more than one" three cat v. three cat<u>s</u>	
7. Possessive the dog tail v. the dog'<u>s</u> tail	
8. A versus *an* an rapper v. a rapper a elephant v. an elephant	
9. Other pattern: _____	
10. Other pattern: _____	

FIGURE 14–11. Code-switching shopping list for differentiated instruction. Modified from Wheeler and Swords (2006). *Code-Switching: Teaching Standard English in Urban Classrooms.* Urbana, IL: NCTE. Used with permission.

To help you keep track of which grammar issues are relevant to which students in your class, use Figure 14–11, Code-Switching Shopping List for Differentiated Instruction. In going through a set of papers, you might find that one group of students consistently uses informal patterns of subject-verb agreement, while another uses informal possessive or past time patterns. The shopping list helps you keep track of which students or groups of students need what grammar attention. One of my collaborating teachers uses this tool to choose which students to call on during relevant class discussions. She also uses the shopping list to help her divide students into small groups based on particular grammar needs during the editing phase of the writing process.

Deciding where to start

While the most frequent pattern you will probably see is everyday English subject-verb agreement, I don't recommend beginning code-switching lessons with that topic, because the standard subject-verb agreement patterns are relatively complex. Instead, begin with possessive and plural patterns, as these most clearly illustrate the whole process of comparing and contrasting "informal" versus "formal" English rules (Wheeler & Swords, 2006). Then move on to teaching minilessons on showing past time. Finally, with that solid foundation, tackle subject-verb agreement.

Of course, once you lead students to compare and contrast an informal with a formal English grammar pattern, you'll want to have them practice switching from informal to formal English (and perhaps from formal to informal English as well). For example, you might have each student make up two sentences using the formal pattern and two sentences using the informal equivalent. Have students justify how they know that a given example is formal or informal.

Making stylistic choices

Grammar usage is relevant throughout the writing process, not just in the editing endgame. When your students are writing their own essays and assignments, have them discuss what kind of language serves their goals and the expectations of their audience. Standard English (Edited American English) is usually appropriate for the reports or test essays students write. However, in narratives with dialogue, vernacular English is surely an appropriate choice. Here is where reading dialectally diverse literature and discussing the effects of language choices create a rich model for students. From Patricia McKissack's *Flossie and the Fox* (1986) to Zora Neal Hurston's *Their Eyes Were Watching God* (1937/1991) and Toni Morrison's *Love* (2003), we see that diverse styles of language are not only appropriate but necessary to create character and voice in literature.

In the editing phase of the writing process, invite students to check their writing for formal English usage. You might give students highlighters and suggest that they highlight their successes in choosing standard English possessives, plurals, subject-verb agreement, and so on. If students find that they've used a pattern from informal or vernacular English, suggest they code-switch into formal English and *then* highlight their success. The Code-Switching Shopping List for Student Editing (see Figure 14–12), which identifies the top patterns I've found in my work with urban students, is a tool that secondary school students find useful after the teacher has indicated which patterns each student typically needs to code-switch. (The form has four columns, allowing you to track a sequence of papers.)

Before you receive your first batch of papers, make a copy of the shopping list for each student. Keep these blank shopping lists by your side as you are grading the papers for the first time. As you comment on a student's paper, responding to the usual matters of organization, focus, elaboration, sentence variety, and so forth, also note whether the student is using informal or formal English grammar. If you see informal grammar, make a note in the margin of the paper, and put a check in the corresponding box on the shopping list for the first paper of the semester. For example, if you notice informal patterns for showing past time or plurality, you might write *past* or *pl* in the margin. Then put a check in the boxes for these grammatical points on the code-switching shopping list. The shopping list then stays in the student's writing portfolio for future reference.

When you return the papers, you'll want to talk with students about their writing. When you come to grammar, tell them that you've begun using a new tool—the code-switching shopping list. Explain that in the first column you've noted instances of informal grammar, so that the *next* time they write a paper, when they get to editing, they should pull out the shopping list to see what grammar issues they will need to address. At that point, students should check their papers for instances of informal English, putting checks in the relevant boxes as appropriate. On the second paper, then, students will self-edit or edit in peer groups, seeking to "flip the switch" from informal to formal English. When you read the class papers after students edit, you might want to check the student's Code-Switching Shopping List to assure that each student is accurately identifying the informal grammar points they need to code-switch.

Grading student writing for standard usage and mechanics

Teachers frequently ask me, "With a code-switching approach, do we grade students' final papers for standard English usage and mechanics?" A quick confirmation is that we most assuredly *do* grade students in part

Code-Switching Shopping List for Student Editing

Name: _____

Do any of the top informal English patterns appear in your paper? If so, put a check in the corresponding box and then *code-switch* to formal English! Put a smiley face ☺ to show when you use formal patterns in your writing. "Flip the Switch!"

Informal v. Formal English Patterns	Paper 1	Paper 2	Paper 3	Paper 4
Verb Patterns				
1. Subject-verb agreement she walk v. she walk<u>s</u>				
2. Showing past time (1) I finish v. I finish<u>ed</u>				
3. Showing past time (2) she <u>seen</u> v. she <u>saw/had seen</u>				
4. A form of the *BE* verb understood (such as *is, are, was, were*) he cool with me v. he<u>'s</u> cool with me				
5. Making negatives she <u>won't never</u> v. she won't <u>ever</u>				
Noun Patterns				
6. Plurality: "Showing more than one" three cat v. three cat<u>s</u>				
7. Possessive the dog tail v. the dog<u>'s</u> tail				
8. *A* versus *an* an rapper v. a rapper a elephant v. an elephant				
9. Other pattern: _____				
10. Other pattern: _____				

FIGURE 14–12. Code-switching shopping list for student editing. Modified from Wheeler and Swords (2006). *Code-Switching: Teaching Standard English in Urban Classrooms.* Urbana, IL: NCTE. Used with permission.

on their level of command of standard English grammar. Our school systems expect it, tests expect it, and our broader society expects it.

How and when we grade for standard grammar is a more intricate matter. A general guideline is that we hold students accountable for and grade them on material we have taught. For example, if the beginning-of-the-year writing diagnostics indicate that students are using vernacular patterns to show subject-verb agreement, past time, possession, plural, multiple negatives, habitual *be* (*we be playing basketball all summer*), or a form of *be* understood (*he kool*), we will want to address these patterns through contrastive analysis and code-switching before we grade students on whether they have mastered the standard English forms. That means that over the course of the school year, we will be increasing the number of standard forms for which students are accountable. Perhaps near the beginning of the school year, after teaching possessives and plurals, we will grade students on whether they choose the appropriate possessive and plural forms to fit the assignment. However, we may not grade on subject-verb agreement or habitual *be* until we have taught those, using contrastive analysis and code-switching.

Questions immediately arise: "Our school system runs K–12. Statewide tests and schools have been attempting to teach standard subject-verb agreement, possessives, plurals, and so forth throughout the grades. Surely students ought to be held accountable for mastery of these standard grammar rules early on."

However, even though statewide planning guides, textbooks, tests, and scope-and-sequences have long required that teachers teach—and tests assess—standard English, the traditional techniques do not succeed in teaching standard English to vernacular-speaking students. Accordingly, at this point, we cannot realistically say that by such-and-such a grade students should reliably command standard grammar points X, Y, and Z. Instead, for the moment, teachers at each grade level may be back at the starting gate when it comes to teaching standard English equivalents. So each teacher needs to assess what standard grammar his/her students know and don't know at the beginning of the year, use that data to plan minilessons in context, and grade for standard equivalents (as appropriate) in sync with the lessons they teach during the year.

Traditional techniques do not succeed in teaching standard English to vernacular-speaking students.

Deciding what comments to make in the margin

After teachers have taught various code-switching lessons (e.g., possession, plural, subject-verb agreement), they need to comment if students use vernacular language patterns when the essay calls for standard English. I recommend that teachers first write *poss* or *pl* or *s-v* in the margin to direct students' attention to the particular code-switching issue. Students can then code-switch during the editing phase of the writing process. As students gain more experience, teachers may simply write CS (for *code-switch*) in the margin, and later they may direct students in peer groups to independently code-switch one another's papers while referring to the code-switching charts posted along the classroom walls.

Linguistically informed responses to reading aloud

During read-alouds, it is very important that teachers not interrupt the student to enforce standard English pronunciation or grammar.

Although our focus is on writing, a word about reading aloud is also appropriate. In particular, insights from linguistics make it clear that a teacher should not "correct" vernacular grammar while the student is reading aloud (Goodman & Goodman, 1978). During read-alouds, it is very important that teachers not interrupt the student to enforce standard English pronunciation or grammar. For example, if the printed text reads, "The cat meows," and the child voices, "Da cat meow," the child has correctly understood the meaning of the text and has voiced it through the sounds and grammar patterns of his or her home language variety. To interrupt the child while he or she is reading is to mix two different tasks— reading, and learning a second dialect—to the disadvantage of both.

Of course, that doesn't mean that the teacher ignores the student's language needs. The teacher should mentally note how the student's pronunciation and grammar differ from the text. It could be that home speech patterns are influencing how the student reads. In our example, that's obviously what's going on with *meow*. Where standard English puts an *s* ending on verbs when there is a he/she/it type of subject, this student's everyday English uses the bare form. So the child's pronunciation follows the pattern of the home language grammar. This pattern will likely be familiar from the students' writing, so the teacher will probably already know that she needs to teach code-switching minilessons in patterns for subject-verb agreement.

What's going on as the child voices *da* is perhaps less familiar to the teacher. She might think that the student is lazy or sloppy in reading the word *the* out loud. Or she might think the student is not paying attention to the letters on the page. But research in second dialect acquisition paints a very different picture. Given what linguists know about the structure of African American English, we know that just as the grammar of that variety contrasts at times with the grammar of standard English, so do the sounds in AAE often contrast systematically with the sounds of the standard variety. In this example, we see one of these sound contrasts. In words like *that* or *this*, standard English pronounces the beginning sounds with what is informally called the /th/ sound (linguists explain that this is a "voiced, interdental fricative"—a voiced rumbling consonant sound with the tongue between the teeth). By contrast, the home dialect this student speaks uses a different sound for the beginning letters of *that* or *this*: /d/ as in *dog* or *dig*. The student is again following a pattern from her home language, this time a sound pattern instead of a grammar pattern. Nonetheless, the same tools apply. As the teacher recognizes that the student may be using the sounds of a different language variety, it's time to use her linguistically informed tools—contrastive analysis and code-switching. Instead of interrupting the student's reading, the teacher should note to herself that she'll need to teach a code-switching minilesson contrasting pronunciation patterns of everyday English with the pronunciation patterns of formal English. In this way, again, we are building on what students know to add the patterns of standard English to the students' linguistic repertoires.

When a child's oral reading shows the influence of sounds and grammar from the home language, the child *does not have a reading disability*. The child is developmentally normal. See the work by Angela Rickford for teaching reading to African American students (Rickford, 1999). See also Charity et al. (2004) for a cogent list of how to distinguish error from dialect influence in the reading classroom.

In conclusion

One day, two of Rachel Swords' eight-year-old students were talking privately in the hallway between classes: "I ain't got nothing to do after school." A teacher, overhearing them, interjected, "You are not to talk like that." Rachel's student stopped, looked at the teacher, and replied, "Oh, I see. You want me to use formal English. Okay. I don't have anything to do after school." The linguistic autonomy and power of this child is inspiring—such presence of mind, such sure-footed, quick analysis, such confidence in her own linguistic understanding.

Stories like these are the nectar that draws teachers to new understanding of what to do about student grammar. We compare and contrast, we analyze and reason, we use the scientific method and critical thinking skills to foster standard English mastery. That is, we teach core foundational skills for citizens of a twenty-first-century society, and we do it by using sociolinguistic approaches to teaching standard English in diverse classrooms.

The Transformative Classroom
Rethinking Grammar Instruction for English Language Learners

15 ❧

JASON ROCHE AND YADIRA GONZALES
REEDLEY HIGH SCHOOL, REEDLEY, CALIFORNIA

We teach English language learners (ELLs), and as part of preparing them to accomplish their goals and achieve their purposes in the larger society, we address the features of their language that mark them as nonnative speakers of English. That comes naturally in our classrooms because we believe in our students and their potential: At the core of our teaching is the conviction that all students have the ability to read, write, view, and think—and to make a difference in the world. We believe that if you create an environment conducive to building community, understand the difference between rigidity and rigor, and generate culturally relevant curriculum that transforms students into inquirers and reflective practitioners—*students will learn.*

It becomes increasingly important that teachers have a solid understanding of how to work successfully with English language learners and the diverse challenges they present, because such students constitute an increasing proportion of our student population, not only locally but nationally.

A challenge to traditional teaching

The pressure for accountability has had a major impact on teacher morale, curriculum quality, and student attrition; at the same time we are experiencing a major shift in the demographics of American students. This shift is exciting because it affords us the opportunity to stop, reflect, and reevaluate American education. To appropriately serve our students, our national priorities and traditional practices must change along with the changing demographics.

Changing demographics

At the time of the 2000 U.S. census, nearly forty-seven million people lived in homes where English was not the primary language. In states with large immigrant populations, this has an enormous impact on schools and on teaching. Eighteen percent of the country's school-age children reside in homes where English is not the primary language. In California, where we teach, that statistic goes up to a staggering 42 percent (U.S. Bureau of the Census, 2000). And because our society has done a woefully inadequate, disgraceful job of integrating America's schools, many schools (including the one in which the two of us teach) have high percentages of ELLs, and many classrooms predominantly include linguistic minorities (Kozol, 2005). It is vital that we take a good, hard look at our instructional practices and priorities if we are going to appropriately serve the needs of the new American student.

It is vital that we take a good, hard look at our instructional practices and priorities if we are going to appropriately serve the needs of the new American student.

The diversity of English language learners

The catch-all phrase *English language learners* does a poor job of defining this diverse population. Yvonne and David Freeman, in their book *Closing the Achievement Gap* (2002), discuss three different categories of English language learners: newcomers with adequate formal schooling in their home country (AFS), newcomers with limited formal schooling in their home country (LFS), and the long-term English learner (LTEL).

The AFS and LFS groups are similar because they have typically immigrated believing that the United States offers "more economic well-being, better overall opportunities, and/or greater political freedom" (Ogbu, 1992, p. 290). These two groups also have fewer identity issues and can typically coexist in the different cultural contexts of school and home.

However, the Freemans argue that those students who arrive in the United States with adequate formal schooling come better prepared for academic success. They have achieved higher levels of literacy and background knowledge in their primary language and have a better understanding of how schools operate. With appropriate support in their second language development, these students quickly "catch up" to their native English-speaking peers (Freeman & Freeman, 2002).

While the LFS students come with the same positive expectations for their life in America, they not only have to learn conversational and academic English, but also have to play catch-up with their academic knowledge and skills and acclimate themselves to the organization and expectations of a formal schooling environment (Freeman & Freeman, 2002).

Long-term English learners have been in the United States for many years, often since birth, but English is usually not the primary language in their home. Often these students have picked up some conversational English, but they have had little exposure to the standard forms of English necessary to be successful in school. Furthermore, unlike the previous groups, LTELs have trouble navigating the different worlds of home and school: They have internalized mainstream values and see themselves as American, but at the same time they understand that they are not an accepted part of that mainstream. This may prevent LTELs from seeing themselves as learners.

Based on our experience, we would like to add a fourth category of ELLs, generational English learners (GELs). Their parents and grandparents speak English, but not the standard English learned in a supportive school classroom. GELs struggle with both the language of their heritage and with English, but are treated by the school system as native English speakers needing remediation.

Toward the transformative classroom

We view our job as not primarily to *transfer* knowledge but to create an environment in which it is possible to *construct* knowledge (Freire, 2000). It is not enough that our students leave our classroom with a lot of learned facts and skills. We want everyone in the classroom community to end the year *transformed*. We want our students to reenvision themselves as learners, redefine and/or refine how they impact their community, and begin thinking about how they can become active and critical members of a democratic society.

In working with our amazing students year after year we have developed six fundamental educational principles we think characterize the transformative classroom:

1. All students want to be connected to a classroom community that is predicated on positive relationships and they crave to be viewed as critical thinkers.

2. All students have value and bring with them funds of knowledge (Moll et al., 1992).

3. All students will thrive in an environment that is transformative and views its members as active seekers of meaning whose voices and opinions matter.

4. All students will flourish in an environment that sees errors as a natural part of the learning process and as a necessary component to growth.

5. All students want to be a part of the literacy club and yearn for a culturally relevant curriculum that brings value to their culture (Smith, 1998; Ladson-Billings, 1995).

6. All students will write and will seek to improve their writing when they see it as purposeful and more than just an academic exercise.

Deficits versus assets

Professor Barbara Flores of California State University at San Bernadino claims that whenever English language learners are discussed, a deficit perspective is usually the frame. In other words, the conversation rarely looks at the strengths of these students but focuses instead on what they lack and what teachers and schools need to "fix." This deficit perspective presupposes that language minorities are at a cognitive disadvantage because they are not native speakers of English.

After years of low expectations, red marks on the paper, and low or failing grades, students begin to see learning as unnatural, teachers as adversarial, and schools as unsafe.

The deficit perspective and its attendant assumptions often lead to what is known as "compensatory education," which attempts to teach the "basic skills" that these students seemingly lack. Diaz and Flores (2001) argue that this "leads teachers to organize instruction for poor and minority students at the 'lower' end of their abilities rather than at a level that maximizes their full potential" (p. 31). In this way, teachers create a cycle of low expectations that perpetuates school failure. Over several years of enduring this deficit perspective, students themselves begin to internalize the assumptions. After years of low expectations, red marks on the paper, and low or failing grades, students begin to see learning as unnatural, teachers as adversarial, and schools as unsafe.

To combat the effects of a deficit perspective, we focus on the strengths that students bring with them. All students arrive with a wealth of complex and valuable knowledge and experience. Moll and colleagues (1992) call this students' *funds of knowledge*. They explain that all households contain "historically accumulated and culturally developed bodies of knowledge and skills essential for household or individual functioning and well-being" (p. 133).

In classrooms that draw on the students' funds of knowledge as valuable classroom resources and that create a community of learners who share their lives and loves, their families and friends and beliefs, it is easy to get students to believe that writing is an important tool that has purpose in their lives. In this environment, with this depth of engagement, students will also begin to believe in the editing process. We think that writing with purpose and getting kids to believe that the process is important are fundamental to getting students to edit. Grades are poor motivators. Red marks are poor motivators. Instead, we work hard to ensure that everything students write not only draws on students' initial and expanding funds of knowledge but is engaging, has purpose, and is more than just something assigned by the teacher.

Lifting the burden of failure

Our learning community views its members as active seekers of meaning who will thrive when learning exists within a nurturing social context. Within our transformative classrooms, we build a love of language and a love of writing, and we discuss editing in the context of what the students are doing. We always begin with the big picture, ensuring that students are connected to something bigger than the task itself. We view writing as something as natural as breathing, and we deem everyone in the room a writer. We share what we write, we discuss what we write, and we actively examine and analyze what it is that great writers do well. Finally, we ensure that everything in our classrooms is positive and that meaning is always more important than form.

Rethinking "errors" and building on what students can do

It would be hard to imagine a time in education where the burden of failure weighed more heavily than it does right now. Unfortunately, the accountability movement has defined academic success as getting the most right answers. We feel that for writers to bloom, temporary "failure" must be seen as a necessary component of growth. When fixing errors becomes the focal point, we miss all the incredible things our students are doing and all the incredible growth they are experiencing. Donald Graves (1994) discusses what he sees as his most "traumatic failure" (p. 9) when, during his senior year of college, his professor failed to see through the errors to appreciate everything Graves had done well. Graves had poured his heart and soul into his senior thesis and the only comments on its pages were thirty-six highlighted errors, a note to change the ribbon on his typewriter, and a grade of D+. There was not a single note about the topic or the content. Graves, like a lot of students, felt "humiliated and defeated."

Graves' story illustrates how important it is to attend to the humanity of the writer—to respond to the writer first, then to the content of the writing, and only later to what might need to be revised or edited.

When we ignore effort, ignore growth, ignore the writer's soul, and place such a high premium on mechanics, the burden of failure becomes too much to bear for many of our students. This is not to say that we ignore the mechanics of language, but only that it is secondary to the message and must be taught with dignity and respect for the writer.

When we ignore effort, ignore growth, ignore the writer's soul, and place such a high premium on mechanics, the burden of failure becomes too much to bear for many of our students.

Connie Weaver (1996a) argues that errors are a natural part of language learning. As students grow older and more confident in their use of language, they begin to experiment with more sophisticated constructions. With more sophisticated constructions come new and maybe even old kinds of errors. English language learners are in the process of acquiring a new language and are going to make a great many errors in convention—errors that must be seen as important and necessary parts of the learning process. This has a major impact on the confidence of a burgeoning writer. Free to make errors, the burden of failure lifted, students will be more open to taking risks and attempting more sophisticated writing techniques and grammatical constructions. Once the writer takes those risks in a draft, we can step in as a mentor to move the writing toward standard conventions. The key is to view writing as a process that involves multiple drafts. It is expected that the first drafts will contain a number of errors because we are encouraging the student writer to experiment with language. This belief in experimentation and the willingness to allow for error will encourage growth (Weaver, 1996a).

Knowing this, we teachers need to reconsider how to deal with what is called "interlanguage" in students' writing.

Interlanguage and students' increasing command of English

English language learners will naturally exhibit interlanguage features—features that differ from, or do not exist in, a "standard" variety of English but that instead reflect the process of acquiring English as a second language (see Chapter 9). These features are evident in all stages of language acquisition and range in level of sophistication from basic features that resemble the early speech of children acquiring English as their first language to more sophisticated features and patterns transferred from ELLs' native language. Many features are creative and idiosyncratic.

As instructors we can respond to these language features and patterns in a variety of ways. First and foremost, we can view these features as either *errors* or evidence of new *learning*. Our stance determines how we guide students to switch to the standard grammatical forms, which in turn either hinders or empowers English language learners and their perceptions of themselves as writers.

Let's examine some interlanguage features of ELLs from a transformative perspective.

Vicky, a sophomore, wrote the following sentence when responding to a story: *She should of thought of the consequentes becaus I think that she was so dumb because I think she was so dumb beccaus why she gave an aborshen*. Her use of *of* instead of *have* is common in ELLs' writing and sometimes in the writing of our monolingual English students. *Because*, although overused, shows a writer who understands the use of conjunctions to introduce subordinate clauses. The sentence gets across the meaning Vicki wishes to convey but, more important, is an attempt at a complex structure. Yes, Vicky is still struggling with standard syntax and needs mentoring, but she is taking risks and it is important that we support those risks so she can continue to grow as a writer.

When asked to write about his name, Benny, a freshman, wrote: *I have a name that usually nobody has. And I like my name because I think is a good name but sometimes I think is emberessed.* The interlanguage features here show he is relying on his linguistic knowledge of Spanish syntax to write in English: *I have a name that usually nobody has.* When translated into Spanish, this is syntactically and grammatically correct, but in English the thought would be expressed as *I have an unusual name.* And again, even though Benny's sentence does not use proper English grammar, it still makes sense to the reader. The second sentence is that of a writer pushing the sophistication of his writing by using conjunctions (*because* and *but)* to craft a sentence with multiple clauses. A newcomer who immigrated to the United States two years ago after receiving adequate formal schooling in Spanish, Benny has shown significant growth in a short period.

Some of the most persistent interlanguage features are the omissions of the third-person singular and the regular past. According to Krashen's (2003) natural order hypothesis, these grammatical morphemes are typically the last to be acquired by second language learners. Musa, an AFS student from Iran whose primary language is Arabic, wrote this in response to Tupac Shakur's poem "The Rose That Grew from Concrete" (1999): *He say's that it grow on a concrete which means he grew up from a rough childhood.* While the sentence exhibits a variety of interlanguage issues, Musa makes three attempts at using the third-person singular. The first attempt (*say's*) suggests he is beginning to grasp the concept that when the noun is singular the verb needs the third-person singular morpheme, an *-s* or *-es* ending, but Benny has used an apostrophe *s*, as if the word were a possessive noun instead of a verb. In the next attempt, he completely abandons the rule and writes *it grow* instead of the standard form *it grows*. In the third attempt, *means,* he once again demonstrates that he is beginning to grasp this grammatical morpheme by using it correctly.

Here's Ricardo—a LTEL student whose primary language is Spanish—on the relationship between rock 'n' roll and racism: *By the way the black were the ones who invented rock-n-roll and jazz and they still didn't even respect them. But then white people start to copy black people by the songs they sanged.* Ricardo is beginning to experiment with using

Vicky and isolated instruction in English

Vicky attended kindergarten in Mexico and first through tenth grade in the United States. She feels most comfortable speaking Spanish and feels insecure when speaking, reading, and writing English. Sadly, Vicky doesn't have an academic grasp of either her primary language or her second language. She is very timid and speaks as little English as possible when participating in collaborative groups and sharing with the entire class. This insecurity is probably directly related to the pull-out instruction she received in English during elementary school. Immersion in her regular classrooms would have been much more effective. Her ELL label will haunt her until she graduates from high school, and she will struggle significantly if she decides to attend college.

The affective filter

Behaviorist approaches that concentrate on errors often lead to an increase in the "affective filter." Krashen's (2003) affective filter hypothesis says that "affective variables" will prohibit comprehensible input from reaching Chomsky's "language acquisition device" in the brain (1975). This means that when confidence is low and when anxiety and/or boredom are high, the ability to acquire language is significantly impaired. Therefore, a nurturing environment and cohesive classroom community are as important as the content and delivery of the lesson.

the regular past tense. In the first sentence, he establishes the tense with the use of the past plural form of *to be* and then correctly uses the regular past with *invented* as well as the correct irregular past didn't. However, in the next sentence he drops the *-ed* morpheme from *start* and overgeneralizes the rule on the irregular verb *sang*.

Both Musa and Ricardo are pushing their use of the English language. Their writing demonstrates that they are beginning to grasp standard forms of English, but they are still exhibiting idiosyncrasies common to ELLs. The stance that we as teachers take when we encounter these digressions is critical to our students' success and their ability to grow as writers.

Behavioral versus transformative approaches to interlanguage

We believe that success with ELL writers is difficult in a traditional setting where teachers see students as empty vessels and learning as memorization. Unfortunately, such principles and a behaviorist model of instruction are pervasive in the teaching of writing and editing. Writing in a behaviorist classroom is often broken down into a number of discrete skills to be memorized and practiced. Errors are emphasized.

Conversely, in a transformative classroom, the teacher is aware that students acquire language at their own pace and that they take risks with writing when they are in a comfortable and inviting environment. The transformative teacher is both a writing coach and a writer who shares his or her own process with the students. Such teachers are open about their own vulnerabilities as a writer and share their own successes and challenges with writing. In this environment, writing is natural and everyone is a writer. Most important, all students aspire to work on their individual craft because the writing is relevant. In this context, students are encouraged to share their writing with peers and grow at their individual pace with their writing.

The writing process

In our classrooms, writers and writing go through several phases, beginning with immersion in literature and literary models and culminating in celebration.

Immersion

For our students to view themselves as readers and writers, we must first immerse them in a literacy-rich environment connected to what we are studying. Writing does not occur in isolation; it involves careful layering of independent, whole-class, and small-group reading, writing, and reflecting (Short, Harste, & Burke, 1996). Immersion enriches student thinking, helps build vocabulary, provides models of writing, and helps students become better speakers, readers, and writers (Krashen, 2003; Allington, 2006).

With this in mind, we begin each year with a six- to eight-week identity unit designed solely to get to know our students as people and as learners. This unit is based on Gloria Ladson-Billings' (1995) theory that instructors must immerse students in reading that connects to their cultures. It incorporates ideas and activities from Linda Christensen's *Reading, Writing, and Rising Up* (2000) that build relationships with students through writing, reading, talking, and presenting based on who the students are—not on who we think they should be. The work done during this unit helps build a tight and safe classroom community, helps us as instructors get to know our students at a deeper level, and helps create the foundation for everything we will do for the rest of the year.

During this time, our students listen to us read aloud; participate in guided and choral readings; and respond to texts via artwork, written reflections, PowerPoint presentations, dramatizations, and group and whole-class discussions (Short, Harste, & Burke, 1996). We begin conversations about an author's purpose and call attention to text patterns they will later be able to recognize when they read independently. Most important, students make the connection that authors write for authentic purposes, and they begin to write their own texts, either emulating one of the mentor texts or venturing out on their own. They too become authors.

Using authors as models for our own writing

Once we have immersed our students in literacy-rich examples, we are ready to select a few to read more closely and use as models. The texts we choose mirror the writing we will ask our students to undertake. Our first reading focuses on the initial transaction that occurs between the reader and the text (Rosenblatt, 1978/1994): Students share their understanding of the text with one another. Then we move into the efferent response, looking at how authors use language in their writing. Katie Wood Ray (*Wondrous Words,* 1999) believes that we must learn to read as writers so we can emulate the author's craft in our own writing. Ray shows how she uses the authors her students read as the teachers of writing in her classroom. She begins the year by helping her students develop a love of reading and writing through the authors that they read. They spend the rest of the school year as critical readers and writers who look at authors as guides for their own writing.

We use these
authors to
celebrate language,
make personal
connections,
have great
conversations, ask
critical questions,
and write with
honesty and zeal.

In our freshman identity unit, we introduce our students to Maya Angelou, Sandra Cisneros, Tupac Shakur, George Ella Lyon, and Francisco Jiménez, among others. We use these authors to celebrate language, make personal connections, have great conversations, ask critical questions, and write with honesty and zeal. Initially, the class reads a piece from one of these authors closely and discusses the connections, thoughts, and feelings generated by the piece. We then reread the piece, asking, *What do we notice?* For example, while reading "My Name" (Cisneros, 1984/ 1991), the students noticed that Hope, the narrator in the piece, uses the words *nine* and *muddy* to describe her name. We created a class T-chart (two-column comparison chart) in which we copied these sentences on the left and identified the technique Cisneros was using—similes—on the right. We then examined other sentences that communicated how Hope truly feels about her name and how Cisneros conveyed this through her writing. At the end of our conversation, our T-chart was filled with numerous sentences that contained examples of the author's craft and the effect these techniques had on the reader.

Then we showed our students examples from Linda Christensen's *Reading, Writing, and Rising Up* and looked at the craft Linda's students used when writing about their name. We wanted our students to have as many examples as possible to refer to when they wrote about their name.

In our sophomore English classes, our students wrote about a particular food from their culture. As a precursor to their culminating piece—a restaurant review—we had them write a recipe for a favorite dish or a poem about something they loved to eat, and respond to various quick-write prompts. Each time we first looked at appropriate models. Before they wrote their recipes, we looked at a number of recipes. We had students read and respond to Jason's "Hot Dogs and Scrambled Eggs" (see Figure 15–1) before they wrote their own poem about their favorite food (Lily's poem, "Posole," is shown in Figure 15–2). While students were working on the recipe and poem, they were also reading restaurant reviews that had appeared in our local newspaper. We spent a lot of time looking at the craft involved in a restaurant review and attempting these techniques in quick-writes before our students wrote their restaurant reviews. (Later, in Figure 15–5, we offer an example of this culminating writing assignment.)

Prewriting/Drafting

After students have taken a deeper look at specific models for a particular kind of writing, they write a similar piece using these authors as their guides. They can rely heavily on the models or venture out on their own. Sometimes, specific prewriting activities are necessary to build their confidence so they feel ready to write an entire piece. Graves (1994) states,

Hot Dogs and Scrambled Eggs for Dinner

Hot Dogs and Scrambled Eggs
Mom, working hard raising three wild boys

Smelled of breakfast and barbecues
The color of Animal Kingdom's leopard
Squishy, hot rubber burning my tongue
Brothers laughing, eggs sizzling, and mom yelling
Tasted like childhood, carefree and innocent

Quick, working-class dinners shared with mom and brothers
Hot Dogs and Scrambled Eggs
      —by Jason Roche

FIGURE 15–1. Jason's poem, "Hot Dogs and Scrambled Eggs for Dinner"

"Sound teaching means that we show our children how to do things through our own demonstrations of learning" (p. 18). Graves prepares his students for success in writing by having them write lists, tap into a memory, and so forth. Once we have finished our prewriting activities, the students draft a written piece they will work on through the rest of the writing process.

Danni, a freshman, was a generational English learner. The primary language in her home was English, but her writing still exhibited some of the interlanguage features of LTELs. Her affective filter was also very high: She did not see herself as a writer and had had little previous success in her English classes. But students like Danni can succeed when their teachers provide enough support.

Danni decided to write her piece about her name without emulating the style of Sandra Cisneros' "My Name" (she needed to feel familiar and safe); nevertheless her first draft had a definite focus (see Figure 15–3). The topic was engaging enough that she wrote almost a full page. Despite her negative perceptions about herself as a writer, the relevance of the topic opened her up and the ideas poured out.

When Danni finished writing her draft, she was the first in her group to share. Her group, moved by what they heard, prompted her to share with the entire class. When she finished, the class clapped. Many students who had known Danni since elementary school were in shock, because they did not know the story of how she got her name. This response from her peers motivated Danni to pour her heart into this assignment and

FIGURE 15-2. Lily's poem, "Posole"

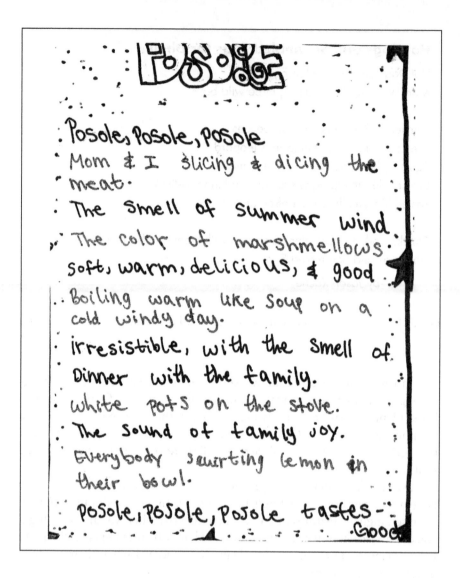

Posole, Posole, Posole
Mom & I slicing & dicing the meat.
The smell of summer wind
The color of marshmellows
soft, warm, delicious, & good.
Boiling warm like soup on a cold windy day.
irresistible, with the smell of.
Dinner with the family.
white pots on the stove.
The sound of family joy.
Everybody squirting lemon in their bowl.
Posole, Posole, Posole tastes—Good

readied her to move with willingness and hope to subsequent phases of the writing process.

A behaviorist model of teaching would have focused only on the grammatical errors in Danni's first draft, perhaps raising her affective filter and reinforcing her negative perceptions of herself as a writer. Fortunately, though, in a transformative classroom, Danni was beginning to see herself as a member of the literacy club and decided (with some nudging and guidance from her teacher) to take a risk and emulate Sandra Cisneros. A previously reluctant writer became the proud architect of her own masterpiece—see Danni's final draft in Figure 15-4.

Mark, a sophomore who had emigrated from the Philippines three years before, had received an excellent formal education there. His famil-

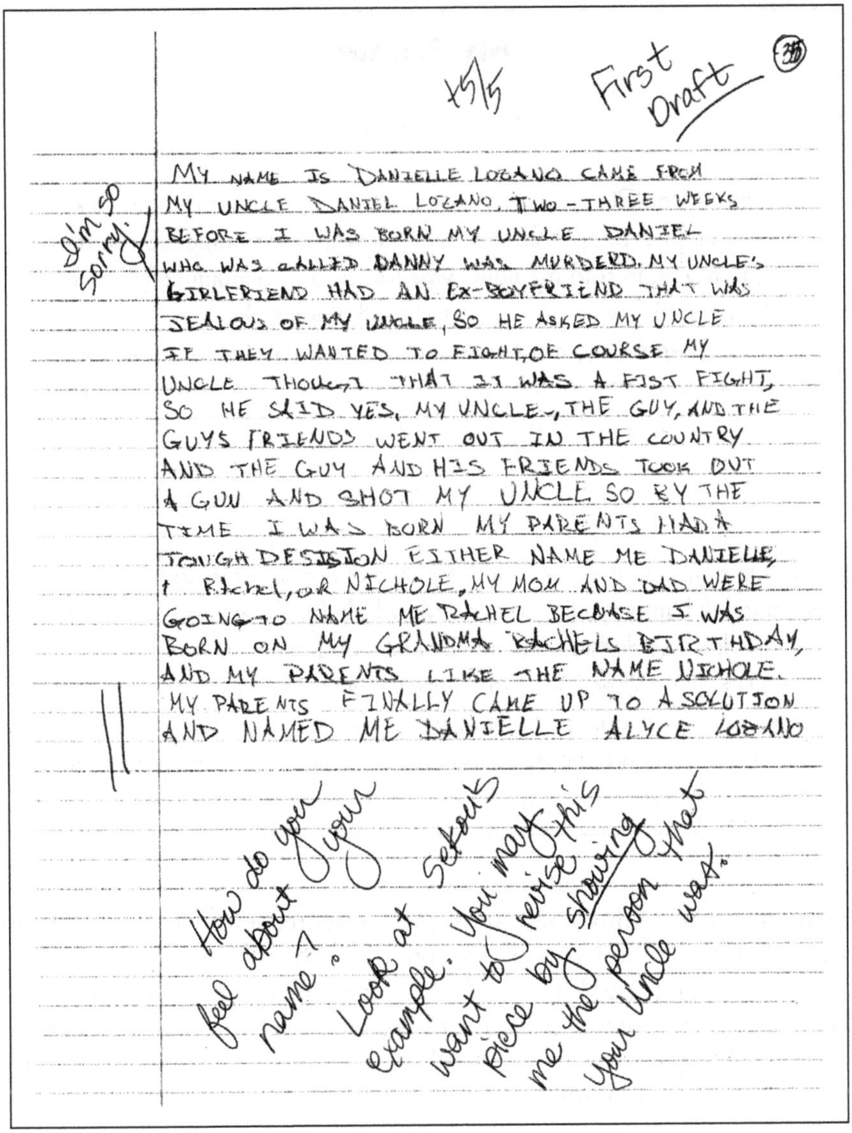

+5/5 First Draft 35

I'm so sorry.

MY NAME IS DANIELLE LOZANO CAME FROM MY UNCLE DANIEL LOZANO, TWO-THREE WEEKS BEFORE I WAS BORN MY UNCLE DANIEL WHO WAS CALLED DANNY WAS MURDERD. MY UNCLE'S GIRLFRIEND HAD AN EX-BOYFRIEND THAT WAS JEALOUS OF MY UNCLE, SO HE ASKED MY UNCLE IF THEY WANTED TO FIGHT, OF COURSE MY UNCLE THOUGHT THAT IT WAS A FIST FIGHT, SO HE SAID YES, MY UNCLE, THE GUY, AND THE GUYS FRIENDS WENT OUT IN THE COUNTRY AND THE GUY AND HIS FRIENDS TOOK OUT A GUN AND SHOT MY UNCLE SO BY THE TIME I WAS BORN MY PARENTS HAD A TOUGH DESISION EITHER NAME ME DANIELLE, Rachel, OR NICHOLE, MY MOM AND DAD WERE GOING TO NAME ME RACHEL BECAUSE I WAS BORN ON MY GRANDMA RACHELS BIRTHDAY, AND MY PARENTS LIKE THE NAME NICHOLE. MY PARENTS FINALLY CAME UP TO A SOLUTION AND NAMED ME DANIELLE ALYCE LOZANO

How do you feel about your name? Look at Sekou's example. You may want to revise this piece by showing me the person that your uncle was.

FIGURE 15–3. Danni's piece on her name, first draft

iarity with formal schooling and his content knowledge helped his English language acquisition considerably, and he performed academically at a level at or above his native-speaking classmates.

Mark and his classmates participated in numerous prewrites intended to prepare the students to write a restaurant review: listing their favorite places to eat, describing the ambience of a restaurant of their choice, drawing a picture of their favorite dish at a particular restaurant, and talking with classmates about restaurants they'd been to. Since we knew some of our students might not be able to afford to eat in restaurants, we included fast food places and our own school cafeteria among places to eat. To push

FIGURE 15-4.
Danni's piece on her
name, final draft

My Name

By: Danni Lozano

My name is Danielle Lozano. When I was a little girl I loved my nick-name Danni then people started saying it was boy's name. so I started hating it. My mom said my name was like a rose, beautiful and perfect, but I thought other wise. I was teased for the name Danni so I wanted to change it. Then my mom sat me down and told me that I had an uncle named Daniel Lozano and he had a nickname too and it was Danny. When she said that I thought, "Oh great I'm named after a boy!" Then my mom said that he was murdered three weeks before I was born. She also said that he was smart, brave, heroic, and loved everyone. My uncle was going to get in a fight for is girlfriend, but the guy that he was going to fight and the guy's friends pulled out guns in the fight and shot him and left him out in the country. My whole family was sad so my mom and my dad decided to name me Danielle and to carry on the name to remember him. When I went to school the next day the kids started teas-ing me again. I told them that they were just jealous because I was named Danielle and people called me Danni because I was named after somebody everybody loved. After that no one teased me again!

their writing to be more descriptive, we presented a minilesson in which we demonstrated how to use descriptive language.

Using what he had learned, Mark incorporated humor and descriptive language in his review (see Figure 15–5). His affective filter was lowered because of the time he got to spend thinking about the assignment and participating in prewriting activities that served as stepping stones. His acquisition of English progressed remarkably.

Revising

Once our students have an initial draft of their writing, we are ready to look at it in depth. Revision deals with changing the meaning, content, structure, or style of writing, and many times students confuse it with editing (Heard, 2003). At the beginning of the school year our students have a hard time revisiting the content of their writing because of their lack of experience in revising. Teaching revising, much like prewriting, involves careful layering of experiences to build student confidence in order to encourage them to take risks. Ultimately, the goal of revision is for the writer

Taco Bell Affordable & commendable

By Mark Labitad

Intro
Not everyone's heard of Taco Bell, except everybody. It's known for its Mexican Vibe, tacos, and burritos. Perhaps you've heard of someone who's "thinking outside the bun" and yelling "I'm full!!!" Taco Bell has always had something new for everybody. They have the new spicy crunch wrap, crunchy burrito, and all sorts of crunchy things.

- **Where is it?**
In front of Save Mart and beside Brook's Ranch. It's by the intersection of Manning and Buttonwillow. (1686 E. Manning Ave.)

- **When is it open?**
Open Late Night.

- **What do they serve?**
You could have the grilled stuffed burrito (chicken or steak) with authentic Mexican spice's that will spice up the night. If you're saving money try the ones in the value menu. For those of you who are on the diet savor the Caesar salad with its enticing ranch dressing. But if you want what I want here's my own combo meal = 1 grilled stuff burrito, 1 nacho and large Baja Blast. Baja Blast is a new soda from "Mountain Dew." This emerald colored drink has its own sweet blast that will refresh you. Baja Blast is only available at Taco Bell.

- **What can I get for 99 cents?**
For 99 cents you can get the half-pound burritos. If you just want to eat a little then try the 89 cents crunchy nachos with a cheesy cheese to go with it. Last but not least you could always stick with crunchy taco or soft taco for 99 cents. Be sure to check out the value menu for more information.

- **How's the drive-thru service?**
The service is of the hook. Your order is right on time. Good food at a fast pace. Taco Bell also has the "No question asks" replacement policy. So if there was a mistake on your order they will happily replace it with the right order.

- **How's the atmosphere?**
Taco Bell is not as crowded as you think it would be. So you could expect that there's a place for you. There's all kinds of people in there old, young, ugly, pretty, players, ballers, skaters and so on. But nonetheless, the atmosphere is always for real. The services are dizzle-grizzle for sizzle.

- **Anything else you should know?**
Do you know that Taco Bell has its own version of a fortune cookie? What you can do is grab a bunch of sauce and read the front side of the sauce pack. They have three kinds—Mild, Hot and Fire. Expect your fortune to make you "think outside the bun."

FIGURE 15–5. Mark's restaurant review

to convey what is in his or her heart to the reader (Heard, 2003), and the instructor's job is to facilitate this for students. Revising is key to student growth and can either empower our English language learners or raise their affective filter, depending on the approach we take.

When we first discuss and demonstrate revision in our classrooms, we make sure students are aware of the struggles that professional writers go through when revising their own pieces. This bolsters our students' self-esteem as writers and invites them to become a part of the revision process. Anne Lamott, in her book *Bird by Bird* (1994), refers to her initial drafts as "shitty first drafts" (p. 21). She believes that as authors we have to go through many drafts in order to reach a final piece. Our students love Lamott's phrase because of the curse word, but they also delight in the discovery that published writers go through the same hardships they do with their writing. Connecting with the struggles of professional writers, students begin to see a similarity between published writing and their own.

It is also crucial for students to see their instructors as writers and for instructors to share their personal struggles. We are honest with our students about how hard we find revision and share with them our numerous drafts of pieces we are writing. Once we have shared these examples, students are more willing to try revising their writing, because they see it as a process that all writers go through.

Once students realize that revision is a necessary component to any and all writing, we need to give them the necessary tools. The way we approach revision will affect the way our students perceive themselves as writers. It is invaluable for all students, especially English language learners, to see themselves as emerging writers preparing for publication. In our classroom we look for patterns in their writing that need revision, make a mental note of them, and develop minilessons that will invite students to look at the content of their piece with a new lens. In these minilessons we reexamine the models that have guided our writing, pay close attention to the craft, emphasize student writing that exhibits a particular skill, and attempt the skill together as a class. Once students have a grasp on the craft that the authors use, they are ready to revise their own pieces.

At the beginning of this school year, we asked our students to write a poem titled "I Come From," an activity suggested in Linda Christensen's *Reading, Writing, and Rising Up* (2000), in which students use items that define them to tell who they are. Leydi, an ELL with limited formal schooling, wrote an initial draft in which she listed items that were important to her. One line in her first draft, "I come from family albums," sounded generic because it was missing the extra detail that would reveal her individuality. Leydi's was not the only piece that lacked this extra detail, so we presented a minilesson in which we all—teachers and students—looked at the nouns in our pieces and how adding an extra detail improved the

It is invaluable for all students, especially English language learners, to see themselves as emerging writers preparing for publication.

writing (as emphasized in Chapters 5 and 6). As part of the minilesson we had the students look closely at George Ella Lyon's poem "Where I'm From" (1999) and the extra details that enhance her writing. We then had students look at the initial draft of a student's "I Come From" poem from the year before and compare it with his final draft, which included extra details. We also handed out a form on which students could write their original stanzas in the left column and their revised stanzas in the right column. The stanzas in the right column of Leydi's form definitely show her attempts at using sensory details (see Figure 15–6). Although there are some interlanguage issues in her revised draft, Leydi is moving through the writing process and showing improvement. Most important, she is taking risks with her writing, beginning to see herself as a writer, and letting go of the burden of failure that has haunted her for so long.

Editing

If the goal of revision is, as Heard (2003) writes, "to help our writing match more accurately what's in our hearts" (p. x), then it seems the goal of editing must be to ensure that our intended audience understands the message. For students to take editing seriously, they have to believe that it has purpose. This is what makes authentic writing tasks so valuable. When student writers have poured heart and soul into a piece that is meaningful to them, they will be more apt to see that editing is not a tedious, superfluous task required by the teacher as punishment, but a vital part of the process that helps the writer convey the intended message. Of course, purpose alone is not enough: Students need to see examples and they need to be taught strategies.

Undoubtedly, editing can be overwhelming, even for the most seasoned writers, and knowing where to begin can be difficult. We start with our students. Reading the students' drafts reveals matters of individual concern but also helps us determine issues that might be worth addressing with the entire class. However, even then it's hard to prioritize. There are so many rules to break and so many mistakes to make, or so it seems. Unfortunately, traditional models of instruction have sought simply to fix as many of those as possible.

Weaver (1996), like many experts in the teaching of writing, believes that we need to go in the opposite direction and narrow our focus to only a few basic grammatical concepts and terms. She also suggests that "it does not seem necessary for students to learn these terms themselves in order to see how to change what they have written to the structure or form expected in Edited American English" (p. 117). In other words, it is more important that students are able to do it than name it.

Furthermore, just because we teach a concept or rule does not necessarily mean that the student writers will be able to apply it in their own

Editing can be overwhelming, even for the most seasoned writers, and knowing where to begin can be difficult.

Original draft	Revised draft
Stanza 1 I am from old photo albums, T.V. from parents, and Toys.	I am from the old brown torned albums, from the black and white t.v. since that we have had for over 10yrs, and the old toys since I was 3yrs old. They are broken.
Stanza 2 I am from water hoes Laying down on the grass like a snake, and a old bike standing in a corner.	I am from water hoes laying down on the grass like a snake, and a bike thats about 6yrs. It just to be green, but now it looks like blue it's being standing in a corner.
Stanza 3 I am from the fights, old car never has moved in 5yrs, and kids playing around the neighborhood.	I am from the gangsters fights around the neighborhood, old car that never moves, it's green, flat tires, and broken windows, and kids playing tag or writing there bikes around the road.
Stanza 4 I am from family history such as my parents, Grandparents, and aunts.	I am from family that comes to the U.S. to have better life such as my parents, Grandparents, and aunts.

Marginal notes:
:)
How old? looks like?
How do they fight? what do they play?
Be specific

FIGURE 15–6. Leydi's original draft and final draft details

Stanza 5	
I am from ~~the sayings of my~~ ~~mom~~ "go and clean up your closet." and	I am from "go to your room and clean up your closet." and "do great in school."
Stanza 6	
I am from the nice smelling ~~carne~~ ~~asada, rice, and~~ ~~the posole.~~	I am from the nice smelling carne asada that we cook in our family reunions, rice that my moms cooks, and the posole my mom and relatives cook.
Stanza 7	
I am from the old photo albums, frames, and letters.	I am from the old photo albums, frames, letters, and
Stanza 8	

Add another line that shows how it applies to you

FIGURE 15–6. Continued

writing. Particularly with English language learners, if the grammatical construct being taught is beyond their level of language acquisition, they may understand the rule in the abstract but still fail to use it. In addition, we need to pay attention to what these writers are attempting. Sentences that on the surface seem to show a struggling writer instead demonstrate young writers taking risks based on their burgeoning understanding of their second language. As with every other part of the writing process, we must attend to our student writers' self-image. If editing becomes all about pointing out the writers' faults and if we fail to accept "failure" as a necessary component of growth, we risk raising the affective filter within the writers, thus stunting their growth.

We approach teaching grammar and/or editing with our young writers in two ways, both within the context of what the students are writing: (1) informal conversations and (2) group or class minilessons.

Informal editing conversations

As our young writers work through a series of drafts on their way to a published piece, we take advantage of critical teaching moments during informal conversations. Here are the procedures we've developed:

1. We read the students' papers, jotting down on sticky notes strengths as well as areas that may need editing. We focus on one or two interlanguage patterns that dominate the writing. With a pencil, we mark the text that we want students to read aloud in a conference.

2. In the conference, we go over the entire paper, making positive comments about the writing. We praise the students for risks they've taken, their attempts at revision, and the overall ideas they have communicated. The focus is on content, and we make it a point to praise students for what they are doing well.

3. We ask the students to read an excerpt from their writing out loud (the part we've chosen beforehand that shows a grammatical mistake or an interlanguage feature). Usually, once students read their writing out loud they notice the feature that needs to be changed and change it right then and there.

4. When students do not recognize the grammatical feature, we have them reread the sentence out loud again and ask: "Does this make sense? Does what you wrote here sound like language?"

5. If students are struggling, we ask, "Is there a way to rewrite this so that it makes sense?" Usually our students are quick to state how they would rewrite the sentence. But if they are still struggling, together we come up with a new way to edit the writing.

6. We then read the initial sentence and the new sentence and ask, "Does the new sentence you [we] came up with make more sense? What do you notice?"

7. Then we usually review the concept we are trying to get across (the use of conjunctions, for example, or the consistent and conventional use of past tense).

We select what we review with our students very carefully. Some students face a seemingly insurmountable number of grammatical issues, but we review only one or two features of their writing during a conference. We want our students to continue to write, and we know some of the desired features will appear naturally as they acquire English over time. We also remind them how important reading is to their English language development and suggest more books for them to read independently. We want to empower our students, not raise their affective filter.

These conversations are fast and easy, but they are important because they are specifically related to the student's own writing. That is not to say that the same student will not continue to make the same kinds of "errors"—or use the same interlanguage features—in the future. We may need to have the same kind of conversation several times over the course of the year before a student begins to apply the rule correctly. In part, this demonstrates that learners must indeed form concepts for themselves.

Group or class minilessons

When we begin to notice a global issue in the writing of many students— a group or the whole class—we develop a minilesson designed to meet that need. The following minilesson addresses the standard use of subordinate clauses. (The format is partially based on Weaver's [2007] "Idealized Framework for Teaching Grammatical Concepts" [see Chapter 4 here] and her lesson on adverbial clauses.)

Minilesson on Subordinate Clauses

1. *Share a model:* Using the front page of *The Fresno Bee*, we pull out a couple of obvious examples of subordinate clauses, write down the sentences and the different clauses on a three-column chart, and ask the students to discuss what they are noticing.

Sentence	Independent Clause	Subordinate Clause

2. *Name it:* At this point, we like to name what it is the author is doing. In other words, we provide the students with the definitions

for the concepts of independent and subordinate clauses. We also discuss the importance of complex sentences.

3. *Create another model:* We provide the students with examples of common subordinating conjunctions. Then as a class, we look for a few more examples from the newspaper (or whatever text has been chosen as a model), eliciting a little more participation from the students. We add to the chart as they find more examples.

Time	Cause	Condition	Contrast
after, as, as soon as, before, since, till, until, when, while	as, because, in order that, since, so that	as if, assuming that, if, in case, unless, when, whether	although, even though, rather than, though, whereas, while

4. *Releasing responsibility:* Students keep working on the chart, in groups or with a partner. We wander from group to group, ensuring that students understand what is being asked of them and answering any questions that arise.

5. *Applying it to writing:* Students (perhaps with a partner) look for examples in their drafts of sentences that use subordinate clauses and determine whether they are written correctly and punctuated conventionally. They might also look for simple sentences to combine into complex ones. Again, we wander through the room, guiding students who have questions or confusions.

The goal of the informal writing conversations and the minilessons is to introduce students to more standard forms of academic English, but we must always recognize that students will acquire these forms when they are ready. We make our decisions based on what we think the students need as opposed to a generic scope-and-sequence chart. And we always teach the constructs in the context of the students' own writing, thus creating a sense of purpose and meaning. Students flourish in this environment and are eager to celebrate their achievements.

Celebrating

The final part of the writing process, sharing and celebrating, is one of the most exciting. Obviously, students' willingness to share has to develop over time. As the community is built week by week, students become more and more comfortable sharing. For many, it is the first time anyone has heard them read their own writing. The room becomes very quiet as the emerging writers expose their thoughts, feelings, and experiences to the class.

At the beginning of the year some students, especially the English language learners, are timid and embarrassed to read aloud. We begin by setting up some guidelines about mutual respect. We also love to quote author and poet Alma Flor Ada who, during her keynote at the California Association of Bilingual Educators, said, "Just because I speak with an accent doesn't mean I think with one." Usually some of the "English only" students are amazed by what the ELLs have written. They might have been in classes with the ELLs for years but never heard them open their mouths. Suddenly they have a voice—and immediately a bond is created. At a Rethinking Schools workshop at UCLA, Linda Christensen told us that one of her students had said, "When you know someone's story, you can't hate them." That quote exemplifies the power of writing with students—especially those who are learning the language or who have been marginalized for too long. They begin to experience and understand this line from Maya Angelou's poem "The Human Family" (1990): *We are more alike my friends than we are unalike.*

Another way to celebrate the author is to create a portfolio. Students have a binder of their finished pieces that stays in the classroom on a bookshelf. (The students' names are on the spines for easy identification.) Students feel like real authors because anyone who visits the classroom can read their writing. For too long, students have felt that their only audience is the teacher. Having their writing accessible to a wider audience encourages students to take pride in their work and experience firsthand the transaction that occurs between the author, the text, and the reader (Mason, 1997).

We'll close by sharing a memorable experience. On the last day of class last spring, we decided to have an "Author's Café." Around a table holding an urn full of hot water, instant cappuccino mix, and pastries, students took turns sharing their final writing piece, a description of an autobiographical incident taking place within a twenty-four-hour period.

We listened to amazing narratives loaded with an explosion of sensory details. We sat quietly as Will, the class clown, read about his grandmother dying of cancer and burst into tears. The class "thug" looked for tissue to give to Will as rest of the class comforted him and shared in his pain. We sat shocked as Jen read about her ex-boyfriend telling her he preferred boys and wanted to break up with her. We thought our ears must be deceiving us when we heard 4.0 student Dee read about her battle with depression and her attempted suicide. The Chinese character for listening includes three symbols—ears, eyes, and heart—and we were listening in all those ways.

This celebration of writing could not have been realized if the focus of our classes had been worksheets, formulaic essay writing, and avoiding errors. It was the result of transformative classrooms in which the teachers believe that all students can read, write, view, and think. In the right environment, all students can be a part of what Frank Smith calls the literacy club.

Allington, R. (2006). *What really matters for struggling readers: Designing research-based programs.* Boston: Pearson.

Alsup, J., & Bush, J. (2003). *"But will it work with REAL students?" Scenarios for teaching secondary English language arts.* Urbana, IL: National Council of Teachers of English.

Anderson, J. (2005). *Mechanically inclined: Building grammar, usage, and style into writer's workshop.* Portland, ME: Stenhouse.

———. (2006, May). "Zooming in and zooming out: Putting grammar in context into context." *English Journal,* 28–34.

———. (2007a). *Everyday editing: Inviting students to develop skills and craft in writer's workshop.* Portland, ME: Stenhouse.

———. (2007b). *The craft of grammar* [DVD]. Portland, ME: Stenhouse.

Anderson, P. (1997). *A Grand Canyon journey: Tracing time in stone.* New York: Franklin Watts.

Andrews, R., Torgerson, C., Beverton, S., Freeman, A., Locke, T., Low, G., Robinson, A., & Zhu, D. (2004a). The effect of grammar teaching (sentence combining) in English on 5 to 16 year olds' accuracy and quality in written composition. In *Research Evidence in Education Library.* London: EPPI-Centre, Social Science Research Unit, Institute of Education.

Andrews, R., Torgerson, C., Beverton, S., Locke, T., Low, G., Robinson, A., & Zhu, D. (2004b). The effect of grammar teaching (syntax) in English on 5 to 16 year olds' accuracy and quality in written composition. In *Research Evidence in Education Library.* London: EPPI-Centre, Social Science Research Unit, Institute of Education.

Angelou, M. (1990). *I shall not be moved.* New York: Random House.

———. (1994). *The complete collected poems of Maya Angelou.* New York: Random House.

Applebee, A. N., Langer, J. A., Mullis, I., Jenkins, L. B., Mullis, I. V. S., & Foertsch, M. A. (1990). *Learning to write in our nation's schools: Instruction and achievement in 1988 at grades 4, 8, and 12.* Princeton, NJ: Educational Testing Service.

Aristotle. (1991). *On rhetoric.* Trans. G. A. Kennedy. New York: Oxford Univ. Press.

Arntz, W., Chasse, B., & Vicente, M. (2005). *What the bleep do we know!?* Deerfield Beach, FL: Heath Communications.

Associated Press. (2002). *Associated press stylebook and briefing on media law.* New York: Associated Press.

Atwell, N. (1996). *In the middle.* Portsmouth, NH: Heinemann.

———. (2002). *Lessons that change writers.* Portsmouth, NH: Heinemann.

Bain, A. (1866). *English composition and rhetoric.* London: Longmans, Green, and Co.

Baker, S., & Yarber, R. E. (1997). *The practical stylist, with readings.* 8th ed. New York: Harper & Row.

Barnes & Noble. (2004). *Webster's guide to English usage.* New York: Barnes & Noble.

Baugh, J. (2000). Racial identification by speech. *American Speech, 75*(4), 362–364.

Beal, J. (2004). *English in modern times: 1700–1945.* London: Hodder.

Beer, E. H. (1999). *The Nazi officer's wife: How one Jewish woman survived the Holocaust.* New York: Harper Perennial.

Bodanis, D. (1986). *The secret house: The extraordinary science of an ordinary day.* New York: Berkley Books.

Britton, J., et al. (1975). *The development of writing abilities (11–18).* London: Macmillan Education.

Brown, H. D. (1987). *Principles of language learning and teaching.* (2nd ed.). Englewood Cliffs, NJ: Prentice Hall Regents.

Brown, R. (1973). *A first language: The early stages.* Cambridge, MA: Harvard University Press.

Calhoun, D. (1999). *Firegold.* Delray Beach, FL: Winslow.

Calkins, L. M. (1980). When children want to punctuate: Basic skills belong in context. *Language Arts, 57,* 567–573.

———. (1983). *Lessons from a child.* Portsmouth, NH: Heinemann.

———. (1986). *The art of teaching writing.* Portsmouth, NH: Heinemann.

———. (1994). *The art of teaching writing.* (2nd ed.) Portsmouth, NH: Heinemann.

Campione, J. (1981). Learning, academic achievement, and instruction. Paper presented at the second annual conference on Reading Research of the Center for the Study of Reading, New Orleans, April.

Carroll, J. A., & Wilson, E. E. (1993). *Acts of teaching: How to teach writing.* Englewood Cliffs, NJ: Teacher Idea Press.

Carroll, L. (1979). *The complete works of Lewis Carroll.* New York: Modern Library. (Original work published 1936.)

Cazort, D. (1997). *Under the grammar hammer: The 25 most important grammar mistakes and how to avoid them.* (2nd ed.). Los Angeles: Lowell House.

Charity, A., Scarborough, H., & Griffin, D. (2004). Familiarity with school English in African-American children and its relation to early reading achievement. *Child Development, 75*(5), 1340–1356.

Chomsky, N. (1957). *Syntactic structures.* The Hague: Mouton.

———. (1965). *Aspects of the theory of syntax.* Cambridge, MA: MIT Press.

———. (1975) *Reflections on language.* New York: Pantheon Books.

Christensen, F. (1965). A generative rhetoric of the sentence. *College Composition and Communication, 16*(3), 144–156. Reprinted in Christensen 1967 and in Christensen & Christensen 1978.

———. (1967). *Notes toward a new rhetoric: Six essays for teachers.* New York: Harper & Row. Included in Christensen & Christensen, 1978.

Christensen, F., & Christensen, B. (1978). *Notes toward a new rhetoric: Nine essays for teachers.* (2nd ed.). New York: Harper & Row. Includes Christensen, 1967.

Christensen, L. (2000). *Reading, writing and rising up*. Milwaukee, WI: Rethinking Schools.

Cisneros, S. (1991). *The house on Mango Street*. New York, NY: Vintage Books. (Original work published 1984.)

College Board. (2006). Strategies for success on the SAT essay. Retrieved December 15, 2006, from: http://www.collegeboard.com/student/testing/sat/prep_one/sat_essay.html.

Collerson, J. (1994). *English grammar: A functional approach*. Newtown, NSW, Australia: Primary English Teaching Association.

Conference on College Composition and Communication. (1988). The national language policy (position statement). Urbana, IL: National Council of Teachers of English. Retrieved from: http://www.ncte.org/cccc/resources/positions/123796.htm.

Connors, R. J., & Lunsford, A. (1988). Frequency of formal errors in current college writing, or Ma and Pa Kettle do research. *College Composition and Communication, 39*, 395–409.

Corder, S. P. (1967). The significance of learners' errors. *International Review of Applied Linguistics, 5*(4), 161–170.

Cruise, R. (1993). *The nuclear disaster at Chernobyl*. Buena Park, CA: Artesian Press.

Culham, R. (2003). *6 + 1 traits of writing: The complete guide grades 3 and up*. New York: Scholastic.

Delpit L. & K. J. Dowty (Eds.) (2002). *The skin that we speak: Thoughts on language and culture in the classroom*. New York: New Press.

Diaz, E., & Flores, B. (2001). Teacher as sociocultural, sociohistorical mediator: Teaching to the potential. In M. Reyes & J. Halcon (Eds.), *The best for our children* (pp. 29–47). New York: Teachers College Press.

Dillard, J. L. (1972). *Black English*. New York: Random House.

DiStefano, P., & Killion, J. (1984). Assessing writing skills through a process approach. *English Education, 16*, 203–207.

Doctorow, E. L. (2005). *The march*. New York: Random House.

Dulay, H., & Burt, M. (1974a). Natural sequences in child second language acquisition. *Language Learning, 24*, 37–53.

Dulay, H., & Burt, M. (1974b). You can't learn without goofing. In J. Richards (Ed.), *Error analysis: Perspectives on second language acquisition* (pp. 95–123). London: Longman.

Dulay, H., & Burt, M. (1975). Creative construction in second language learning and teaching. In M. Burt & H. Dulay (Eds.), *On TESOL '75: New directions in second language learning, teaching and bilingual education* (pp. 21–32). Washington, DC: Teachers of English to Speakers of Other Languages.

Dupré, J. (1997). *Bridges: A history of the world's most famous and important spans*. New York: Black Dog & Leventhal.

Ehrenreich, B. (2001). *Nickel and dimed*. New York: Henry Holt.

Elley, W. B. (1991). Acquiring literacy in a second language: The effect of book-based programs. *Language Learning, 41*, 375–411.

Elley, W. B., Barham, I. H., Lamb, H., & Wyllie, M. (1976). The role of grammar in a secondary English curriculum. *Research in the Teaching of English, 10*, 5–21.

(Reprinted from *New Zealand Journal of Educational Studies*, May 1975, *10*, 26–42.)

Elley, W. B., & Mangubhai, F. (1983). The impact of reading on second language learning. *Reading Research Quarterly, 19*, 53–67.

Erskine, J. (1946). *Twentieth century English.* (A 1970 edition, edited by W. Knickerbocker, was published by Ayer, Manchester, NH.)

Fairclough, N. (1989). *Language and power.* New York: Longman.

Farrell, E. J. (1971). *Deciding the future: A forecast of responsibilities of secondary teachers of English, 1970–2000 A. D.* (Research Report No. 12). Urbana, IL: National Council of Teachers of English.

Fletcher, R. (1993). *What a Writer Needs.* Portsmouth, NH: Heinemann.

———. (1996). *A Writer's Notebook.* New York, NY: Harper Trophy.

Fogel, H., & Ehri, L. C. (2000). Teaching elementary students who speak Black English Vernacular to write in standard English: Effects of dialect transformation practice. *Contemporary Educational Psychology, 25*, 212–235.

Francis, W. N. (1958). *The structure of American English.* New York: Ronald Press.

Freedman, R. (1991). *The Wright brothers: How they invented the airplane.* New York: Holiday House.

Freeman, Y. S., & Freeman, D. E. (1998). *ESL/EFL teaching: Principles for success.* Portsmouth, NH: Heinemann.

Freeman, Y. S., & Freeman, D. E. (2002). *Closing the achievement gap.* Portsmouth, NH: Heinemann.

Freire, P. (2000). *Pedagogy of the oppressed.* NY: Continuum.

Fries, C. C. (1952). *The structure of English.* New York: Harcourt, Brace.

Fu, D. (1995). *"My trouble is my English": Asian students and the American dream.* Portsmouth, NH: Boynton/Cook.

Gámez, L. A. (2006, September–October). The fabricated cosmonaut and the nonexistent prophecy. *Skeptical Inquirer, 30*(5), 12

Garner, B. (2002). *The Oxford English dictionary of American usage and style.* Oxford: Oxford University Press.

Gass, S. M., & Selinker, L. (2001). *Second language acquisition: An introductory course.* (2nd ed.). Mahwah, NJ: Erlbaum.

Gee, J. P. (1992). *The social mind: Language, ideology, and social practice.* New York: Bergin & Garvey.

Gillette, J. L. (1997). *Dinosaur ghosts: The mystery of coelophysis.* Illus. D. Henderson. New York: Penguin.

Goodman, K., & Goodman, Y. (1978). *Reading of American children whose language is a stable rural dialect of English or a language other than English.* Final report, Project NIE-C-00-3-0087. Washington, DC: U.S. Department of Health, Education, and Welfare.

Graves, D. H. (1994). *A fresh look at writing.* Portsmouth, NH: Heinemann.

Graves, D. H.(2006). *A sea of faces.* Portsmouth, NH: Heinemann.

Green, L. (2002). *African American English: A linguistic introduction.* Cambridge, UK: Cambridge University Press.

Griswold, E. (2006, September) American gulag: Prisoners' tales from the war on terror. *Harper's, 313*(1876), 41–50.

Hairston, M. (1981). Not all errors are created equal: Nonacademic readers in the professions respond to lapses in usage. *College English, 43*, 794–806.

Halliday, M. A. K. (1985). *An introduction to functional grammar*. London: Edward Arnold.

Harris, M., & Rowan, K. E. (1989). Explaining grammatical concepts. *Journal of Basic Writing, 8*(2), 21–41.

Hartwell, P. (1985). Grammar, grammars, and the teaching of grammar. *College English, 47*, 105–127.

Hartwell, P., & LoPresti, G. (1985). Sentence combining as kid watching. In D. A. Daiker, A. Kerek, & M. Morenberg (Eds.). *Sentence combining: A rhetorical perspective* (pp. 107–126). Carbondale, IL: Southern Illinois Press.

Haussamen, B. (2000). *Revising the rules: Traditional grammar and modern linguistics*. (2nd ed.). Dubuque, IA: Kendall/Hunt.

Haussamen, B., with Benjamin, A., Kolln, M., & Wheeler, R. S. (2003). *Grammar alive! A guide for teachers*. Urbana, IL: National Council of Teachers of English.

Heard, G. (2002). *The Revision Toolbox*. Portsmouth, NH: Heinemann.

Hillocks, G., Jr. (1986). *Research on written composition: New directions for teaching*. Urbana, IL: National Council of Teachers of English.

Hoffman, E. (1989). *Lost in translation: A life in a new language*. New York: Penguin.

Hunt, A. (2006, December 19). Brandon Banks is 6 years old: He's trying to save his sister's life. *Detroit News*.

Huntsman, J. F. (1983). Grammar. In D. LO. Wagner (Ed.), *The seven liberal arts in the Middle Ages* (pp. 58–95). Bloomington: Indiana University Press.

Hurston, N. Z. (1991). *Their eyes were watching God*. New York: HarperPerennial. (Original work published 1937.)

Juriaan, J. (2007). Stylistic writing. Retrieved January 2007 from: www.jjuriaan.com/Stylistic_Writing.htm.

Kantz, M., & Yates, R. (1994). Whose judgments? A survey of faculty responses to common and highly irritating writing errors. [Online]. Paper presented at the Fifth Annual Conference of the NCTE Assembly for the Teaching of English Grammar. Retrieved May 20, 2006 from: www.ateg.org/conferences/c5/kantz.htm

Killgallon, D., & Killgallon, J. (2006). *Grammar for middle school: A sentence-composing approach*. Portsmouth, NH: Heinemann.

———. (2007). *Grammar for high school: A sentence-composing approach*. Portsmouth, NH: Heinemann.

King, M. L., Jr. (1997). *I have a dream*. Illus. Kathleen A. Wilson. New York: Scholastic. (Speech presented August 28, 1963.)

King, S. (2000). *On writing: A memoir of the craft*. New York: Pocket Books.

Kinneavy, J. (1980). *A theory of discourse*. New York: Norton.

Kiviat, B. (2006, September 11). Investing by the numbers. *Time, 168*(11), 83.

Klein, G. W. (1995). *All but my life*. New York: Hill and Wang. (Original work published 1957.)

Kohl, H. (1991). *I won't learn from you! The role of assent in learning*. Minneapolis: Milkweed Editions.

Kolln, M. (2006). *Rhetorical grammar: Grammatical choices, rhetorical effects*. (5th ed.). New York: Longman.

Kozol, J. (2005). *The shame of the nation*. New York: Pantheon Books.

Krashen, S. D. (1981). *Second language acquisition and second language learning*. Oxford: Pergamon Press.

———. (1982). *Principles and practice in second language acquisition*. New York: Pergamon Press.

———. (1985). *The input hypothesis: Issues and implications*. New York: Longman.

———. (1997). *Foreign language education the easy way*. Culver City, CA: Language Education Associates.

———. (2003). *Explorations in language acquisition*. Portsmouth, NH: Heinemann.

———. (2004). *The power of reading: Insights from the research*. Westport, CT: Libraries Unlimited.

Kroll, B., & Schafer, J. (1978). Error analysis and the teaching of composition. *College Composition and Communication, 29*, 242–248.

Kroll, S. (1994). *Lewis and Clark: Explorers of the American West*. Illus. R. Williams. New York: Holiday House.

Labov, W. (1972). *Language in the inner city: Studies in the Black English Vernacular*. Philadelphia: University of Pennsylvania.

Lacayo, R. (2006, September 11). As sharp as it gets. *Time*, 77–78.

Ladson-Billings, G. (1995). Toward a theory of culturally relevant pedagogy. *American Educational Research Journal, 32*(3), 415–421.

Lamott, A. (1994). *Bird by bird*. New York: Pantheon Books.

Larson, M. (1996). Watch your language: Teaching standard usage to resistant and reluctant learners. *English Journal, 85*(7), 91–95.

Lasky, K. (1994). *The librarian who measured the earth*. Illus. K. Hawkes. Boston: Little, Brown.

Lester, M., & Beason, L. (2005). *The McGraw-Hill handbook of English grammar and usage*. New York: McGraw-Hill.

Levi, P. (1996). *Survival in Auschwitz*. New York: Touchstone.

Lippi-Green, R. (1997). *English with an accent: Language, ideology, and discrimination in the United States*. New York: Routledge.

Loban, W. D. (1976). *Language development: Kindergarten through grade twelve*. (Research Report No. 18). Urbana, IL: National Council of Teachers of English.

Lowry, L. (1993). *The Giver*. Boston: Houghton Mifflin.

———. (2000). *Gathering blue*. Boston: Houghton Mifflin.

———. (2004). *Messenger*. Boston: Houghton Mifflin.

Lowth, R. (1967). *A short introduction to English grammar: With critical notes*. Menston, England: The Scholar Press Limited. (Original work published 1762.)

Ludlum, R. (2001). *The sigma protocol*. New York: St. Martin's.

Lunsford, A. A. (2003). *The St. Martin's handbook*. (5th ed.). Boston: Bedford/St. Martin's.

Lyon, G. (1999). *Where I'm from: Where poems come from*. Spring, TX: Absey.

Macauley, W. J. (1947). The difficulty of grammar. *British Journal of Educational Psychology, 17*, 153–162.

Mack, J. (2006, December 17). Kalamazoo school superintendent, Smooth handoff essential. *Kalamazoo Gazette*, A1.

Mackey, A. (1999). Input, interaction, and second language development. *Studies in Second Language Acquisition, 21*, 557–587.

MacLure, M. (2005). "Clearly bordering on stupidity": Where's the quality in systemic review? *Journal of Educational Policy, 20*(4), 393–416.

MacNeil, R., & Cran, W. (2005). *Do you speak American? A companion to the PBS television series*. New York: Doubleday.

Macrorie, K. (1988). *The I-search paper.* (Rev. ed. of *Searching writing.*) Portsmouth, NH: Boynton/Cook.

Maddox, B. (2006, October) Who's freaky now? How abhorrence and attraction affect our bioethical judgment. *Discover*, 28–29.

"Magnificent animals." (2006, December 17). *Kalamazoo Gazette*, A4.

Magorian, M. (1981). *Good night, Mr. Tom.* New York: HarperCollins.

Mailer, N. (1975). *The fight.* Boston: Little, Brown.

Marzano, R., Pickering, D., & Pollock, J. (2001). *Classroom instruction that works: Research-based strategies for increasing student achievement.* Alexandria, VA: Association for Supervision and Curriculum Development.

Mason, R. J. (1997). *An inquiry into the transactional nature of text: The learning edge binder.* Fresno, CA: Fresno Pacific University.

Mason, W. (2006, December 18). The master of Malgudi: The fiction of R. K. Narayan. *The New Yorker*, 86–91.

McCrum, R., Cran, W., & MacNeil, R. (2003). *The story of English.* New York: Penguin Books.

McKissack, P. C. (1986). *Flossie and the fox.* Illus. R. Isadora. New York: Scholastic.

McQuade, F. (1980). Examining a grammar course: The rationale and the result. *English Journal, 69*, 26–30.

Menand, L. (2004, June 28). Bad comma: Lynne Truss's strange grammar. *The New Yorker.*

Michigan Educational Assessment Program. (1997). Released anchor papers, High School Proficiency Test. Communication arts: Writing. ED 429 317.

Michigan State Board of Education. (1994). *Assessment Frameworks for the Michigan High School Proficiency Test in Communication Arts. Part I: Writing.* Prepared by the Michigan Council of Teachers of English. E. H. Brinkley, Project Manager. Lansing. (Printed in the *Michigan English Teacher*, May 1993, a publication of the MCTE.)

Moll, L., Amanti, C., Neff, D., & Gonzalez, N. (1992). Funds of knowledge for teaching: Using a qualitative approach to connect homes and classrooms. *Theory into Practice, 31*(2), 132.

Monaghan, C. (1998). *The Murrays of Murray Hill.* Brooklyn, NY: Urban History Press.

Morrison, T. (2003). *Love.* New York: Knopf.

Munsch, R. N. (1980). *The paper bag princess.* Illus. M. Martchenko. Toronto: Annick Press.

Murray, L. (1795). *English grammar.* York, England: Wilson, Spence, and Mawman.

National Assessment of Educational Progress (NAEP). (2002). *The Nation's Report Card.* Retrieved from the National Center for Education Statistics: http://nces.ed.gov/nationsreportcard/.

Nelson, N. W., Bahr, C. M., & Van Meter, A. M. (2004). *The writing lab approach to language instruction and intervention.* Baltimore: Paul Brookes.

Nickell, J. (2006, September/October) Ghost hunters. *Skeptical Inquirer, 30*(5), 26.

Noden, H. (1999). *Image grammar: Using grammatical structures to teach writing.* Portsmouth, NH: Boynton/Cook.

———. (2007). *Image grammar activities book.* Logan, IA: Perfection Learning.

Noguchi, R. R. (1991). *Grammar and the teaching of writing: Limits and possibilities.* Urbana, IL: National Council of Teachers of English.

O'Conner, P. T. (2003). *Woe is I: The grammarphobe's guide to better English in plain English.* (2nd ed.). New York: Riverhead Books.

O'Donnell, R. C., Griffin, W. J., & Norris, R. C. (1967). *Syntax of kindergarten and elementary school children: A transformational analysis.* (Research Report No. 8). Urbana, IL: National Council of Teachers of English.

Ogbu, J. (1992). Adaptation to minority status and impact of school success. *Theory into Practice, 31*(4), 287.

Olson, J. (1992). *Envisioning writing: Toward an integration of drawing and writing.* Portsmouth, NH: Heinemann.

Paulsen, G. (1991). *Hatchet.* New York: Puffin.

———. (1999). *Dogsong.* New York: Bradbury Press.

Payne, L. V. (1975). *The art of lively writing.* New York: Penguin.

Pearson, D., & Gallagher, M. C. (1983). The instruction of reading comprehension. *Contemporary Educational Psychology, 8*(3), 317–344.

Pilkey, D. (1997). *The adventures of Captain Underpants.* New York: Scholastic.

Pinker, S. (1994). *The language instinct: How the mind creates language.* New York: HarperCollins.

Plait, P. (2006, September/October). Name dropping: Want to be a star? *Skeptical Inquirer, 30*(5), 51–54.

Poe, E. A. (1843/1975). The tell-tale heart. In *The complete tales and poems* (pp. 303–306). New York: Viking.

Provost, G. (2001). *Make your words work: Proven techniques for effective writing.* Lincoln, NE: iUniverse.

Pullman, P. (2005, January 22). It's time English teachers got back to basics—less grammar, more play. *The Guardian.* [Online]. Retrieved October 6, 2006, from: http://www.guardian.co.uk.

Pullum, G. (1999). African American Vernacular English is not standard English with mistakes. In R. S. Wheeler (Ed.), *The workings of language: From prescriptions to perspectives* (pp. 59–66). Westport, CT: Praeger.

Putnam, J. (2006, December 17). Impact of affirmative-action ban unfolding. *Kalamazoo Gazette*, A1.

Putz, M. (2006). *A teacher's guide to the multigenre research project: Everything you need to know to get started.* Portsmouth, NH: Heinemann.

Raimes, A. (2005). Language guide to transfer errors. In *Keys for writers: A brief handbook.* (4th ed.) Boston: Houghton Mifflin. Retrieved from: http://college.hmco.com/english/raimes/keys_writers/3e/instructors/esl/transfer.html.

Ray, K. W. (1999). *Wondrous words: Writers and writing in the elementary classroom.* Urbana, IL: National Council of Teachers of English.

———. (2001). *The writing workshop.* Urbana, IL: National Council of Teachers of English.

Richards, J. C. (1971). A non-contrastive approach to error analysis. *English Language Teaching 25*, 204–219.

Rickford, A. (1999). *I can fly: Teaching narratives and reading comprehension to African American and other ethnic minority students.* Lanham, MD: University Press of America.

Rickford, J. (1996, December 26). The Oakland Ebonics decision: Commendable attack on the problem. *San Jose Mercury News.* Retrieved April 3, 2006, from: http://www.stanford.edu/~rickford/ebonics/SJMN-OpEd.html.

———. (1999). *African American Vernacular English*. Malden, MA: Routledge.

Rickford J. R., & Rickford, R. J. (2000). *Spoken soul: The story of black English*. Indianapolis: Wiley.

Rickford, J. R., Sweetland, J., & Rickford, A. E. (2004). African American English and other vernaculars in education: A topic-coded bibliography. *Journal of English Linguistics, 32*, 230–320.

Roberts, P. (1956). *Patterns of English*. New York: Harcourt Brace Jovanovich.

Romano, T. (1995). *Writing with passion*. Portsmouth, NH: Heinemann.

———. (2000). *Blending genre, altering style: Writing multigenre papers*. Portsmouth, NH: Boynton/Cook.

Rosen, L. M. (1987). Developing correctness in student writing: Alternatives to the error-hunt. *English Journal, 76*, 62–69. Reprinted in C. Weaver (Ed.), *Lessons to share: On teaching grammar in context* (pp. 137–155). Portsmouth, NH: Boynton/Cook. 1998.

Rosenblatt, L. (1994). *The reader, the text, the poem: The transactional theory of the literary work*. Carbondale, IL: Southern Illinois University Press. (Originally published in 1978.)

Rowling, J. K. (2000). *Harry Potter and the goblet of fire*. New York: Arthur A. Levine/Scholastic.

———. (2005). *Harry Potter and the half-blood prince*. Arthur A. Levine/Scholastic.

Rozakis, L. E. (1997). *The complete idiot's guide to grammar and style*. New York: Alpha Books.

Sagan, C. (1997). The gaze of God and the dripping faucet. In Sagan, *Billions and billions: Thoughts on life and death at the brink of the millennium* (pp. 31–44). New York: Random House.

Salinger, J. D. (1991). *The catcher in the rye*. New York: Little, Brown. (Original work published 1951.)

Samway, K. D., & McKeon, D. (1999). *Myths and realities: Best practices for language minority students*. Portsmouth, NH: Heinemann.

Schuster, E. H. (2003). *Breaking the rules: Liberating writers through innovative grammar instruction*. Portsmouth, NH: Heinemann.

Scott, C. M. (1999). Learning to write. In H. W. Catts & A. G. Kamhi (Eds.), *Language and reading disabilities* (pp. 224–258). Boston: Allyn & Bacon.

Scott, P. (2006, April 2). Kid rock: How a group of Australians turned an ed-school project into a multimillion-dollar toddler supergroup. *New York Times Magazine*, 36–41.

Selinker, L. (1972). Interlanguage. *International Review of Applied Linguistics, 10*, 201–231.

Shakur, T. (1999). *The rose that grew from concrete*. New York: Pocket Books.

Shaughnessy, M. P. (1977). *Errors and expectations: A guide for the teacher of basic writing*. New York: Oxford University Press.

Sheaffer, R. (2006, September/October). Time flies like an arrow, but fruit flies like bilked bananas. *Skeptical Inquirer, 30* (5), 31–33.

Short, K., Harste, J, with Burke, C. (1996). *Creating classrooms for authors and inquirers*. Portsmouth, NH: Heinemann.

Sís, P. (1996). *Starry messenger: Galileo Galilei*. New York: Farrar, Straus, Giroux.

Smith, F. (1998). *The book of learning and forgetting*. New York, NY: Teachers College Press.

Smitherman, G. (1972). English teacher, why you be doin' the thangs you don't do? *English Journal, 61,* 59–65.

———. (1999). *Talkin that talk: Language, culture, and education in African America.* New York: Routledge.

Spandel, V. (2003). *Creating young writers.* Boston: Pearson.

———. (2005). *Creating writers through 6-trait assessment and instruction.* Boston: Allyn & Bacon.

Strong, W. (1994). *Sentence combining: A composing book.* (3rd ed.). New York: McGraw-Hill.

———. (1996). *Writer's toolbox: A sentence-combining workshop.* New York: McGraw-Hill.

Strunk, W., Jr., & White, E. B. (2000). *The Elements of Style.* (4th ed.). New York: Longman. (Original work published 1935.)

Sweetland, J. (2006). *Teaching writing to African American students: A sociolinguistic approach.* Dissertation, Department of Linguistics, Stanford University.

Taylor, H. (1991). *Standard English, Black English, and bidialectalism: A controversy.* New York: Peter Lang.

Tchudi, S., & Tchudi, S. (2001). *The English language arts handbook: Classroom strategies for teachers.* (2nd ed.). Portsmouth, NH: Boynton/Cook.

Ten Boom, C., & Scherrill, J. (1971). *The hiding place.* New York: Bantam.

Terrell, T. D. (1991). The role of grammar instruction in a communicative approach. *Modern Language Journal, 75,* 52–63.

Troutman, D. (1998). The power of dialect: Ebonics personified. In C. Weaver (Ed.), *Lessons to share: On teaching grammar in context* (pp. 209–227). Portsmouth, NH: Boynton/Cook.

Troyka, L. Q. (2004). *Simon & Schuster handbook for writers.* (7th ed.). New York: Simon & Schuster.

Truss, L. (2003). *Eats, shoots and leaves: The zero tolerance approach to punctuation.* New York: Gotham/Penguin.

Twain, M. (1985/2001). *The adventures of Huckleberry Finn.* Berkeley, CA: University of California Press.

U.S. Bureau of the Census. (2000). Table 2: Language use, English ability, and linguistic isolation for the population 5 to 17 years by state: 2000. Census 2000, Summary File 3, Tables P19, PCT13, and PCT14.

Van Allsburg, C. (1990). *Just a dream.* Boston: Houghton Mifflin.

Vygotsky, L. S. (1986). *Thought and language.* Ed. A. Kozulin. Cambridge, MA: MIT Press. (Original work published 1934.)

Waldman, A. (2006, October). Prophetic justice. *The Atlantic Monthly,* 82–93.

Warriner's English grammar and composition (textbook series). (1986). New York: Holt, Rinehart & Winston.

Warriner's high school handbook. (1992). New York: Holt, Rinehart & Winston.

Weaver, C. (1979). *Grammar for teachers: Perspectives and definitions.* Urbana, IL: National Council of Teachers of English.

———. (1982). Welcoming errors as signs of growth. *Language Arts, 59,* 438–444.

———. (1996a). *Teaching grammar in context.* Portsmouth, NH: Boynton/Cook.

———. (1996b). Teaching grammar in the context of writing. *English Journal, 85*(7), 15–24.

————. (Ed.) (1998). *Lessons to share on teaching grammar in context*. Portsmouth, NH: Boynton/Cook.

————. (2003). *Reading process and practice*. (3rd ed.). Portsmouth, NH: Heinemann.

————. (2007). *The grammar plan book: A guide to smart teaching*. Portsmouth, NH: Heinemann.

Weaver, C., Bush, J., Anderson, J., & Bills, P. (2006, May). Grammar intertwined throughout the writing process: An "inch wide and a mile deep." *English Teaching: Practice and Critique, 5*(1). Retrieved from: http://education.waikato.ac.nz/research/files/etpc/2006v5n1?pdf.

Weaver, C., McNally, C., & Moerman, S. (2001). To grammar or not to grammar: That is *not* the question! *Voices from the Middle, 8*(3), 17–33.

Wheeler, R. (2005). Code-switch to teach Standard English. *English Journal, 94* (5), 108–112.

Wheeler, R., & Swords, R. (2004). Code-switching: Tools of language and culture transform the dialectally diverse classroom. *Language Arts, 81,* 470–480.

————. (2006). *Code-switching: Teaching Standard English in urban classrooms.* Urbana, IL: NCTE.

Wiesel, Elie. (1969). *Night.* New York: Bantam.

Williams, J. M. (1981). The phenomenology of error. *College Composition and Communication, 32,* 152–168.

Wolfram, W. (1969). *Detroit Negro speech.* Washington, DC: Center for Applied Linguistics.

Wolfram, W., Adger, C., & Christian, D. (1999). *Dialects in schools and communities.* Mahwah, NJ: Erlbaum.

Wolfram, W., & Schilling-Estes, N. (2006). *American English: Dialects and variation.* (2nd ed.). Malden, MA: Blackwell.

Woltjer, S. (1998). Facilitating the use of description—and grammar. In C. Weaver (Ed.), *Lessons to share: On teaching grammar in context* (pp. 95–99). Portsmouth, NH: Boynton/Cook.

Wong, B. Y. L. (2000). Writing strategies instruction for expository essays for adolescents with and without learning disabilities. *Topics in Learning Disorders, 20*(4), 29–44.

Woods, G. (2001). *English grammar for dummies.* New York: Hungry Minds.

Woods, W. F. (1986). The evolution of nineteenth-century grammar teaching. *Rhetoric Review, 5*(1), 4–20.

Wright, R. (1978). *Richard Wright reader.* Ed. E. Wright & M. Fabre. New York: Harper & Row.

Writer's choice: Grammar and composition, Grade 7. (1996). New York: McGraw Hill.

Yoder, R. B. (1996). Of fake verbs and kid words: Developing a useful grammar. *English Journal, 85*(7), 82–87.

Yoshida, J. (1985). Writing to learn philosophy. In A. Gere (Ed.), *Roots in the sawdust: Writing to learn across the disciplines* (pp. 117–136). Urbana, IL: National Council of Teachers of English.

Jeff Anderson, a teacher of writing and reading for eighteen years, has written articles for NCTE's *Voices from the Middle* and *English Journal*, as well as ASCD's *Educational Leadership*. NCTE recently awarded Jeff with the Farmer Award for his *English Journal* article on teaching grammar in context. He is the author of two books—*Everyday Editing: Inviting Students to Develop Skill and Craft in Writer's Workshop* (2007a) and *Mechanically Inclined: Building Grammar, Usage, and Style into Writer's Workshop* (2005)—as well as a DVD, *The Craft of Grammar* (2007b).

Jonathan Bush is an associate professor of English education at Western Michigan University, where he teaches courses in teacher education and composition studies. He is also the coordinator of the basic writing program and a codirector in the Third Coast Writing Project. He is coauthor (with Janet Alsup) of *"But Will It Work with Real Students?" Scenarios for Teaching Secondary English Language Arts* (NCTE, 2003), and the former editor of the Language Arts Journal of Michigan.

Patricia Bills is a faculty specialist in the Department of English at Western Michigan University. She teaches elementary writing methods and grammar pedagogy with a focus on linguistic diversity. She is a teacher consultant with the Third Coast Writing Project and has served as a site coordinator for TCWP's New Teacher Initiative. Her other professional interests include teacher induction, language ideology, critical pedagogy, and urban education.

Yadira Gonzalez has been a high school instructor for seven years in California's Central Valley. She currently teaches English at Roosevelt High School in Fresno, California, and is earning a master's degree in reading and language arts at Fresno Pacific University. As a second language learner herself, Yadira is a tireless student advocate and is passionate about ensuring the success of all her students.

Emily Mihocko is a first-grade teacher at Round Elementary School in Hartland, Michigan. She has taught first grade for three years and has had experience in kindergarten and preschool as well. Emily recently graduated with a Master of Arts in Reading from Eastern Michigan University and is considering a career as a reading specialist.

Sharon Moerman has taught eighth-grade English language arts at Watervliet (Michigan) Middle School for eleven years. She discovered she loved being a literacy coach while working with at-risk students, which prompted her to get her teaching certificate. She is passionate about teaching kids to love reading and writing. She graduated from Western Michigan University and is a teacher consultant with the Third Coast Writing Project.

Jason Roche has been a professional educator in California's Central Valley for nine years. He currently teaches English at Roosevelt High School in Fresno. Having already received his Master of Arts in Education in curriculum and instruction, he is currently working on a second master's degree in reading and language arts at Fresno Pacific University. Jason believes that schools need to be safe, authentic environments that build on and focus on the strengths and varied perspectives of all students.

Rebecca Schipper is a ninth-grade English language arts teacher at the Hudsonville Freshman Campus in Hudsonville, Michigan. She received her master's degree in educational leadership from Grand Valley State University. During her time in Hudsonville, she has served as a mentor teacher, worked on the district curriculum council, and been a school improvement chairperson. Rebecca has also helped with coordinating data from common exams and worked on unit development that incorporates best practice research and aligns with the Michigan High School Content Expectations. The work on unit development led her to be a part of the Michigan Department of Education's unit development team.

Rebecca S. Wheeler works with literacy coaches, communication specialists, and K–12 classroom teachers who want to know "what to do about all those missing -*ed*'s and -*s*'s" in minority students' writing. An associate professor of English language and literacy at Christopher Newport University in Virginia, she offers teachers linguistic insights and classroom strategies to address the grammar needs of African American students. Her book, *Code-Switching: Teaching Standard English in Urban Classrooms*, was published by NCTE in 2006.

Index

AAAWWUBBIS, 133–138
Absolutes, 106, 115, 225–226
    examples of, 106, 120–121,188
    functions of, 107–109
    teaching of, 109–111, 204
Accountability, 259–260
Action absolutes, 107, 108
Acquisition. See Language acquisition
Adjectival clauses, 112, 197
Adjectival phrases, 98–99
Adjectivals, xvii, 17
    examples of use of, 71–72, 186–188
    free modifying, 112–118
    out-of-order, 75, 97–103, 105, 118, 129, 165
    punctuation with, 17, 75, 143, 144, 197, 205
    See also Appositives;
        Participles/participial phrases
Adjectives, xvii–xviii, 204–205
Adverbial clauses, 112, 196, 271, 278–279. See also AAAWWUBBIS
Adverbial phrases, 112
Adverbials, xviii, 17, 204–205
    defined, 189
    examples of use of, 189–190
    placement in sentence, 210–211
Adverbs, xviii, 189, 204–205
    conjunctive, 193, 194–196, 204
Affective filter, 157, 266
Affective hypothesis, 266
African American Vernacular English
    (AAVE), 44
    also called AAE, 241
    code-switching to language of wider communication, 146–148, 235–239, 251, 253
    grammatical patterns of, 240–241
Agreement, subject-verb, 205, 253, 255, 265
and, to start a sentence, 175
    in creative and expository writing, 177–180

in journalism, 176–177
    in standardized tests, 180
Appositives, 90
    examples of, 118–120, 165–166
    function of, 103
    and out-of-order adjectives, 105
    teaching of, 103–105
Argumentative writing, 160
Assessment
    cautions regarding, 215–216
    chart as guide for, 204–205
    examples of, 216–226
    of grammatical effectiveness, 207–212
    of organization and structure, 208
    of punctuation and usage, 214–215
    of word choice, 212–214
Authentic reading, 32–33
Authentic writing, 32

be, forms of, 214
Behaviorism, 151
    approaches to errors, 152–153
    and English language learners, 152–154, 266
"Between the World and Me," 112
"The Big Guy," example, 124–126
Bound modifiers, 75
but, to start a sentence, 175
    in creative and expository writing, 177–180
    in journalism, 176–177
    in standardized tests, 180

Celebrating, of writing completion, 280–282
"Choices," sample essay, 198–200
Christensen, Francis, 3, 4, 17, 74, 75, 90, 91, 106, 112, 169, 225
Clauses, xviii, 204
    adjectival, 112, 197, 131, 197
    adverbial, 112, 196, 279
    defined, 192

dependent, xix
essential, 197
independent, xix, 192, 193
nonessential, 197
noun, 197–198
subordinate, xix, 192–193, 196–198, 204
Cleft sentences, 204, 211
"Coaches," example, 163–170
Code-switching, 146–148, 238–239, 250–256
    checklist for, 147, 251, 254
    and contrastive analysis, 242–245
    defined, 242
    and grading and comments, 253, 255–256
    and grammar patterns, 240–241
    minilessons for, 248–250
    and reading aloud, 256–257
    setting stage for, 245–248, 252
    sociolinguistic concepts relevant to, 239–240
    in student editing, 253–254
Cohesive devices, 169–170, 191, 204
    choice of, 198–200
    and traditional connectors, 171
    types of, 191–198
Colons, 194, 205
Combining sentences, 34–35, 89, 109–110, 124–127
Commas
    with coordinating conjunctions, 194, 205
    modifiers set off by, 17, 75, 97, 205
Complex sentences, xx, 204
Compound sentences, xix, 204, 205
Conjunctions
    coordinating, xviii, 169, 193–194
    correlative, 193, 194
    in independent clauses, 194–195
    punctuation with, 194, 204–205
    to start a sentence, 175–180
    subordinating, xviii, 133–138, 196

Conjunctive adverbs, 193, 204
    described, 195
    list of, 195–196
    punctuation with, 194–195
Connectors, 169, 204
    cohesive devices and, 171
    types of, 169, 191–192
Constructivism, 151–152
Constructivist approach to errors,
    152–153, 266
Content words, 11
Contrastive analysis, 242, 243
    and code-switching, 242–245
Conventions, 5, 7–9, 31–33, 35–40,
    163, 167
    assessing use of, 205, 207, 228
    importance of, 67
    mainstream vs. dialect, 40–45
    teaching in isolation, research on, 7,
    14–15, 26, 36–37
    teaching through writing and editing,
    38–40, 139
    teaching in writing workshop, 67–68
Coordinating conjunctions, xviii, 169,
    193, 204–205
    list of, 193–194
    punctuation with, 194
    See also and and but
Correction, 7, 37, 68, 139, 142,
    157–158, 215, 236–239, 250
Correlative conjunctions, 193
    list of, 194
Coverage approach to grammar
    instruction, 201
    alternatives to, 201–202
Cumulative sentences, 119–120

Demographics, of United States, 260
Descriptive absolutes, 108
Descriptive grammars/rules, 10, 13
Details, in writing, 202
Developmental patterns, 48–49,
    203–205, 215
    in acquisition of English, 152,
    154–156
Developmental readiness, 7, 31–32, 155
Developmental sequence in drawings,
    46
Dialects
    appropriateness of, 43–44
    attitudes toward, 240
    defined, 239
    respect for, 41–42, 146, 240–247, 252
    and usage "errors," 40–41, 145, 215,
    235–239
Drafting, 5, 6, 51–52, 58, 65, 69, 124,
    268–272

Edited American English, 42–43
    features of, 43
    See also Mainstream English
Editing
    AAAWWUBBIS in, 133–138
    "Bugaboo," 68, 141
    deciding which skills to teach,
    142–146
    difficulty of teaching, 68, 131–132,
    141–142
    error hunt in, 132–133
    focus of, 275–278
    informal conversations for, 278–279
    as a positive experience, 138–139
    and teaching of conventions, 38–40
    teaching in writing workshop, 67–68
    in writing process, 133–138
English language learners
    affective filter of, 157, 266
    behavioral and constructivist
    approaches to, 151–154
    deficit perspective of, 262–263
    diversity of, 260–261
    "errors" by, 145–146, 263–264
    interlanguage of, 152, 156–157,
    264–266
    lifting burden of failure from, 263
    and second language acquisition,
    150–151
    studying vs. acquisition, 148–149
    teaching grammar during editing,
    275, 278–280
    teaching grammar to, 149, 155,
    156–157, 259
    teaching principles for, 157–158
    teaching writing process to,
    266–282
"Errors"
    AAVE interpreted as, 235–239
    attitudes toward, 144–145
    behavioral vs. constructivist approach
    to, 152–153, 266
    changing approach to, 227–233,
    263–264
    by English language learners,
    145–146, 263–264
    vs. error patterns, 214–215
    illusory, 171–180
    vs. interlanguage features, 152–157,
    264–266
    as signs of progress, 45, 47–49, 80
    and status marking, 145–146
    teacher's pet peeves, 142–145
    traditional emphasis on, 18–19,
    36–38, 132–133
    transformative approach to, 266,
    275–280

unsuccessful approaches to, 14–15,
    37–38, 122–123, 236–239, 263–264
    See also Editing; Rules; Research
"Errorwocky" poem, 49
Essential clauses, 197
Ethos, 129, 167, 168
Evaluation, 160. See also Assessment
Expanding, sentence, 80, 124, 127–129.
    See also Generative rhetoric
Expository writing, 159–160
    definitions of, 160
    forms of, 160–161
    rhetoric in, 167–169
    stylistic issues in, 165–167
    teaching of, 180–184
    traditional vs. nontraditional, 161–169
    traditional perspective on, 161

Fragments, 169, 204–205
    effective use of, 171–175
    and standardized tests, 175
Framework for teaching grammar
    concepts, 62–64
Free modifiers, 17, 75, 76, 90, 97, 99,
    112
    in nonfiction, 115–118
    in poetry, 112–115
Function words, 10, 11
Functional linguistics, 13

General-to-specific order, 73–74
Generative rhetoric, 3, 74, 169. See also
    Ideas, grammar to generate
Gerunds, 209–210
Gradual release of responsibility model,
    64
Grammar
    definition, xvii–xx, 1, 12
    developmental patterns and. See
    Developmental patterns
    emerging, 27–31, 106–107
    to enhance writing, 4–5
    to enrich writing, 3–4
    history of instruction, 18–20
    patterns in, 27, 203–205. See also
    African America Vernacular
    English; Interlanguage
    playing with, 58–62, 99
    on standardized tests, 180, 202
    types of. See Grammars
    usage. See Usage
Grammar instruction
    analyzing students' papers for, chart,
    204–205
    coverage approach to, 201
    developmental readiness for, 31–32,
    203–205

Grammar instruction (*cont.*)
  examining options, 57–62, 204, 207
  framework for teaching, 62–62
  gradual release of responsibility in, 64
  in language-rich environment, 27–31
  patterns and examples vs. rules, 27,
    137
  principles of, 7–8
  priorities in, 201–202
  purpose of, 6–7
  through reading, 32
  research on. *See* Research
  traditional, 13–23
  during the writing process, 5–6,
    25–26, 32, 50, 52, 202
  in writing workshops, 66–68
Grammars
  descriptive, 10, 13
  operational, 10, 12
  prescriptive, 10
  structural, 13
  traditional, 10, 12–13
  transformational/generative, 13
Grammatical conventions. *See*
  Conventions; Edited American
  English

"I am" poems, 60–61, 76–83
Ideas, grammar to generate, xii, 3, 4, 6,
  30, 37, 74, 202, 215
Imitating, sentence, 89, 124
  value of, 35, 53, 57, 110
Independent clauses, xix, 192, 193
  conjunctions and, 194–195, 204–205
Infinitives, 112, 209–210
  examples of, 210
Inflectional word endings, 10, 11
Informal/formal speech, 147, 160, 198.
  See also Code-switching
Informational writing, 115, 120, 144,
  160, 181
-ing words. *See* Participles/participial
  phrases
Interlanguage, 152–157
  behavioral and transformative
    approaches to, 152–153, 266
  and English grammatical patterns,
    156–157
  and English language learners,
    264–265
Inverted sentences, 210–212
"I-search" papers, 182

Krashen, Stephen, 32–33, 148, 149, 150,
  151, 155, 156, 157, 158, 265, 266

Language acquisition. *See* Second
  language acquisition

code-switching to, 146–147
Language transfer features, 152
Language varieties. *See* Dialects
Language of wider communication, 5,
  40
Lessons and lesson plans
  on absolutes, 109–110
  on adverbial clauses, 133–138,
    279–280
  on editing skills, 133–138, 233,
    278–279. *See also* Code-switching
  on "I am" animal poems, 76, 78–79
  on out-of-order adjectives, 101
  on present participial phrases, 89
Life map, 227, 231
  rubric for, 231
Linguistic grammars, 13
Linguistics, 13
Linguists, 13
Literature as models for writing,
  267–268
Logos, 119, 167, 168, 208
Low affective filter, 157

Main clauses, xix
Mainstream English, 5, 41–42, 44, 51,
  146, 157–158, 192, 235, 240
Metaphors, appositives as, 104–105
Minilessons
  for code switching, 248–250
  for grammar skills, 279–280
Models of writing, 6, 68–70
Modifiers
  adding, 74–76
  bound, 75
  free, 17, 75, 97, 112–118
  in nonfiction, 90–91
  See also Adjectivals; Adverbials
Morphemes, 152, 154, 156, 265–266
Multigenre papers, 182–184

NAEP assessment of writing, 238
Noden, Harry, 17, 28, 35, 37, 57, 75,
  121, 124, 135
Nominals, xvii, 17, 197–198
Nonessential clauses, 197
Noun clauses, 197–198
Nouns, xvii–xviii, 15–19, 154–156,
  204–205

Operational grammar, 10, 12
Organization
  assessing, 204, 208
  patterns and rhetorical effects of, 161,
    166, 182, 204
  See also Cohesive devices;
    Connectors; Transitions
Out-of-order adjectivals, 98–99

and appositives, 105
single-word, 118
teaching of, 99–103

Parallelism, 165
  assessing, 204, 208–209
  examples of, 209
Participles/participial phrases, 73–74,
  98–99, 116–118, 204
  definition of present, *-ing* form, 75
  examples of, 28, 30, 60–61, 73,
    74–75, 79–82, 83–85, 90–91,
    98–99, 112–114, 116–118,
    128–129, 165
  lessons on, 59–61, 76, 78–79, 83,
    86–88, 90–91
  in nonfiction, 90–91, 116–118
  in poetry, 112–114
Parts of speech, xvii–xviii, 17
Pathos, 119, 129, 167, 168, 181
Periods, separating clauses, 194, 195
Persona, 3
Persuasive writing, 160
  ethos and pathos in, 167–168
  formulaic example of, 161–163
  nontraditional example of, 163–165
  stylistic choices in, 165–167
Phrases, xx
  See also Absolutes; Adjectivals;
    Adverbials; Appositives; Out-of-
    order adjectivals;
    Participles/participial phrases,
    Prepositions/prepositional phrases
Playing with language, 99
Predicates, xix
Prepositions/prepositional phrases, xviii,
  190, 204
  examples of, 191
  functions of, 191, 204
Prescriptive, defined, 10
Prescriptive rules, 13, 20; *See also* Rules
Prewriting, 268–272
Pronouns, xvii, xviii, 9, 15–19, 61
  as appositives, 103
  conventions involving, 63, 69, 143,
    145, 174, 204
  relative, 197–198
Punctuation, 38–39
  to enhance writing, 214–215
  and grammatical constructions, 192,
    205
  patterns of, 204–205
  research on teaching and learning of,
    36–39
  teaching through writing and editing,
    39–40
  third graders' use of, 38–39
  See also Colons; Commas; Semicolons

Reading
 authentic, 32–33
 grammar learned through, 32–33
 importance of, 32
 to model for writing, 267–268
Red-pen syndrome, 37
Register, defined, 239
Relative pronouns, 197
Research
 on contrastive approach to code-
 switching, 244
 need for more, 14–15, 51
 on sentence combining, 34
 on teaching grammar in context,
 38–40
 on teaching grammar in isolation, 7,
 26, 14–15, 36–37
 on usage errors, 16–17, 38–39,
 40–42, 143–145
Research writing, 160
Restructuring, of sentences, 86, 87, 89,
 110, 124
Revision, 123–124, 272–275; See also
 Sentence combining; Sentence
 expanding; Sentence restructuring
Rhetoric
 choices of, 182–183
 defined, 169
 in persuasive writing, 167–168
Rules
 arbitrary, 1, 10–13, 18, 20–22
 in African American English. See
 African American Vernacular
 English
 for expository/persuasive writing,
 161–163, 166–168, 175, 191
 "Jonathan Edwards syndrome," 37
 prescriptive, 12–13, 18, 20, 41
 that don't rule, 12, 17, 21–22, 43,
 171, 175
 See also Informal/formal speech

Sarcasm, 174
Second language acquisition, 148–156
 acceleration of, 155
 developmental aspects of, 154–155
 distinguished from studying language,
 148–149
 explicit instruction for, 151,
 155–156
 first language patterns in, 151–152,
 154
Semicolons, 194, 205
Sentence

chunking, 93–96, 188
combining, 34–35, 89, 109–110,
 124–127
expanding, 88, 124, 127–129
imitating, 35, 53, 57, 88, 110,124
restructuring, 86, 87, 89, 90, 110,
 124
Sentences
 cleft and inverted, 210–212
 complex, xx, 204
 compound, xviii, 204
 cumulative, 119–120
 parts of, xix
 simple, xix, 193
Sequencers, 169, 191
Signal words, 10
Simple sentences, xix, 193, 204
Six traits of writing, xii, 25, 72,
 201–202
Sociolinguistic concepts underpinning
 code-switching, 239–240
Sociolinguists, 13
Standard American English, 42
 as misnomer, 240
 See also Mainstream English
Standardized tests
 attitudes of toward fragments, 175
 and coordinating conjunctions
 beginning sentences, 180
 grammar on, 202
Structural grammar, 13
Structure words, 10
Style, xii, 3–4, 7, 21, 25, 168, 169, 175,
 182, 204–205, 242, 272
 defined, 239
 Engfish, 182
 See also Informal/formal speech
Subjects, xix, 204
Subject-verb agreement, 205, 254, 255,
 265
Subordinate clauses, xix, 192–193
 types of, 196–198
Subordinating conjunctions, xviii
 introducing, 134–135
 list of, 196
 reinforcing, 136–137
 in transitions, 137–138

Traditional grammars/grammar
 instruction, 10, 12–13
 archaisms in, 20–22
 coverage approach in, 201
 current state of, 14
 disadvantages of, 23

emphasis of, 18–19
 inconsistencies in, 15–16
 ineffectiveness of, 14–15, 26–27,
 36
Transactional writing, 160
Transformational/generative linguistics,
 13
Transformative classroom,
 characteristics of, 261–272
Transitions, 204
 subordinating conjunctions in,
 137–138
 types of, 191–192
 See also Cohesive devices;
 Connectors

Usage, 19, 20–21
 "correct," 9
 to enhance writing, 214–215, 252
 grading, 228, 253, 255
 See also Research; Rules

Verb phrases, xvii
Verbs, xvii, xix, 11, 16, 18, 99, 118,
 142, 154, 203–205, 212, 214, 216,
 256
Vernaculars, 43–44
 code-switching to and from. See
 Code-switching
 defined, 240
Voice, xii, 7, 9–10, 25, 182, 200, 202,
 204–205, 239, 243, 252
 examples, 3, 44, 56, 128–129, 142,
 162–164, 167–169, 172, 224–225,
 227–228
 rhetorical choice of, 4, 9–10, 25

Word choice, 202, 205, 212–214
Word endings, 10, 11
Word order, 10
Writing process
 adapting to ELLs, 266–282
 contrasted with workshop approach,
 65
 grammar in, 5
 recursive model of, 6, 69–70
 waves as metaphor for, 69–70
Writing workshop, 65
 conventions and editing in, 67–68
 demonstrations in, 67
 focus lessons, 66
 grammar in, 66
 minilessons, 66
 teacher conferences, 67